Off to College

Chicago Guides to Academic Life

Off to College

A Guide for Parents

Roger H. Martin

The University of Chicago Press
Chicago and London

Roger Martin served as president of Moravian College in
Bethlehem, Pennsylvania, and Randolph-Macon College in
Ashland, Virginia. Today, he serves on the Board of Education
in Mamaroneck, New York, and is president of Academic
Collaborations, Inc., a higher education consulting firm.

The University of Chicago Press, Chicago 60637
The University of Chicago Press, Ltd., London
© 2015 by The University of Chicago
All rights reserved. Published 2015.
Printed in the United States of America

24 23 22 21 20 19 18 17 16 15   1 2 3 4 5

ISBN-13: 978-0-226-29563-3 (cloth)
ISBN-13: 978-0-226-29577-0 (e-book)
DOI: 10.7208/chicago/9780226295770.001.0001

Library of Congress Cataloging-in-Publication Data

Martin, Roger H., 1943– author.
    Off to college : a guide for parents / Roger H. Martin
        pages cm
    Includes bibliographical references and index.
    ISBN 978-0-226-29563-3 (cloth : alkaline paper) —
ISBN 978-0-226-29577-0 (ebook) 1. College freshmen—
United States. 2. College student orientation—United States.
3. College student parents—United States. I. Title.
    LB2343.32.M37 2015
    378.1′98—dc23
                                            2015003599

♾ This paper meets the requirements of ANSI/NISO
Z39.48–1992 (Permanence of Paper).

Dedicated to my daughters Kate and Emily
who I hope will benefit from this book when
my grandchildren head off to college

Contents

10
Growing Up 191

A College President Comments on the First-Year Growing-Up Process 192

A Personal Story of the First Year 195

Preface

Off to College is the indirect result of sabbatical leave I took in the fall of 2004. Over the eighteen years I had been a college president, initially at Moravian College in Bethlehem, Pennsylvania, and then at Randolph-Macon College in Ashland, Virginia, I had become intensely interested in what happens during the first year of college. Indeed, I had come to the conclusion that going off to college is one of those potentially life-transforming events that if done well can have far-reaching consequences.

So instead of flying off England to write yet another monograph in my field of nineteenth-century British history, I enrolled for six months as a first-year undergraduate at St. John's College, the Great Books school, in Annapolis, Maryland. I survived orientation there along with 135 eighteen-year-olds who were starting their college careers at this venerable but unusual seventeenth-century college. I took the first-year course of study, reading and discussing Greek writers like Homer, Plato, and Herodotus and reexperienced the joys of the college classroom. I hung out at the college coffee shop trying (with varying degrees of success) to connect with my teenage class-mates, hearing firsthand about their hopes, dreams, and aspirations. Once they had more or less accepted the fact that I was a first-year student like themselves they even invited me to some of their parties, which I cheerfully attended with my wife, Susan. And, of all things, I relived my glory days as a college athlete by joining crew and rowing in an eight-person shell with a bunch of high-testosterone first-year

men. I ended up writing an often-humorous book about this experience titled *Racing Odysseus: A College President Becomes a Freshman
Again* (University of California Press).

In 2006, I retired as a college president and moved back to my
childhood home in Mamaroneck, New York, where today I volunteer
with the Mamaroneck High School (MHS) Counseling Department
helping rising juniors and seniors navigate the college admissions
process. One August morning, not long after I arrived in Mamaroneck, a woman I did not know entered the Starbucks where I do
most of my writing, introduced herself as the mother of an MHS
senior, and then after some small talk exclaimed rather plaintively,
"Dr. Martin, I don't want to be a helicopter parent. But I really need
to know what my daughter will be going through after she leaves
home for college next week." She had heard from her daughter about
the former college president working with the counseling office and
wanted to get an insider's perspective on the first year. Above all she
wanted to be appropriately responsive to her daughter and not end
up becoming one of those parents we hear about all too often who
cannot let their child go. Soon moms were queuing up each morning
at my table seeking advice. I was no longer getting any writing done!

And then a light went on. After spending my entire professional
career in higher education and, perhaps more important, after
recently reliving the first year myself at St. John's College, I was in a
pretty good position to give some helpful advice and encouragement
to parents concerned about whether their children could survive the
first year of college without them. And so I decided to write a sequel
to *Racing Odysseus* in the form of a proper college guide for parents
and families.

A few comments before I begin.

Some readers might wonder why I chose the five colleges and universities I did to illustrate what happens first year. My response is
that I wanted to write about a diverse group of institutions—public
and private, large and small, elite and nonelite, located in different
parts of the country—that represent four-year residential colleges
and universities generally. But I needed to find campuses that would
allow me to interview the faculty and staff most familiar with the first
year. Few colleges or universities would permit an anonymous person to wander on campus and, without invitation, randomly inter-

view faculty, staff, and students for a book like this. So I chose institutions whose presidents trusted me and who would give me unfettered access to their campuses. I also wanted to include colleges that do the first year well. I ended up choosing five colleges and universities that met my criteria: Queens College of the City University of New York, a large public university; Tufts University, a smaller, elite private university located near Boston; Vassar College, a national liberal arts college located in suburban Poughkeepsie, New York; Washington College, a small liberal arts college located in rural Chestertown, Maryland; and Morningside College, a regional church-related comprehensive college located in Sioux City, Iowa, the heartland of the Midwest. All the faculty and staff I interviewed were proven, seasoned professionals in their respective fields.

Readers might also ask why I am qualified to write specifically about the first year beyond the fact that I was a college president. First, I want to emphasize that I am not a social scientist who has studied the first year using empirical data and analysis. Nor do I claim to have a solution for all the pressing issues facing first-year students and their parents, like how to bring down the cost of a college education or how to deal with sexual assault. Instead, I write as a student of the first-year experience starting from when I was a first-year college student myself to when, after retiring as a college president, I started counseling college-bound high school juniors and seniors.

Because of a learning disability, my own first year at an otherwise wonderful college was an unmitigated disaster. The first year is often problematic for students with a learning or physical disability and so I write with some knowledge but also compassion about this subject. After college, my involvement with first-year students continued as a graduate student at Yale University, where I was a master's assistant in one of Yale's undergraduate colleges and wrote a master's thesis on, in part, the effect of coeducation on an (until then) all-male undergraduate population, including first-year students. Later, at Middlebury College, one of my jobs as assistant to the president was to field telephone calls from disgruntled parents who were calling the president's office to complain about one thing or another. And perhaps most important, I was a parent of first-year students myself and can vividly remember the day each of my daughters left for college.[1]

As my readers will discover, this book is largely about "best practices" in higher education, namely, what *should* happen first year. But sometimes colleges fail their first-year students, and so I will often allude to what I call "educational malpractice"—not at the colleges I write about (they were selected in part because they do the first year well) but elsewhere. When I do this, I will make some suggestions about what your first-year student can do should things go wrong.

Finally, when talking about how the colleges I write about in this book deal with particular issues—say, how they deal with a bad roommate situation or when a first-year student gets caught doing drugs—I will often say that this is also what *other* colleges do. Obviously, I can't know how every college in America deals with a particular concern or problem; but with a general knowledge of over one hundred colleges in the Annapolis Group of liberal arts colleges (of which my college is a member), I have a pretty good sense of how other colleges and universities address common first-year challenges.

Some additional comments by way of introduction:

The gold standard of data on first-year students is produced every year by the Cooperative Institutional Research Program of the Higher Education Research Institute at UCLA. Unless otherwise indicated, when I refer, throughout the book, to data regarding first-year students, it is to this survey. The 2014 report is based on a survey of 9,168 full-time first-year students attending American four-year colleges and universities. I would like to thank Professor Kevin Eagan, director of the Higher Education Research Institute, for providing me with this report.

Perhaps the leading American scholar of the first year is John Gardner, president of the John N. Gardner Institute for Excellence in Undergraduate Education. After reading a proposal for this book, he reminded me that many first-year students these days do not attend traditional four-year colleges and universities but instead are part-time students and/or attend community colleges and thus live at home with their parents or on their own. He therefore suggested I focus my book on first-year students who attend traditional four-year colleges and universities and not give the misleading impression that I was writing about *all* first-year students. With Dr. Gardner's helpful comment in mind, this book is dedicated to the parents and families of the approximately 1.2 million high school students who will go off to a four-year college or university this year.[2]

Dr. Gardner also pointed out, quite correctly I think, that we should stop using the term "freshmen," which might suggest that all college students are males, and instead refer to "first-year students." I have done this throughout the book *except* when I am quoting others who still use this term. I deeply appreciate Dr. Gardner's helpful suggestions and advice.

For obvious reasons, while I use real names and identities for all the faculty and staff I interviewed for this book, I have protected the identities of most of the students I write about. In the few instances where I use real names, I have received permission to do so.

Introduction

I'm sitting in an extremely hot and very crowded auditorium at Mamaroneck High School where fifty years ago, almost to the day, I received my high school diploma. Surrounding me are 250 high school seniors attending what is called Senior Seminar, a half-day retreat that is supposed to get them thinking about the next big step in their lives, namely, going off to college. Just a couple days ago, as they finished their final exams, these kids exhibited the confident look of accomplished high school seniors. This morning they look apprehensive and very nervous. The reality that they will soon be leaving the familiarity of home and high school for the uncertainty of an unknown college campus is beginning to sink in. Those who achieved some prominence or distinction in high school are panicked, wondering what it will be like to start all over again as humble first-year college students.

To my right, and four seats in front of me, I spot Nathan, one of the kids I will soon be joining at Tufts University for orientation. I turn around and see Phoebe just entering the auditorium. She's going to Tufts as well. Both have agreed to let me interview them with their parents at summer's end. I want to know what's on their minds as they head off to college.

Helene Fremder, MHS's substance abuse counselor and social worker, approaches the podium. The idle chatter subsides. Senior prom is next week and so Ms. Fremder admonishes the seniors to act responsibly and not show up at the prom drunk or on drugs undoing everything they have worked so hard to achieve. Alcohol abuse is a topic of great concern on college campuses, so I listened with particular interest to Ms. Fremder and the next speaker to take the podium.

Bernie McGrenahan, a well-known comedian in the area, is introduced as the keynote speaker. He tells lots of corny jokes about his own youthful fling with alcohol and drugs. I'm beginning to wonder where this is going, but he ends by telling the seniors that because of the bad choices he made as a high school senior he ended up in the county jail doing time on a charge of driving under the influence instead of going to college. He urges the seniors not to follow his example.

The students depart to surrounding classrooms for various workshops on different aspects of college life. The themes revealed in the workshop titles are instructive: "Avoid the Freshman 15." "Sexuality in the New Millennium: Sexually Transmitted Diseases, Birth Control, Date Rape, and Drugs." "Relaxation and Guided Meditation: Coping with Stress." Nobody would have publicly talked about these things when I was leaving Mamaroneck High School for college fifty years ago!

After forty-five minutes of getting oriented to the brave new world they are about to enter, the seniors reconvene back in the auditorium for a session titled "So, What's It Really Like: Seniors Come Back to Share Their Secrets." Sitting on the apron of the stage are eight confident-looking MHS graduates who have just completed their first year of college. They are going to field questions from their former high school classmates. The audience is riveted. The questions from the seniors come hot and heavy.

MHS Senior: "How did you get along with your roommate?"

Lew from Williams College: "My roommate is my best friend."

Wally from Springfield College: "My roommate got to orientation a few hours before I did and took the best bed and most of the closet space. Needless to say, we didn't get along. Then again, I had a night job, so I hardly ever saw him."

MHS Senior: "What about seeing your parents?"

Sarah from Washington University in Saint Louis: "If you get homesick, you can always go home and visit your family."

Marissa from Yale University: "Avoid going home at all costs. If you do, it won't be easy."

MHS Senior: "Any advice on classes to take?"

Samantha from Wake Forest University: "Take afternoon and evening classes so you can sleep in the morning."

Tim from the University of Rochester: "Take classes in the morning so you have the rest of the day free and can party at night."

MHS Senior: "What *about* parties?"

Samantha from Wake Forest University: "Bring plenty of wild clothes for theme parties."

Lew from Williams: "Know your limits. You can't party every night. If you do you'll flunk out."

Tim from the University of Rochester: "Don't worry about drinking illegally at parties. Nothing will happen."

What are these high school seniors to make of all this conflicting advice? And what about their parents?

Since retiring several years ago as a college president, I have begun conducting mock college interviews with MHS juniors and seniors pretending that I am the dean of admissions at a college they plan to visit. I love doing this because it keeps me in touch with young people. I often also meet the parents of the students I interview. Now, you would think that these parents, most of them college graduates themselves, would have a clear picture of what happens first year. Think again. No matter who I talked to—parents of first-year students who are well adjusted, parents of first-year students who have learning disabilities, parents of first-year students who are homesick, and especially parents of high school juniors and seniors who are planning to attend college—no one completely understands how the first year works or how parents are supposed to relate to their children. Many parents don't understand the rationale behind general education requirements, whether taking on a campus job will compromise grades, how to deal with a child who is calling home every day and seems depressed, what to do when their student athlete is warming the bench, what the special challenges are for a child who is the first in their family to go to college, and whether it's a good idea to report a child's learning disability to college officials.

I wrote *Off to College* to answer these and many other questions that are on the minds of parents. The answers I give are based on my almost forty years of experience in higher education, twenty of them as the president of two liberal arts colleges. The answers, however, are not just my own. They also come from the professionals (professors, deans, campus safety personnel, and health care professionals) who work in the trenches with first-year students at the five very different colleges and universities mentioned above. While it would be impossible to write about the first-year experience from the perspective of all the four-year colleges and universities in the United States, the faculty, staff, and students at these five places are fairly representative of the colleges and universities your child is or will be attending.

So join me for a guided tour of the first year!

1

Making the Transition

High school students have a somewhat fanciful notion of what col- lege will be like once they arrive at orientation. Disneyland with a beer garden readily comes to mind. All they know is that their lives as college students will be a vast improvement over their lives in high school.

To begin to get a sense of what the transition is like for high school students as they go off to college, I make a plan to interview Phoebe and Nathan—the two MHS seniors I had recently met at Senior Seminar—as they prepare to leave for orientation at Tufts University, a medium-size, highly selective university in Medford, Massachusetts, only a few minutes from downtown Boston. I will interview them again next June to find out what they learned as new students. Their parents have agreed to join us, so I'll have an opportunity to know what's on their minds as well.

Nathan has been accepted into Tufts School of Engineering. Not only does he want to be an engineer, he already knows he wants to be a mechanical engineer because, he says, "I've been tinkering with mechanical objects all my life." Phoebe, in contrast, doesn't have a clue what she will major in. Maybe math. Maybe Spanish. All Phoebe knows is that she will be taking lots of different courses in the School of Arts and Sciences. She is bubbling over with enthusiasm and is proudly wearing a brand new Tufts sweatshirt. According to Dr. Fritz Grupe, founder of MyMajors.com, only 20 percent of incoming college students, like Nathan, know what they want to major in. Phoebe is more typical, as part of the 80 percent who have no clue.[1]

I ask Nathan and Phoebe how they hope college will be different from high school. Nathan says with self-assurance that he hopes he can take courses that he wants to take rather than being told what to take. I don't have the heart to tell him that most undergraduate engineering programs are extremely proscribed, even more so than high school! Phoebe agrees with Nathan. With great confidence, she tells me that she is also looking forward to making her own decisions, but when she notices that her parents are looking at her in a strange way she checks herself and adds, "Not that I don't have freedom at home right now. I mean, I'm a very independent person and mom and dad have given me plenty of leeway. But at college I will *really* be on my own." Both Nathan and Phoebe agree that with all this newfound freedom and independence, college will be just short of achieving Nirvana.

Indeed, most high school seniors will publicly claim they no longer need their parents, but privately they aren't too sure about this. I ask Nathan and Phoebe how they plan to survive without their parents telling them what to do. Before Nathan can answer my question, his father assures me that his son will do just fine. "I'm not sure about that, dad," Nathan jumps in with a grin, "Who's going to do my laundry?" Everyone laughs, especially Nathan's mother.

Phoebe's mother, who is obviously struggling with the fact that her daughter will soon be leaving for college puts a different spin on my query. She says that the real question is how she and her husband are going to survive without Phoebe. "She is the tech support in our house," Phoebe's mother says. "I'm not sure how we're going to cope without her." Phoebe picks up on her mother's distress and declares with obvious affection that she's going to miss her parents greatly and might even be a little homesick for awhile. And then, not wanting to be too sullen, adds a bit of levity: "Actually, I'll miss Mayzie the most." Mayzie is Phoebe's dog.

I ask Phoebe and Nathan how often they plan to come home during the school year to visit their parents or how often their parents plan to visit them at Tufts. Both are planning only for the major holidays, but Phoebe adds that she will be seeing her parents at some of her soccer matches. She is hoping to play on the varsity team.

I then ask them how, outside of home or campus visits, they plan to stay in touch with their families. The average college student is in contact with their parents via all means of communication an unbelievable 13.4 times per week![2] "Tough question to answer," Phoebe's mom volunteers. "We're a close family and we've always had great conversations around the breakfast and dinner table. This will obviously have to change. With Phoebe away at college maybe we'll text each other." I half-jokingly ask Phoebe's mom whether she can text as fast as her daughter. "You better believe it!" she boasts.

I turn to Nathan's mother. She says that she plans to stay in touch with Nathan by calling him on his cell phone. "And she'll do this every hour," Nathan laughs. "Also by e-mail and texting," Nathan's mom continues, ignoring her son.

First-year college students are notorious for packing far more than they really need—such as a year's supply of coffee filters—so I am curious to know what Nathan and Phoebe are planning to take with them to college the next day. Phoebe tells me that since she shares half her wardrobe with her mom this will be a challenge. "You mean, dear, since you *use* half my wardrobe this will be a challenge," Phoebe's mother affectionately corrects her daughter. "Also, I plan to take my 'bankie' and the pillow my brother Liam made me for my eighteenth birthday. You know, the brown and light blue pillow with 'TUFTS' crocheted into it." Phoebe pauses to give the question a bit more consideration and then says, "And the disco lights grandpa gave me. Also lots of alarm clocks because I have trouble waking up." When Nathan says he is only planning to take a bed set with sheets, his mom blanches. "Nathan, do you *really* think that will be enough?" It seems Nathan's family still has more packing to do that night.

The hour is growing late and everyone has to get up early the next morning for the drive to Tufts, so I ask Nathan and Phoebe what they think their biggest challenge will be as first-year college students. Similarly, I will ask them the following June what their biggest challenge was. Phoebe reveals that because she's a very social and positive person she is nervous about who her roommate will be. "I just hope she isn't a negative person," she says shaking her head. "If she is, getting along with her will be my biggest challenge." Nathan is worried he will get involved in a million different activities and struggle to keep up his grades. He hopes to get involved with groups like Engineers Without Borders and the Tufts Emergency Medical Services. "But I'm wondering," Nathan says, "Will I be overextending myself? Can I manage my time effectively?"

And what do Nathan and Phoebe's parents hope for their kids as they leave for college? Phoebe's father says that he hopes his daughter will remain a happy, well-rounded young woman. "She's into music and athletics," he says. "We just hope that she continues to develop these talents." Nathan's mom hugs her son. She hopes Nathan will excel academically and enjoy his classes. She pauses. "I also hope Nathan fits in socially."

What Happens When Your Child Arrives for Orientation?

It's move-in day, and almost overnight Tufts University has been transformed. Whereas only the day before this place was like a ghost town, on this morning the streets and parking lots are jam-packed with cars and trucks as families deliver their children to the residence halls that surround the campus. Upper-class students are putting up signs advertising various clubs and organizations, hoping to get an early start on recruiting new blood. Orientation leaders in their blue shirts are patrolling the quads in groups of three or four, giving directions to lost parents and otherwise trying to be helpful.

Yolanda King, the director of Residence Life, has let me know that I've been assigned to Houston Hall to observe a first-year residence hall meeting later in the day and that Tommy Travis, the sophomore resident assistant (RA), is expecting me.

New students are signing in and getting their room keys from upper-class RAs in Houston's ample lounge. The RAs look confident; the first years look nervously expectant and unsure of themselves. Down a hallway a father is straining to get a huge refrigerator through the narrow hallway doors. The mother follows with an equally large window fan. It's amazing to me the amount of junk families bring to college for their children! What I know from experience is that most of this stuff will return home two weeks from now when moms and dads are back on campus for Parents and Family Weekend. I think of Phoebe who must be arriving on campus about now with her collection of alarm clocks and disco lights and wonder whether she, too, is realizing that she brought too much.

A young man with a 1950s-style crew cut greets a new student and her parents, and then introduces himself to me. It's a busy day for Tommy Travis, who is working hard to put both students and parents at ease. Only a few minutes prior, Tommy says, he had to deal with an impatient mother who decided to stand in the registration line in place of her son who had inexplicably wandered off. When she was told by an RA staffing the table that she couldn't register in her son's place, she called her son's cell phone but didn't get an answer. Uttering some choice expletives under her breath she marched off in a huff. Hopefully, this mother will learn that she can no longer take care of her son's business. He will now have to do this for himself and face the consequences if he screws up.

Tommy excuses himself to answer another parent's question. In the entryway, a campus police officer is trying to untangle a mini traffic jam that is developing in front of the building. When things are sorted out I strike up a conversation with him. Sergeant McCarthy has been on the Tufts University Police Force for thirty-seven years, and I'm glad to be able to talk with him about a concern that all of us in higher education have, namely, the safety of the new students. He says that this week will be pretty quiet, but by the end of next week at least three or four first-year students will probably end up in the hospital with alcohol poisoning. As a former college president I know the scene all too well.

At about 11 A.M., families are asked to take a break and walk down the hill to Cohen Auditorium, where new students and their parents will get a pre-matriculation warm-up from Bruce Reitman, the dean of Student Affairs and Jim Glaser, dean of Undergraduate Education. The matriculation ceremony will follow.

Dean Reitman begins his address by saying that while some parents are worried about what their children will do without them, others are preparing to pop the cork on the champagne bottle, thankful that their sons or daughters are finally out of the house and on their own! Nervous laughter from the audience. He then gets serious. He says that he knows what some of the students in the auditorium are thinking—or maybe it's the parents who are thinking this—that because Tufts is a competitive place, better to focus on academics and put off joining clubs or teams. "But what I want you to know," he continues, "is that what you will learn *outside* the classroom is just as important as what you learn inside." He encourages the new students sitting before him to take advantage of the cultural and campus activities that are available at Tufts. "Get involved now. You'll be happy you did!" he says. Turning briefly to campus safety, he then urges students to use the university's communication system. "I know that most of you have gmail or hotmail accounts, but we don't always know these addresses. If there is an emergency or if we need to get in touch with you we must do this via your university e-mail address and phone messaging system. If you don't use the system you're going to be in trouble."

Jim Glaser, dean of Undergraduate Education, is up next. His advice to the new students is profound, and I notice several of them taking notes. Glaser tells them not to be passive about their education, to take their professors out to coffee ("It's free at the library," he says). He goes on to say that they should learn from their peers, especially since many of them come from rather incredible backgrounds; to take advantage of all the things that are happening on campus including meeting and hearing from campus guests like Colin Powell, George Bush Senior, Stephen Sondheim, Bill Clinton, Tony Blair, Salman Rushdie, and Bill Richardson. (He says that the last-mentioned celebrity, the governor of New Mexico, is a Tufts's alum). He suggests, furthermore, that students not let problems overwhelm them but instead address these problems immediately and, if necessary, use the counseling center. "Seek help," he says. "If you hide, you will get lost. Students who have balance in their lives will be successful." Finally, he encourages the students to glory in the power of the liberal arts and sciences because the BA and the BS are practical degrees. "Knowledge will always change," he says "but skills like writing, talking, thinking—all things the liberal arts will teach you—are constant."

The matriculation ceremony, when this incredibly diverse collection of recent high school graduates will officially become college students, will soon take place. So everyone briskly marches from Cohen Auditorium back up the hill to the Green, a large area in the center of campus. I find a seat among parents and families under the shade of a large elm tree just in front of Ballou Hall. As 1,313 new students file to their seats, I spot Phoebe and Nathan together in the procession and wave to them. They smile and cheerfully wave back.

President Larry Bacow is introduced by Dean Glaser, who tells us that he is a graduate of MIT where he was professor of environmental studies and chancellor before coming to Tufts, that each year he runs in the Boston Marathon, and that he has a passion for sailing. I have met Bacow and he is, indeed, a very impressive person.

Having been a college president myself, I can imagine what is going through President Bacow's mind as he approaches the podium and the excitement he likely feels at the start of a new academic year, see-ing so many eager young men and women and their parents sitting before him. I wonder whether he will make the comment that was standard fare for my college generation and that terrorized practi-cally everyone: "New students, look to your right. Now look to your left. One of you won't be here at graduation!" But Bacow doesn't do this. Instead, he begins his address by playing an audio of Bob Dylan's tune from the 1960s, "The Times They Are a-Changin'." Cleverly using the theme of this song, he compares his college generation— the same generation as most of the parents in the audience—with the college generation represented by the 1,313 students sitting before him. When he and his wife went to college in the late sixties, he says, it would have been impossible to imagine an African American pres-ident or a Latina Supreme Court justice, a global economy turned upside down by financial crisis, and a nation challenged by climate change and health care. "What makes Bob Dylan's words so true today," he says, "is the fact that change seems to be the only constant." He then suggests how these new students should take advantage of the next four years. He recommends that they play to their weak-nesses not their strengths, that they take at least one course every semester in a subject they know nothing about, and that they read voraciously. "You cannot expect to get all your information from tweets and texts," he says. President Bacow next touches on a key to college success, specifically, the importance of time management. He points out that many students fall into the trap of staying up too late, dragging themselves out of bed just in time for their first class. They then hang out with friends until dinner and don't start doing their homework until 11 P.M. Before they know it, it's 3 A.M. and they still haven't gone to bed. A few hours later they get up and repeat the same cycle. "Treat school work like a 9:00 to 5:00 job," he says. Many parents are nodding in agreement.

After encouraging the students to get to know the faculty, to get off campus ("Go to Fenway Park. Even Yankee fans are welcome!"), and to get involved, President Bacow gets very serious. He says that if they look hard enough they will find many temptations on a college campus. "We admitted you because we thought you had good judgment," he says. "Please do not prove us wrong. If you would not be comfortable explaining to your parents why you did something, *don't do it*." He then turns to a topic that is current on all college campuses, which is to say, the dangers of drinking. "Let me give you some blunt advice about drinking," he says. "Nothing good ever happened to anyone while they were drunk. Tufts is not a consequence-free zone. Your Tufts ID does not entitle you to flout the law."

He has an equally serious message for the parents—namely, to let go. Their kids will never chill out unless they do, and they need to let them fight their own battles. If the refrigerator breaks in their suite they shouldn't be calling the president's office to get it fixed. "Learning to deal with large organizations is another useful life skill that your sons and daughters will master at Tufts, *if you let them*."

President Bacow ends his matriculation address with a touching reference to the good-byes that will soon take place all across the campus. "I hereby grant you a special presidential release from all commitments to avoid emotional good-byes. When the time comes, hold your kids close, give them a big hug, and cry if you want. I guarantee that no one will notice because they will all be doing the same thing!"

Matriculation ends with more of the Dylan song, poignant as the parents in the audience contemplate saying good-bye to their sons and daughters in a few minutes:

> Come mothers and fathers
> Throughout the land
> Don't criticize
> What you can't understand
> Your sons and your daughters
> Are beyond your command
> Your old road is
> Rapidly agin.'
> Please get out of the new one
> If you can't lend your hand
> For the times they are a-changin'.

For parents who can't quite tear themselves away yet, Tufts has devised a special post-matriculation program. I drop in on a session that focuses on mental health. The copresenters are Julie Ross, director of the Counseling and Mental Health Service, and Marilyn Downs, director of outreach at the counseling center. Surrounding them are some somber-faced and concerned parents. Questions flow in a torrent. "How do I stay involved with my child?" "Who do we contact if we start to worry about our son?" "Is it a bad sign if my daughter starts coming home every weekend?"

Julie Ross says that the students these parents will soon be saying good-bye to are going through multiple and complex emotional feelings right now: excitement, relief, nervousness, worries, missing friends and siblings. She suggests that these feelings are natural but nonetheless can be stressful and require support and good coping skills. "Your kids have worked hard to get to this day," she says. "Just think of all the essays and interviews they went through in the college admissions process. This day is a culmination of that effort and their success in the process. And yet now that they are here, everything that seemed familiar just a few hours ago is gone. They are in a new environment with social, academic, and daily living challenges. They have both increased freedom and increased responsibility, and they are faced with many new choices and demands."

Marilyn Downs notes that in many cases these kids are experiencing the "small fish in a big pond" syndrome. They excelled in high school. But everyone at Tufts excelled in high school, so they face the prospect of not being perfect, of competing with kids who might be smarter than they are. Pointing out that 25 percent of young people have experienced clinical depression by age twenty-four and three-quarters of lifetime mental disorders begin by that age, she says that multiple developmental transitions and stressors can add up and may contribute to mental health difficulties. For these students, counseling services can be an important resource.

"My son has a history of depression," one mother reveals. "Should I share this information with Tufts?" Marilyn Downs answers that it can be helpful for the Counseling and Mental Health Service to be aware beforehand of a student's prior mental health difficulties if the student plans to use its services or if he or she needs assistance with a referral to other resources in the community. She says that, ideally, this type of information is shared by the student or with the students' knowledge and permission. Although sometimes students and families hope that mental health problems will resolve with the "fresh start" of college, this is often not the case.

"Well, what if my child goes into counseling. Can't counseling services tell me what's up?" a mother sitting next to me asks. Marilyn Downs answers that counseling services are confidential, and outside of an emergency, she and her colleagues cannot share any information about students without their permission. She says this is important, not only because of legal and professional guidelines, but also because students are more likely to use counseling services if they trust that they are confidential. But parents and other family members can always contact counseling services if they are concerned about their student. A staff clinician can provide general guidance about available resources or about how to talk with a student about mental health–related concerns. Though they hope to never use them, the parents in the room carefully note Julie Ross's and Marilyn Downs's names and phone numbers.

What Happens after You Have Driven Off into the Sunset, Leaving Your Child Behind?

Time for families to go home! Banished from campus! From now on these first-year students are on their own. As I walk back across campus to Houston Hall, I see families taking President Bacow's presidential pardon seriously. A grown man and his daughter hug and sob on the corner of Packard Avenue in front of the Olin Center. But as I get closer to Houston, I see pairs of students—probably roommates whose parents have already left—happily walking around campus together, exploring their new home, talking nonstop. They are relieved that the "saying good-bye" ordeal that they and their parents have been dreading for weeks is finally over. And there, on the large playing field in front of Houston, RAs and their charges have started an ultimate Frisbee game. No parents are in sight. Just students. Freedom at last!

Tommy Travis is gathering new students for their first-floor meeting so they can learn the ropes of residence hall living. Between today and tomorrow, Tommy says, everyone will have to complete a formal contract with their roommate: an agreement on when music can be playing in their room, what time the lights go out at night, and so forth. For many of these students, this is the first time they will have to share a room with someone other than a brother or sister. Indeed, many of these kids come from privileged families with large homes and have never had to share a room with anyone. For them, having a roommate will be an education in itself. Tommy encourages his charges to read *Habitats*, Tufts's manual for community living, but just in case they don't he goes over some of the more important rules. Quiet hours on weekdays start at 11 P.M., on weekends at 1 A.M. This means no loud music or parties after these hours. He admonishes the students sitting before him to keep the hallway clear and not disarm the fire alarm system located in every room. He cautions them not to hang their clothes or decorations on the sprinklers and to know where the closest exit is.

Conversation next turns to the subject of drinking. With the previous student generation—the so-called Generation X that was in college most of the time I was a college president—eyes would be rolling at this point. Generation X hated to be lectured, especially on drinking; they just wanted to know what the rules were. Tommy tells the first years that the residence halls are dry for those under twenty-one and that it is a serious offense to break the university's drinking regulations. He goes on to mention that under Tufts's new judicial system underage students caught drinking for the first time receive a level-one sanction, which is a stern warning. A second offense results in a level-two sanction, meaning that their parents will be called and they might not be eligible for an athletic team. A level-three sanction may mean expulsion. "You don't have to go to parties where there is alcohol," Tommy says. "There are *many* other things to do on campus and in Boston besides getting crazy all the time."

Tommy pauses, knowing that most of these students will eventually drink despite the law. "If one of your friends gets dangerously drunk, call TEMS. They will pick up your friend and take him to the hospital." He says that as Good Samaritans they will not get in trouble even though they might have been drinking as well. The goal of the Tufts Emergency Medical Service—or TEMS—is to save lives. Some of the kids write down the TEMS emergency number on the back of their hands.

Having heard a rumor that Tufts is a dangerous place because of the surrounding neighborhood and its proximity to Boston, someone wants to know what the "truth" is. Tommy dispels the rumor but adds that students shouldn't do stupid things like going out alone in the middle of the night. If they think they are in danger, students should call the Tufts escort service, who will pick them up and deliver them safely back to Houston. Or if they are on campus and near one of the blue-light telephones they should just push the red emergency button and the Tufts Police will show up within minutes. Tommy gives the police emergency number. The backs of hands are beginning to look like telephone books! "And remember," Tommy adds, "The Tufts police are on your side. They are not the enemy. They are basically good guys." He suggests that if students are polite and respectful to the police, they will be respectful in return.

Most of the questions have been answered and dinner time is approaching. As the group gets up to leave Tommy has one last word. "Listen up, everybody," he says, almost as an afterthought. "Houston is a great place to live and study. We are a solid community and we respect each other. But for goodness sake, don't get involved with Blakeley Hall next door." Tommy is pointing to a residence hall just to the left of where we have been sitting. "They seem to be partying all the time. Just stay away from them. They're trouble."

As we leave the meeting I pull Tommy aside. "Do you know what Blakeley Hall is?" I ask.

"Yeah, it's a Tufts residence hall, isn't it?"

"Well, sort of," I answer, "but it's the residence hall for the Fletcher School of Diplomacy and Law, the place where many of America's ambassadors are trained."

"Get out of here!" Tommy utters in disbelief. "Graduate students party that hard?"

Some Orientation Safety Concerns Parents Probably Don't Want to Know About

Before dinner, I sneak over to the basement of Dowling Hall to meet with John King who oversees campus safety at Tufts. I want to find out from him how orientation is going from the perspective of the

Tufts police. I know from personal experience that, free from family, some first-year students go berserk almost immediately after they arrive on campus and do reckless things that land them in the dean of student affairs office—or worse. It's the university police who initially have to deal with these issues.

Like the state and community police, Tufts officers have the power of arrest. But King tells me that his force really focuses on the Tufts campus, only getting involved in the outlying communities when requested. He says that even in the communities surrounding the university, including Somerville and Medford, the local police prefer that his force handle Tufts students who are disruptive in their neighborhoods. But he still has to keep reminding Tufts students that they are not above the law and that if they break town ordinances or do something more serious like drugs they can go to jail like anyone else.

John King's department is involved in many campus safety initiatives besides normal police work. These include creating liaisons with the residence halls so that students get to know who the Tufts police are, coordinating with Emergency Medical Service, overseeing the blue-light telephones around campus recently mentioned by Tommy, and, after the Virginia Tech massacre—in which a student at Virginia Polytechnic Institute shot and killed thirty-two people and wounded seventeen others on April 16, 2007—constantly planning emergency alert strategies. "Students need to remember that while Tufts is a safe place to go to school," King says, "we are an open campus. So we all have to be extra vigilant." He then repeats what Sergeant McCarthy told me earlier today: this week will be quiet, but next week, when the upper-class students return, some of the first-year students will get drawn in, discover where the parties are being held (either at the fraternities or in off-campus housing), and where they can get alcohol. Most problematic incidents happen off campus, where there are few controls.

King has three main safety concerns for first-year students. The first is alcohol and everything that comes with excessive drinking. The second is situation awareness: knowing where you are and how to get back to campus, especially since Tufts is so close to Boston. Finally, there is sexual assault, which often goes back to alcohol and drugs. All of these concerns, he says, are connected.

In light of this heavy topic, I ask King whether he enjoys his job. "Yes I do," he says. "And the big payoff for me is when, at commencement, a few graduating students will give some of my officers a big hug. They obviously have a significant impact on lots of students."

What Are Your Kids Talking about After You Have Gone?

I hike down to the President's Lawn, a massive open space in back of the president's house, for the community dinner. The entire first-year class, all 1,313 of them, seem to be converging on this spot at the same time. I spot Nathan chatting with some new friends. Contrary to his mother's concerns, he seems to be fitting in just fine!

I grab some food and join a group of first-year Houston Hall residents sitting on the lawn in a circle with Marcus and Kate, two Houston RAs. Kate, a junior and a member of the Tufts women's varsity basketball team, is engaged in animated conversation with Megan, a new student who is trying out for field hockey tomorrow. I overhear Kate ask Megan what position she plays. Megan reveals that she usually plays the midfield position, something she's been doing since middle school, but says that she is really worried about whether she can balance athletics with her courses and also whether she will make the first cut. She says that ten freshmen are trying out for the team, but there are only five places. Kate tells Megan not to worry about getting cut. "Just do the best you can," she counsels, adding that playing a sport actually forces her to better manage her time— that during basketball season, for instance, she gets her work done by spending all day Sunday in the library studying. "Of course it's sometimes difficult seeing my roommates chilling out on Sunday when I have to work," Kate admits.

Unable to mind my own business I turn to Megan and remind her that even if she makes the team she'll probably have to spend time on the bench first year. Megan rolls her eyes as teenagers often do when an adult says something obvious. "*Of course* I know that, Roger. You pay your dues. *Everyone* starts out this way." Wanting to quickly change the subject, I ask Megan what she plans to major in. Probably international relations or political science, she says, but she also plans to take plenty of Spanish because she wants to do a junior year abroad in Spain. She mentions that she picked a Division III college because it's often difficult to do a junior year abroad at most Division I universities when you are on an athletic scholarship.

Marcus, one of the RAs sitting with us, has been listening in on our conversation. He asks Megan what other courses she plans to take. "What do you recommend?" Megan asks. Marcus, now a sagacious sophomore, suggests that Megan shop around by signing up for five courses and dropping the one she doesn't like. "Everyone does this at Tufts," Marcus says. "I learned the hard way. I thought that once you attended the first class you had to commit to it." The kids in our circle are really listening to Marcus's advice because orientation officially begins tomorrow.

2

Orientation

What happens during orientation is an inscrutable mystery to most parents. You made the long drive home and are beginning to enjoy being empty nesters but now are wondering what your kids are up to as they begin their new lives as college students. Are they getting up on time? Are they pigging out on junk food now that they are no longer getting home-cooked meals? Are they getting to their orientation sessions on time without you hounding them? In short, how are they surviving without you constantly pestering them as you did when they lived at home?

Parents really don't know much about these things because they are usually barred from attending orientation, and there is nothing they can do about it. But I have been invited by Tufts University to attend the part of orientation you can't. For the next couple days, I will serve as your guide as I sit in on most of the orientation sessions, talk to the professors and administrators in charge, and touch base with some of the first-year students themselves. Along the way I will share my own perspectives on orientation because, as a college president for twenty years, I have given the subject plenty of thought.

Orientation, Day 1: The Curriculum
(including the Use of Advanced Placement
Credits), Time Management, and Eating Well

The purpose of the first day's orientation session on the academic program is to give first-year students a sense of what courses are offered in each of the university's four curricular divisions: the natural sciences, the social sciences, the humanities, and the arts. Students are expected to attend faculty panels representing the four divisions. There is also a session for first-year engineering students like Nathan. These panels are scheduled repeatedly throughout the day so that new students have additional opportunities to taste the endless variety of courses Tufts has to offer.

Like the student organizations hawking their wares across campus, the job of the faculty panel is to tell the first-year students in attendance why their departments are special and why, therefore, they should consider signing up at registration this coming Saturday for one of their courses. Tufts, like most liberal arts colleges, subscribes to a competitive free marketplace when it comes to choosing classes, but while some colleges allow preregistration over the Internet during the summer, almost all want first-year students to meet with their advisers before making a final selection. After registration, as in the case of Tufts (and per Marcus in the previous chapter), many colleges allow students to "shop around" during the first week of class and change a course if so desired.

Professor Anne Gardulski of the Geology Department, who is chairing the science panel, offers up some practical advice. She tells the sea of young faces before her that when they go to class they should sit in the front row so they can hear their professors and see what they are writing on the blackboard. Repeating President Bacow's recent admonition at matriculation, she continues: "Take challenging courses, but don't overreach yourself. You want to do well first year but not burn yourself out." She also urges the students to not blow off introductory courses, especially in the natural sciences, simply because they bring with them advanced placement (AP) credits from high school.

At most colleges, high school AP courses with a score of four or five count as actual college credit, so that when students go to college they can take fewer courses, graduate earlier, and save money in the process. Indeed, with the goal of early graduation in mind, AP courses have proliferated, with 1.8 million high school students taking 3.2 million of them. This number represented 71 percent of all incoming first-year college students in 2011.[1] Since almost all new students at selective colleges like Tufts graduated at the top of their high school class and therefore took loads of AP courses, the temptation is to prematurely blow off introductory courses. The problem is that many college professors question whether high school AP courses are truly the equivalent of a college course. And since there often is a progressive course sequence to the science majors they offer, they feel that skipping the introductory course by using an AP credit might put students at a serious disadvantage. Professor Gardulski is suggesting that, even if first-year students have science AP credits to burn, they might be better off taking an introductory science course designed for those who did plenty of high school science—even though the goal of graduating from college early might have to be sacrificed.

Professor Gardulski starts off the departmental reviews by saying a few words about geology, after which the other members of the panel representing biology, chemistry, physics, and premed give brief descriptions of the courses they are offering to first-year students. The meeting is then open for questions.

One student wants to know whether he must major in a science in order to go to medical school and is told by Carol Baffi-Dugan, program director for Health Professions Advising, that while a good grounding in science and math will be necessary she can just as easily major in a nonscience discipline such as history or English. Another student asks about undergraduate research opportunities, a hot activity at selective colleges, and is told that many Tufts science professors have students involved in their research but mostly during junior and senior year.

The new students are now told that later this afternoon they will join their faculty advisers at various venues around campus to discuss the registration process that will take place on Saturday. I will be joining Professor Gardulski's group.

The next orientation session takes place up campus in Barnum Hall, named after P. T. Barnum, the circus impresario and Tufts benefactor. The presenters are Nicole Anderson, assistant director of the

Career Center, who will talk about time management, the Achilles heel of many first-year students, and Julie Lampie, a nutrition expert with the Tufts food service, who will talk about the notorious freshman 15.

Nicole Anderson starts out by asking the assembled students to respond to her questions by putting their hands up. She asks how many of them did sports in high school. Almost everyone's hands go up. How many did two sports? Still lots of hands. Three sports? Maybe a quarter of the students. Four sports? Just one or two. The questions continue with clubs as the focus. At "four clubs" half the students still have their hands raised!

"Now, what you are telling me," Anderson says, as she surveys her hushed audience, "is that as high school students you were involved in everything. You probably thought this would help you get into a selective college. OK, so you made it! But college is really about depth, not just breadth. You are going to be encouraged to get involved, but you don't have to be involved in a million different activities. It's just not possible in this kind of demanding academic environment. So time management becomes really important." The students are riveted.

Anderson continues by suggesting some helpful strategies:

- not to sacrifice sleep because if they fall asleep in class their professors won't be happy;
- to know what their resources are, for example, how to use time features on their smartphone;
- to invest in a daily planner, electronic or paper;
- to be proactive and, for example, not wait until April of their sophomore year to start thinking about what they might choose for a major;
- to set smart, manageable goals for themselves and not think they have to do everything;
- to look into the future but begin with what they hope to achieve this semester;
- to set aside a time for reflection and relaxation.

"Remember, no one is perfect," she concludes, "so forgive yourself when you screw up. Plus it's OK to start over." She ends by suggesting that the students ask staff for advice, noting that the Career Center employs time management consultants and career counselors like her.

Next up is Julie Lampie from the dining service. At Tufts, all new students are required to be on the premium meal plan, which means that they have unlimited access to all the dining halls, seven days per week between 7 A.M. and 9 P.M. In other words, they can eat all they want almost from morning 'til night! Lampie tells us that according to a recent survey 77 percent of Tufts students say they want to eat healthfully. "But guess what their top food choices actually are?" Hands go up. One student declares macaroni and cheese. Another, chicken nuggets. Several say "fried foods" in unison. "Correct. So where's the idealism?" Lampie asks. She points out that the dining centers at Tufts serve all the foods just mentioned. But they also serve turkey in place of pork, egg whites in place of regular eggs, whole grain breads, yogurts, steamed vegetables, and plenty of fresh fruit. She mentions that the dining centers also have a vegetarian section and suggests that they don't have to be among the 10 percent vegetarians and 1 percent vegans to enjoy these offerings.

Lampie now launches into one of my favorite subjects. "You know how in America, portions at restaurants are *huge*?" she says as she pulls two plates out of a brown paper bag she has placed on the podium. She holds both of them up for everyone to see. In her right hand is the standard plate restaurants used in 1957. It's 10.5 inches in diameter. In her left hand is the plate most restaurants use today. It's 12.5 inches. "No wonder we are an obese nation!" she remarks.

Next she pulls out of her bag two muffins and places them on the podium. The first is a huge muffin sold in any number of commercial coffee shops and the other is a smaller muffin available in the Tufts dining halls. As she holds up the larger muffin, she asks the students how many calories they think are in this typical retail six-ounce muffin. One young women shouts out "350 calories," another "450 calories." "Nope," Lampie says. "The retail muffin has six hundred calories, 30 percent of the daily caloric requirement for the average woman!" She then holds up the smaller muffin. "This one contains only two hundred calories."

Lampie tells the students that experiencing the so-called freshman 15 should not be the norm as some of them might think because research indicates that the average weight gain for first-year students is more like six pounds. So in order to prevent weight gain, she suggests that, instead of eating the large muffin or taking one of the larger plates and piling it up with food, they eat the smaller muffin and use the smaller plates that are also available in the dining hall. "If you are eating a fresh salad," she quickly adds, "then absolutely use the larger plate!"

Lampie gives the students a helpful rule of thumb. She suggests that for each plate they carry through the serving line, fill half with fruit and vegetables, a quarter with whole grains, and a quarter with protein. "And reduce the amount of sodas and juice you drink." She then asks the students how much sugar there is in each twelve-ounce can of Coke or Pepsi. The students don't have a clue. "Well, it's this much," she announces as she pulls ten packets of sugar out of her magic brown bag. I hear gasps of disbelief.

On the way to the dining hall for lunch, I overhear some interesting cell phone conversations. "But mom, I saw you two days ago. [*Pause*] I miss you too, but I plan to come home for the weekend. Can't it wait until then? [*Pause*] OK, OK. Let's have lunch. I'll meet you at the Campus Center in five minutes." And there on the corner of Talbot Avenue and Latin Way, a first-year student embraces her parents as though they had not seen each other for ages.

Time for lunch. I load my plate with garbanzo beans, fresh organic carrots and celery, and plenty of lettuce (Julie Lampie has inspired me!), and I sit next to the only kid who is not with a group, hoping to strike up a conversation. After introducing myself I ask him where he comes from. He says New Hampshire. But before I can ask the next question, he tells me that he must leave immediately to—you guessed it—meet his mother in a few minutes! I thought the parents had gone home yesterday. Stupid me!

Outside the dining hall, a group of women are sitting on the patio wall in animated conversation, all of them puffing away on cigarettes. At their feet are a pile of cigarette butts from the hundreds of students who preceded them. I first started noticing this when I was a college president—the phenomenon of first-year women, in particular, smoking in groups and trying to look sophisticated and cool. A survivor of cancer myself, this has been hard for me to witness, and I've often been tempted to say something, but then chicken out at the last moment. Is it any of my business? Will they listen if I lecture them? But then I wonder whether our concern about dangerous drinking has obscured an equally dangerous teenage activity, namely, smoking? I wonder if we'll hear any mention of smoking during orientation, but since it is legal, my guess is no.

In the late afternoon I join Professor Gardulski and her ten advisees arranged around a large seminar table. We are in the geology department where the room's shelves are piled high with assorted rocks. Professor Gardulski opens the meeting by saying that it's OK to call her Anne, but not to make the assumption that they can address all their professors this way. She then amplifies on the advice she gave at the natural science panel. "This is not high school," she declares, "and the courses you will take here are very demanding. Examinations and papers won't just be on the lectures you attend and the books you read. You will also be expected to *apply* what you have learned." She then repeats what many others have been saying throughout this orientation: "Don't get overwhelmed. You don't need to be involved in eight or nine extracurricular activities as many of you were in high school. Focus on one or two things outside the classroom. Make sure these activities complement rather than detract from your academic program."

Professor Gardulski next talks about registration. As she does this, a sign-up sheet is circulated allowing her advisees to choose a time when they will meet with her to review their proposed course of study for first semester. She encourages them to have backup courses in mind when they meet; because upper-class students have first choice, some courses might be oversubscribed.

Like most colleges, Tufts requires students to complete what are called foundation courses (sometimes known as general education courses) and distribution requirements, usually in their first and second years. At the School of Arts and Sciences, for example, foundation courses include college writing, foreign language and culture, and world civilizations. In addition students must take at least two classes in each of five academic areas, specifically, the humanities, the arts, the social sciences, the natural sciences, and the mathematical sciences.[2] First-year students who have scores of 4 or 5 on high school AP courses can avoid some of these requirements, but as Professor Gardulski counseled at the presentations earlier today, using AP credits to avoid introductory courses in the sciences is generally discouraged. "Don't worry if you don't get every course you want," she says. "When we meet we will go over your high school transcript and come up with some good courses that interest you. No course choice will be a bad one."

Professor Gardulski next introduces her two upper-class assistants who have been quietly sitting with me in the back of the room. They will work on a more individual basis with her advisees, meeting with them in the computer lab on Saturday morning to help with the registration process. "It will take about a minute to do this," one of them says.

Professor Gardulski winds up the meeting by suggesting that her advisees plan ahead but not to the point of planning *all* four years. The key is to keep their options open. As the meeting ends, a first-year advisee is just entering the classroom. Visibly embarrassed, he says by way of a lame excuse that he was on the phone with his mom and forgot what time it was. "That's OK," Professor Gardulski gently responds. "Since everyone has already signed up for their meeting with me you get the only open slot. See you tomorrow morning at eight."

I take a break from orientation to talk with Laura Doane and Joe Golia, Tuft's orientation directors, about the biggest challenges they face with first-year students. To me, Joe and Laura look like college students themselves!

"Most of the new students here at orientation were big shots in high school and sometimes feel they don't need advice," Joe says, "but believe me they really do. When they get overinvolved at Tufts, as many of them will, or lose their way, they need us to help them get back on track."

And the parents: Laura gets more e-mails and phone calls about orientation from parents than she does from their children, with questions that can easily be found on Tufts's website. Joe wants to gently tell these parents to let their student call if they have questions. Let them take responsibility for themselves. Let go. Laura agrees: "Well before they arrive at orientation and meet with their advisers, fully one-third of these new students have been told by their parents what courses they should take. This isn't helpful either."

Knowing that parents are often in the dark about what goes on at orientation, I ask Laura and Joe what they want these new parents to know. "That there is support here for their kids," Laura quickly responds. "We don't have all these eighteen-year-olds come to orientation and then abandon them." Joe nods. "We understand that becoming a college student can be overwhelming. And that's OK. Being overwhelmed is part of life. Financial issues, in particular, can be overwhelming. But there are people here who can help if their children just ask." Laura adds that it's natural for kids to make mistakes and that the college experience won't be perfect. "Some kids will want to return home the first time things go wrong. Parents need to discourage this behavior."

Because some kids think orientation is a waste of time, they blow it off and go drinking instead, which can get them into trouble—such as engaging in inappropriate sexual behavior—before the school year has even started. So Joe and Laura focus on training their orientation leaders around these issues by, for instance, requiring them to read the website "mystudentbody.com." Laura also says that one of the things they do during orientation, besides helping first-year students make good choices, is to exhaust them. "As you can see, we run our programs all day long and well into the evening. There is little time for students to get into trouble."

"And so far, knock on wood," Joe declares, "there have been no major problems."

Orientation, Day 2: Plagiarism, Campus Jobs, and Date Rape

Like many of the orientation sessions, this morning's talk on academic integrity is student-run, this time by juniors and seniors who are Writing Fellows at Tufts. Writing Fellows are upper-class students, usually nominated by the faculty, who are available to help students improve their writing skills. Because academic integrity defines the academy, students are required to sign in for this session. Those who fail to show up will be required to attend a repeat session later in the week. The requirement is more than justified. According to a survey of fourteen thousand college undergraduates, 61 percent admitted cheating on assignments and exams, slightly more than the 59.4 percent of all high school students who admitted the same thing.[3]

Harold, a senior from New Orleans, tells the group that the session is not just about plagiarism but about maintaining the high ethical standards Tufts expects of its students. The students present are handed a booklet titled *Academic Integrity*, an exhaustive treatment of academic honesty as applied to papers, projects, and exams and of the consequences when students violate the rules. It gives examples of the use and misuse of sources such as word-for-word plagiarism, borrowed language, and paraphrasing.

The audience is cautioned against thinking that they can somehow game the system and are then given some examples of real Tufts first-year students who tried to do this. One first-year student got his roommate's help and handed in a perfectly written paper but was then called into his professor's office after taking the final exam in which his writing—his own without help—was deplorable. Another student received a bad grade on her midterm paper because of errors in punctuation but then altered the paper so that the punctuation was corrected. Thinking that he wouldn't notice, she then confronted her professor claiming that *he* was in error, not she, and showed him the altered paper. What this student didn't realize is that many professors photocopy corrected papers before they are returned to the student. Both of the students in these examples were suspended after adjudication by the Judicial Affairs Office.

The nuclear weapon in the faculty arsenal is Turnitin.com, a website to which many faculty require student papers be submitted. The search engine at Turnitin is linked to millions of sources, including published and unpublished papers together with books and manuscripts that will detect almost any attempt at plagiarism including paraphrased sentences and quotations. The papers come back to the professor either with a clean bill of health or with a notation that they contain plagiarized material. This service, used at many other colleges and universities, not only catches academic dishonesty but is a great deterrent to cheating. According to Turnitin, 1.6 million college teachers worldwide use its services.

The session ends with a panel member reading a letter from an alumna and parent whose first-year daughter got suspended for plagiarism. "'My daughter was an A student in high school,'" Eliza reads from the letter. "'She came to Tufts to study premed, but she overextended herself. Not only was she taking six very difficult courses but she was into a million different activities in addition to a robust social life. She simply didn't have time to write two papers and study for four exams and so she completely plagiarized the papers. She was discovered and suspended, her plans for medical school ruined.' JUST DON'T DO IT!"[4]

The economy is slowly recovering from a past recession, and college costs have skyrocketed over the years, so it shouldn't be surprising that students are hanging from the rafters in Pearson Hall's large first-floor amphitheater to hear about Work Study and jobs in general. This will be the first of two sessions on this topic, and maybe three hundred students are in attendance. Pat Reilly, director of financial aid, makes it clear that new students are not required to work, but if they qualify for the Federal Work Study program they can earn some extra money, which goes directly to them and not necessarily for their tuition. "So if you need some extra cash and you're willing to work a few hours each week," Reilly says, "I am interested in hearing from you." I suspect, however, that since many families are stressed out financially, campus jobs aren't just for extra pocket change! Indeed, according to a survey commissioned by Sallie Mae (largest issuer of federally insured student loans), as the economy was coming out of recession, 11 percent of all families in 2011 needed an average of $1,712 in Work Study money to help pay the tuition bill.[5]

Those considering jobs are advised to work between six and eight hours a week (twelve hours at the most) and to think about on-campus jobs rather than jobs in the community. Joanne Grande, manager of the Student Employment Office, tells the students that the advantage to working on campus is that university employers understand that first-year students might need flexible hours. This might not be the case if they work at Starbucks or Baskin Robbins in Davis Square. Consequently, first-year students are encouraged to check out Tufts's job website, where work can be found in the dining halls, computer labs, and athletic offices. "You don't have to make your minds up right away," Pat Reilly suggests, "but don't take too long to decide. Jobs fill up quickly." Sensing how tight things are financially for many of these students, my bet is that the best jobs will be gone by tomorrow.

So far we have seen the faculty only in the context of the various divisional panels. This afternoon we have an opportunity to sample the teaching skills of some of Tufts's best known professors in an orientation program called Faculty Forums. I choose to attend a lecture being given by Roger Tobin, professor of physics and chair of the department. Tobin is not only a world-renowned physicist but, more importantly, one of Tufts's most engaging teachers as well. The title of his topic is catchy: "Sox and Drugs: Baseball, Steroids, and Physics."

It is silent in the room as we wait for Professor Tobin. He enters, pulls a Boston Red Sox baseball jersey out of his dog-eared briefcase, and puts it on. Everyone laughs. He then introduces his presentation by saying that physicists are always involved in scientific investigation and that this morning he is going to do some sleuthing and try to answer an important question on the minds of many people, such as whether there is a relationship between steroids and all the home runs we were seeing from the likes of Barry Bonds and Mark McGwire.

After creating a line graph with "home runs" on the vertical axis and "years" on the horizontal, Professor Tobin labels a modest bump-up at the beginning of the line as "1927—Babe Ruth," a second modest bump-up a quarter of the way along as "1961—Roger Maris," and then the two huge bump-ups at the end as "1998—Mark McGwire" and "2001—Barry Bonds." "So, is there a correlation between steroids and home runs?" he rhetorically asks the class, answering his own question by saying that he cannot say so definitively but that physics can suggest some answers.

Professor Tobin next presents a series of physics equations, graphs, and correlations involving gravity, air drag, lift, and spin that seem to be understood by most of the students in the audience, especially those among the ballplayers who recently took high school calculus and physics. Their eyes are riveted on the graph. Professor Tobin's conclusion is that the effects of steroids could be large enough to account for McGwire's and Bonds's achievements and those of other elite athletes, but that average players will not get much of an advantage by using them. The session ends with an especially robust question-and-answer session.

What I like about this presentation is that it takes a difficult and sometimes arcane subject like physics and relates it to the world in which we live. Were I a first-year student who wasn't necessarily going to major in physics but wanted to broaden my horizons, I would definitely take Professor Tobin's course to fulfill one of my distribution requirements in science. What I also like is that the class is small. Too many first-year courses, especially at large universities, have as many as two hundred or more students packed into a large lecture hall. Even with teaching assistants meeting with students in smaller break-out groups for such classes, I'm not sure how much learning really takes place in a congested and impersonal environment. Moreover, being able to ask the professor a follow-up questions right after class can't happen when lots of students are trying to get to the professor at the same time. Professor Tobin would agree that when in doubt it's always important to talk to the professor and that sometimes these informal conversations after class are as important as the class itself.

On my way to lunch before the afternoon orientation programs begin, I overhear a noteworthy cell phone conversation between a first-year student and his father. "Dad, I just heard this awesome Faculty Forum lecture by Professor David Locke called New Technology for Old Music and want to take his course. [*Long silence*] I know you want me to take economics dad, but I really don't want to go into the family business. I want to do something with music. I love music."

Some parents can't let go!

I am joined at lunch by Serena, an African American student I met at the Houston residence hall meeting the other day. She is the first member of her family to go to college, what we call a first gen. I ask Serena about her impressions of Tufts so far. She tells me that at first she thought she would be the only black student enrolled at the Tufts and wondered whether she would fit in. But then, at the orientation picnic the other night, she saw other students who look like her and felt a bit more comfortable. Serena's roommate comes from Boston's North End ("I guess she didn't go too far away to college!") and seems a bit eccentric, but so far they haven't had any arguments. Serena thinks her roommate's family is Italian American. "Her parents seemed really surprised when I met them yesterday," Serena says. "I don't think they thought that their daughter would be rooming with a black student."

I ask Serena about the others students she's met. She tells me that most of her classmates have parents who went to college, some to Tufts, so she feels a little out of place. At the same time, orientation has made her realize what a wonderful chance she has not only to get a great education but also to meet people who are different. She tells me that tonight she's going to the Shabbat dinner at Hillel. "My father would probably be shocked because he's a devout Baptist," she says. "But what a great opportunity. Plus I *love* kosher food!"

"You seem to be happy you came here?"

"So far yes," Serena responds. "The place is kind of overwhelming.

At my high school the options were very limited. Here I have almost too many options. I really don't know where to start. Kind of frightening. But it's a good kind of frightening."

Cohen Auditorium is packed for the last formal session of orientation. And with good reason. It's about sex. And sex is *the* topic of conversation on college campuses across America just as it was when I started college. The only difference between now and then is that students today are much more open (and graphic) when they talk about this decidedly personal subject.

Tonight's session, with the provocative title "In the Sack," takes place in the context of theater. The upper-class students responsible for this part of the orientation program will role-play various sexual situations that they want the students in the audience to be aware of. To get our attention, they first give us some rather startling statistics:

> On U.S. college campuses, thirty-five rapes are committed each year per thousand female students.
> One out of six college women will experience rape or attempted rape.
> The number of college men who rape is very small, but most have predatory histories and some average fourteen attempted rapes per year. These men tend to be well liked and charming.
> First-year women are the most vulnerable, and most rape attempts are made within the first six weeks of college.
> Nine out of ten rapes are done by men their victims know.
> Eighty-four percent of all rapes go unreported.
> Seventy-five percent of male students and 55 percent of women involved in date rape were drinking.

As the audience absorbs this disturbing information, student actors begin to assemble on the stage. They will now narrate or enact scenarios developed from anonymous student testimonies.

"I was drinking all night," one actor, a senior woman, reveals, using the very words of an anonymous classmate, "and this guy invites me back to his room. We start making out and it's getting pretty hot and heavy. So he pulls out his dick and starts playing with it. 'What are you doing?' I ask. 'Isn't it obvious?' he whispers. 'I don't want to do this,' I say. 'Put it away.' He isn't listening. While he pushes me down on the bed, he pulls his pants off, yanks my panties down and then starts thrusting. 'I don't want to do this," I scream at him. 'Oh come on, you know you want it.' I finally push him off me but it's too late. Later I realized that I've been raped. So when I run into him later in the week I confront him. 'You raped me,' I say. 'I told you no but you did it anyway.' 'I didn't rape you,' he replies. 'You were giving me mixed signals and besides, we were both drunk.'"

The action now shifts to a male actor standing on the opposite end of the stage. He provides an analysis of what just happened. "Is this rape?" he asks the assembly of new students. "It *is* because she said 'No.' And being under the influence is no defense in a court of law." He then asks the women in the audience how many of them have ever been in a situation like this. An alarming number of hands go up. "OK guys, how many of you have seen one of your friends making the move on a drunken women at a party you were attending?" Again, lots of hands go up. "And how many of you intervened?" Just a couple hands this time. "We are a *community* at Tufts," he yells out to the crowd as if he were leading a cheer at a Tufts football game, "and if we see something that is not right, we have a responsibility to *intervene.* DID YOU HEAR ME?" Subdued yeses are heard from the sober-faced crowd. "Be *proactive*," he continues. "If you see a classmate who seems to be in trouble, ask her if she's OK. If she indicates that she isn't, then do something about it!"

Five different student actors now take over the stage. Three male actors stand on one side. They are seniors observing two other actors, a senior classmate and a first-year woman standing closely together. They all appear to be at a party. The woman is clearly drunk. As the classmate tries to kiss her, she staggers forward and almost falls down. It is obvious to the three senior men who are observing this situation that the first-year woman is not in control. And they know very well what their classmate has in mind. The three men decide they must take action. Two of them approach their classmate and convince him that what he is contemplating is wrong. As they do this, the other senior quickly removes the drunken woman from the party. The session ends with a review of what we have just observed: That consent cannot happen if you are drunk or on drugs. That sex can never be forced. That "no" means "no." And that being a community means intervening when you see a classmate in trouble.

Tonight marks an end to orientation and a tradition that, in various forms, goes back to Tufts founding 157 years ago: the candle-lighting ceremony, an event that will be repeated four years from now when these students are seniors and about to graduate.

It's 9 P.M., and I'm standing on the roof of the library, which is on the top of a steep hill. In the distance is a magnificent view of downtown Boston with its skyscrapers all lit up and glowing in the dark like the candles on a huge birthday cake. Below me 1,313 new students are assembling on the President's Lawn, the same venue at which Wednesday's community dinner had been held. As the new students arrive, they are handed candles.

I move off the library roof and slowly walk down to a hollow below to be nearer the students. I sit down at the base of a large oak, maybe twenty feet from the edge of the crowd. The cacophony of the human chatter reminds me of the katydids one hears on a warm summer evening. Phones occasionally sound with their various ringtones. This time the calls are not from parents but instead from newfound friends trying to locate each other so that they can enjoy this tradition together. As some new students approach the event from across the President's Lawn, the sprinkling system suddenly comes alive. I'm sure President Bacow would frown to see this snafu in back of his house, but to these teenagers, getting soaked is just part of the fun. They howl with laughter as they skip and dance through the torrents.

Dean Reitman shares with the assembled students the traditions that make Tufts unique, the president of the Student Senate spins off several pithy pieces of advice, and two representatives of the alumni association, recent graduates themselves, take the mike. They talk about Tufts being one big family, then each lights a candle and, using their flames, light the candles of the students standing in front of them. Slowly the entire hill begins to glow, like the city in front of them, as 1,313 candles are lit. As the alma mater is being sung, I get up from my outpost under the oak tree, walk around the back of the crowd, and make my exit.

I spot both Nathan and Phoebe as I am leaving. They seem quite happy.

3

Teaching and Advising

One of the least understood aspects of the first year is the rationale behind the overall academic program. Many parents think that the sole purpose of a college education is to prepare their children for jobs, often particular jobs.[1] And so they sometimes don't understand why their children are required to take general education courses in the first and second year that feature various areas of human knowledge or why they have to complete a foreign language requirement even if they are going into a more vocationally oriented undergraduate program such as engineering or nursing. Why can't they just take courses in engineering? What does art or a foreign language have to do with nursing? The problem is that when my father went to college the expectation was that he and his generation would have only one career in their lifetimes. But because of the highly technological and global world in which we live today, some say that an individual might have as many as seven or eight completely different careers or job responsibilities before they retire.[2]

So how does the academic program in a modern college or university begin to address this very different world the children of today will be entering? Why is college advising so important? What are first-year general education courses really like? What is the rationale behind the curriculum they will be studying and what are some of its challenges? And, finally, why in this age of smartphones and tweets is good writing still critical to a college education and, indeed, success in life?

Why Is Advising So Important?

The first year is not just about taking courses. It's also about receiving quality advice from skilled mentors. Colleges usually don't throw a course catalog in front of students and then ask them to make hit-or-miss choices about what courses to take. Instead, they assign them an adviser, ideally a senior professor or a professionally trained staff member who is skilled at helping first-year students navigate the curriculum and make informed choices.[3] But advising is more than just about academics. Good advisers look at students holistically. Are they successfully adjusting to their new learning and social environment? Are they attending class regularly? Are there signs of depression? Whether or not your child succeeds in college will in good part depend on the quality of the professional advice they receive.

Most colleges have a key administrator who oversees first-year academic advising. At Vassar College, a medium-sized selective liberal arts college in Poughkeepsie, New York, where I have been given permission to observe the first-year academic program and advising, this person is Joanne Long, dean of freshman, who is also a faculty member and an adviser herself. Along with other advisers, her job is extremely varied. Most days she deals with the ordinary challenges of the first year, for example, helping new students cope with missed deadlines or adding and subtracting courses. But she also deals with more serious issues. These fall into several categories.

First, Dean Long and her fellow advisers see students who are not doing well academically. Only a few months ago first-year students were in a highly structured high school environment. Now they are basically on their own without parents or teachers telling them what to do. Many aren't sure how to handle this newfound freedom and are overwhelmed.

A second group of students that Dean Long and her colleagues deal with are those that didn't disclose that they have a learning disability and are now struggling in class. Most colleges are absolutely clear in their preorientation literature that, if a student has a learning disability, he or she needs to let the college's disability and support services office know well in advance so that accommodation can be provided.

A third category of first-year students Dean Long sees are those that come to college facing some kind of domestic crisis. Maybe there is an illness at home. Or a parent has died. When this is made known, she will follow these students closely, looking out for their best interests.

Finally, there are first-year students who, after being in college a semester or so, are considering transfer and seek advice. Maybe they are having problems with their roommates. Or they are not making friends. Or they figure out that what they really wanted was a large university. "This college is what it is," Dean Long says, "namely, a small liberal arts institution with a very demanding academic program, and some first-year students, really a very small number, come to the conclusion that this is not where they want to be. What I tell them is, 'Before you leave, stay positive and get as much out of Vassar as you can.' In the end, most decide to stay."

Dean Long tells me that, in addition to her own group of first-year advisees, she coordinates 170 faculty advisers, working most closely with them during orientation and the first two weeks of classes when students can add or drop courses. It's often during this period of time that these faculty advisers will share with Dean Long the names of students who aren't attending class or who are performing inadequately. When this happens, she will usually invite such students to meet with her. "I go over their class schedule and their grades," she says. "I then suggest strategies to help them improve, maybe to work more purposefully with their professors or perhaps to go to the Writing Center for help." Parents often don't realize that many colleges carefully monitor the progress of their children by encouraging faculty and staff to report early signs of attrition, such as missed classes or abnormal behavior, like never leaving their residence hall room or frequently getting into fights.

Many parents wonder how first-year advisers are chosen, especially since their children might not yet know what they will major in. Dean Long tells me that, just before orientation, first-year students must fill out a fairly lengthy questionnaire that tries to get at their academic interests. She then uses this information to select a faculty adviser in a department that aligns with the students' interests. "Of course, if they keep saying 'economics, economics, economics,' we get the message and assign them an adviser from the Economics Department."

A lot of parents are no doubt curious about the kind of advice their children are receiving from their advisers and would love to eaves-drop on an advising session, so I have arranged with Dean Long to do this later in the week. But parental curiosity can sometimes be a mixed bag. On the plus side, parents can be extremely helpful when they know that something is seriously wrong (when, for example, their child is not adjusting well to academic life) and communicate this awareness to the college. Dean Long tells me that, recently, a first-year student she had been advising unexpectedly left Vassar before Thanksgiving break. The student's mother later told Dean Long that, when she was on campus for Freshman Families Weekend in September, she sensed that there was something terribly wrong with her daughter, that she seemed unfocused and disconnected from her classes. "Well, I wish this mother had told me this earlier," Dean Long says, "because maybe we could have intervened and helped her daughter better manage in college."

But on the deficit side, there are times when parents should probably back off and not get too involved, such as when, for example, they are in the dark about their children's grades. The principle most colleges work with is that their primary relationship is with the student, not with the parent. So it is difficult when a parent directly calls an adviser or a professor and says, "I'm paying the bills, so why can't you tell me what my kid's grades are?" When this happens, parents are usually told that the Family Educational Rights and Privacy Act, commonly known as FERPA, forbids the college sharing confidential information of any student over eighteen unless the student gives permission. This is the law that all colleges and universities must follow. In most cases, parents are then encouraged to get their children's permission to release this information, especially if they are concerned about how well their child is doing academically. "Of course, when we talk with students experiencing academic difficulties," Dean Long says, "we *always* encourage them to talk to their parents."

Probably foremost on parents' minds is whether their child is surviving the first year. Attrition is not only a fear that parents share with their students but a primary concern of colleges as well. Again, effective advising plays a huge role in assuring that students succeed and stay in college. So, what are the signs of attrition that advisers are looking for? Dean Long tells me that not going to class or being late with work is a red flag. When either happens, advisers will intervene early and try to get to the root of the problem. Sometimes not going to class is a symptom of depression. If this is the problem, they will encourage the student to meet with a staff psychologist for counseling. If the problem is poor study habits or writing skills, they might be referred, at Vassar, either to the Learning, Teaching, and Resource Center or to the Writing Center. The goal is to help students figure out how to take responsibility for their own learning, with lots of guidance about where to find resources.

First-Year Class, Part One: Classroom Policy, Grades and Grade Inflation, Strategies around Teaching First-Year Students, More on Plagiarism, and Time Management

Many parents wish they could sit in on a first-year class being taken by their child—if for no other reason than to see what their tuition dollars are paying for. Well, we are about to join one of Vassar's Freshman Writing Seminars, and I think you will be pleasantly surprised by three things. First, many colleges have moved away—far away—from the lecture format that has defined classroom instruction in the past. Second, these seemingly arcane first-year courses can actually be decidedly relevant to the wider world students will soon enter. And finally, you might be surprised at how small many first-year classes are.

Ten men and six women are seated in a large circle in the upstairs classroom of Olmsted Hall, one of Vassar's science facilities. They have elected to take The Science and Fiction of Mind, one of several Freshman Writing Seminars. Professor Ken Livingston begins the class precisely at 7 P.M. He introduces himself as a cognitive scientist, then hands out blank sheets of yellow paper and announces the class's first assignment. He asks the students to put their names on the top of the sheet of paper and the title, "My Life So Far." He writes this on the white board. "You can write this essay anyway you want," he continues. "Take a few minutes to reflect and then start. You will have fifteen minutes to complete the task."

Professor Livingston surveys the class as they begin writing their essays. At 7:20 he announces, "Ok, let's call it quits." He now asks the students sitting next to each other to exchange papers, silently read each other's essays, and then discuss with each other questions they might have about what was written. There is a low-volume buzz in the room as pairs of students confer with each other. After a few minutes of reading, Professor Livingston interrupts the chatter. "OK, let's come back together. Now, I want each of you to introduce your partner to the class and then summarize from memory the essence of your partner's essay." The seminar jumps to life.

FIRST STUDENT: This is Brendon. He comes from Queens, New York. He ran track in high school and grew up watching *Sponge Bob*.

FIRST STUDENT'S PARTNER: This is John from Vermont. He was hit by a car when he was little. He has played the violin for fourteen years.

SECOND STUDENT: This is Ruth. She comes from an evangelical family but went to a Catholic high school, where she got involved in drama. She has been dating the same boy since she was fourteen.

SECOND STUDENT'S PARTNER: This is Sarah from Los Angeles. She has a bunch of cats at home she misses. She has played soccer since she was five. She lives very much in the present and really likes her dad. [*Ruth breaks into an explosion of nervous laughter*]

THIRD STUDENT: This is Neville. He was born in Johannesburg, South Africa, where his dad works for ABC News. He came to the United States in fifth grade. He plans to study math and philosophy.

THIRD STUDENT'S PARTNER: This is Kevin. He was born in Boise and mentions this fact six times in his essay! He was a newscaster in high school and might want to be a TV anchor someday. He is single and if there are any ladies in the room who would like to date him, his phone number is 208-777-1644.

"Well that last introduction was a first!" Professor Livingston admits with a big grin as he walks around the inner circle. "Now, we have accomplished two things," he continues. "First, I have a writing sample, so please hand in your essays. Second, although you had to write these essays quickly, I think everyone can see not only how multidimensional characters can be, but also how to write about these characters."

Professor Livingston next goes over the nuts and bolts of the course:

You will be doing lots of essays in which you not only write about some aspect of science but also write fictional stories based on this science. The trick is to make the stories you have in your head grab people's attention when you put them on paper. So keep a small notebook with you at all times so you can jot down your ideas. Later in the semester, I'm going to encourage you to choose one of your better essays and submit it for publication. It could be to a Vassar literary publication like *Helicon*. But there are other options. Several years ago I had a student in this seminar who came in fourth at the national Science Fiction Short Story Writers Contest! Just to make sure you are on track, I will meet with everyone individually after you have completed the draft of your first essay.

Professor Livingston now makes a plug for the Writing Center located in the library. "They won't write papers for you, but they can help you work out your writing issues. But don't show up the night before an essay is due! If you are having problems, get to them sooner rather than later."

After briefly describing the books the class will be reading Professor Livingston shares his classroom policy. "*Always* come to class. Of course if you are sick or have a family emergency, I will understand. But just doing the readings is not enough. You need to *actively* participate in class, and that means you must be here. No phones and no texting in class. Finally, how many people read this little pamphlet?" Professor Livingston holds up *Originality and Attribution*. One hand goes up. "OK, *everyone* read it! Plagiarism is a serious offense at Vassar. Any questions?"

One student asks the BIG question on everyone's mind. It's about grades. "Thank you for reminding me," Professor Livingston says as he passes around a handout. "What I am giving you is Vassar's standard guide on grades plus a couple additional paragraphs on what I believe grades mean. At Vassar, we make an important distinction between work that is excellent and work that is unsatisfactory or merely satisfactory. I believe that there is nothing particularly informative in a grade by itself. But grades are an important way for me to communicate to you how well you are doing in relationship to what I think is possible. OK let's take a five-minute break." It's 8:00 P.M.

As I ruminate on Professor Livingston's comment on plagiarism, I remember the orientation session at Tufts when this subject was discussed. Honesty is the currency of the realm in colleges and universities and using someone else's ideas without attribution is a cardinal sin that some parents don't completely appreciate. I can no longer count the number of times as a college president I got phone calls from indignant parents whose first-year students were penalized because they were caught plagiarizing—like the call I once received from a parent concerning her daughter who had copied a paper wholesale from the Internet and then denied that she had done anything wrong. "So what's the big deal?" this mother acidly exclaimed over the phone. "Everyone does it!" Whenever this happened, I would sometimes e-mail the parent part of a letter Thomas Jefferson wrote to his nephew, Peter Carr, on becoming a first-year student at the College of William and Mary in 1785. What Jefferson said over two hundred years ago rings true today: "It is of great importance . . . never to tell an untruth. There is no vice so mean, so pitiful, so contemptible; and he who permits himself to tell a lie once, finds it much easier to do it a second and third time, til at length it becomes habitual; he tells lies without attending to it, and truths without the world believing him. This falsehood of the tongue leads to that of the heart, and in time depraves all its good dispositions." Students who are caught plagiarizing and are bounced out of college for a semester or receive a failing grade learn an important life lesson that might very well save them down the road. This is what I call tough love.

When the students return, Professor Livingston hands out two short essays, one about real science and the other a science fiction piece. After they read the essays, a lively discussion ensues, expertly steered by Professor Livingston's questions and comments. As the clock nears 9 P.M., he sums up the purpose of the exercise. "These stories bring up several important writing strategies," he tells the class. "One of the challenges faced by people who write science fiction is plausibility. If you go too far, the reader will stop paying attention. So the trick is how to make science fiction plausible and engaging but not out of bounds."

As the class files out, I join Professor Livingston at the front of the classroom because I am eager to know more about the strategies he employs teaching first-year students. I'm also impressed by the fact that he has chosen to teach one of Vassar's Freshman Writing Seminars. At many colleges and universities, general education or introductory courses are often taught by junior faculty, adjuncts, or even graduate students, leaving upper-level courses and the major to be taught by more senior colleagues. Professor Livingston is not only a full professor but one of the most well respected members of the Vassar faculty as well.

As we sit in two chairs around the circle, we talk about what appeals to him about teaching first-year students. His enthusiasm is contagious. He leans back in his chair, finally relaxing after teaching, and tells me that he finds first-year students to be endlessly fascinating. "Every year the students are different, and so over time I get a microscopic view of how teenage culture in America is evolving. It's quite intriguing." He also mentions that he loves the fact that first-year students aren't yet jaded, that they are still wide-eyed and in awe of almost everything around them. "These kids are smart and they know it. But they are still coping with uncertainty as new students. First semester is a unique moment when they have a chance to figure things out and I enjoy watching this happen." Because he has these students only four hours a week, he isn't sure what impact he has on them, but still feels that small nudges can accumulate over time and maybe make a difference in their lives.

Does Professor Livingston teach and advise first-year students differently than he teaches and advises upper-class students? "This is a hard question to answer," he admits,

> because this is the only class where I just have freshmen. So what I do with them is somewhat different from classes where I have a mix of freshmen and upper-class students or no freshmen at all. But thinking about it, with possibly one exception, I really treat them like I treat sophomores, juniors, and seniors. Indeed, most of the time I don't think of them as freshmen. The exception is that with freshmen I tend not to get into substantive issues of content. For example, in this writing seminar we will talk a lot about identity, consciousness, and free will. These are the issues that loom large with teenagers, most of whom are leaving home for the first time and are just beginning to develop a concept of themselves that is independent from their families. As a cognitive scientist I have my own views, of course, on what identity and consciousness are all about, but I avoid getting into long, drawn-out arguments about how these issues affect them personally. Doing so can sometimes be premature and involve overkill. So in freshman year I just *raise* the questions and then wait until they are juniors and seniors before I challenge some of their preconceptions.

We talk about advising. Professor Livingston has been a faculty adviser for many years and has been able to watch the great changes he sees in first-year students. But some of what he sees he doesn't like. "These kids come from the No Child Left Behind generation, which, for various reasons, has been moving away from activities that encourage initiative and independence. Increasingly, they are used to being told by their teachers and their parents exactly, and in detail, what they must do in order to complete a project or an assignment. For instance, when I assign a paper, instead of just taking the initiative and doing it, I often find some of these kids in my office wanting to know exactly what should be included. As a result, I have to spend much more time on process rather than on content. But when this happens, I often ask them whether this is the way they really want to live their lives. 'When you graduate from college, do you still want to be told how to do *everything*?'"[4]

I noticed that Professor Livingston spent some time talking to the class about how he will grade them and express curiosity as to whether he grades first-year students easier than upper-class students. He tells me that on balance he's probably tougher on new students than on upperclassmen because he wants to set the bar high for them from the beginning and push them to perform at their very best. "Unfortunately, this is not always the case in higher education," he says. "I fear that there is a creeping loss of integrity in the grading process as witnessed to by widely reported incidents of grade inflation on America's university and college campuses." Professor Livingston has hit on a sore point that is very much in the media—grade inflation. At Harvard, his own undergraduate alma mater, eight out of every ten students not long ago graduated with honors and nearly half received As in their courses. Elite colleges like Harvard and Vassar are trying to address this aberration.[5]

What does Professor Livingston think are the biggest challenges first-year students face as they adjust to doing college-level work? His response is not altogether surprising, considering what I heard at Tufts's orientation and what I know from my own experience as a college president. He tells me that, with the exception of first-year students who come to college from boarding schools, the biggest single challenge is time management. First-year students live in residence halls where no one is telling them what to do. Moreover, they are confronted by an overwhelming number of activities that compete with their studies. And they often don't know how to handle this freedom. "But there is a flip side to this," Professor Livingston admits. "There is another kind of freshman I encounter who has lived such a scheduled life since nursery school that *every* hour is accounted for. You know who these freshmen are when they show up for an advising session with their iPad in hand and they can tell you *exactly* what their schedule is down to the second. And I wonder: Are they missing moments of serendipity because they are so overscheduled?"

What's a Typical Advising Session Like?

Because quality advising can mean the difference between, as mentioned, a successful first year and one that turns sour, many parents will wonder what an advising session might entail. With the permission of Dean Long and one of her first-year advisees, Carla, I sit in on an advising session in order to describe an average appointment.

Carla sits in a chair facing Dean Long's desk. First semester is almost over, and the plan is to discuss her first year so far and what she plans to do second semester.

"So, how are you doing Carla?" Dean Long asks.

"Oh, I love Vassar," Carla responds with genuine enthusiasm.

"What about your social life?" Dean Long continues.

"Good. The residence hall I'm in is especially good."

"How about your roommate?"

"Oh, my *gosh*," Carla responds, her face lighting up. "She's wonderful. We get up in the morning at the same time, enjoy the same music."

"So tell me about your classes so far?"

"Oh, I love my *Moby-Dick* course," Carla exclaims with fervor. "It's so good that I've recommended it to my friends. From the get-go the professor was *sooo* enthusiastic. I mean, my friends back at high school were telling me how terrible *Moby-Dick* is. But my professor makes the book come alive. She has us keeping a journal as we read the book."

"What about chemistry?"

"Ok, I guess," Carla says. "Labs take up a good amount of time. But the professor is very approachable. I think she's new here."

"Any disappointments?"

"Well, the Freshman Writing Seminar I'm taking isn't exactly a disappointment. I mean I enjoy the readings we do. But we have only written two papers, and I was kind of hoping to be doing a lot more writing. So next semester I'd like to take a writing-intensive course. Writing is very important to me."

"What about English 101 or English 170?" Dean Long says as she pulls a list of special topic courses offered by the English Department from one of the files on her desk. "There are six sections, all very different, but each section involves extensive writing."

Carla scrutinizes the handout.

"Are you thinking about majoring in English?" Dean Long asks as an aside.

"I'm clueless," Carla responds. "I really don't know what I want to major in. Do I have to declare now?"

"No, no, you have plenty of time," Dean Long says. "You will need to declare at the end of sophomore year. But it's good to start thinking now about what courses you might take to test out your ideas about a major."

Too often, students come to college thinking they know exactly what their major will be, usually something their parents suggest like economics or computer science. Parents often think that these majors will help their children find well-paid jobs after graduation. But a study done by the National Bureau of Economic Research suggests that giving students some time to think about what they might major in ultimately results in their making better career choices down the road.[6] Indeed, one of the virtues of a liberal arts education is that it gives students at least two years to discover—for themselves—what their passion is, and this might or might not be what their parents had in mind for them. The reality is that most teenagers don't have a clue what they will major in when they first come to college. According to a recent study, over 34 percent of first-year students who thought they knew what their major would be when they entered college reported changing their minds by the spring semester of their first year.[7]

"How is French going?" Dean Long continues with her questioning.

"Oh I love my French professor," Carla responds. "The only problem is that I feel I should be speaking out more in class. And I'm not sure why I don't. In high school I had a pretty good command of French, and so this was never a problem. But here at Vassar, I sometimes choke up. Maybe it's because there are lots of juniors and seniors in the class who speak French better than I do." Carla is expressing the frustration many new students experience at highly selective colleges like

Vassar. In high school they were the overachieving minority. Here, everyone is an overachiever!

"I was going to ask you if you felt intimidated in class," Dean Long says. "I remember a course I took on Byron in graduate school. One day I made a comment about something the professor had just said. But in the back of my mind were all the PhD students sitting around the room. I was intimidated, too. Don't be intimidated, Carla. Speak up. Say to yourself, 'Today I'm going to ask one question and I don't care what my classmates think.'"

After more discussion of Carla's current courses, Dean Long shifts gears. "Time to talk about next semester," she says, as she hands Carla an up-to-date list of courses that will be offered second semester.

"Oh, my gosh," Carla exclaims as she scans the handout. "There's so much to choose from. I'll never be able to decide!"

Dean Long is unsurprised by Carla's astonishment at the variety of courses. Most of her advisees say the same thing, but she is here to help. "So from our conversation, I expect that you will continue with French."

"Yes," Carla replies, "but do you think I can get into this class?" Carla points to an upper-level French course on the handout.

Dean Long spins her chair around and checks the online schedule of classes. "I'm afraid not. The course has limited enrollment, and my bet is that upper-class students will have preference. It's a very popular course, you know. You might e-mail the professor and ask her permission, but meanwhile, I'd look for an alternative." First-year students, of course, are low persons on the totem pole and therefore often lose out to upper-class students when popular courses like this one are being offered. "What about French Lit and Film?" Dean Long asks, suggesting an alternative.

Carla looks at the syllabus. "No, it meets Wednesday and Friday at 2 P.M. This conflicts with chemistry."

"Then what about Studies in Genre, which is a French department course that meets Tuesday and Thursday at 10:30 A.M.?"

"Perfect," Carla says.

"What about the classics?" Carla asks. "Last week I went to the Vassar College Majors Fair. Everyone was talking about Professor Olsen's History of the Ancient Greeks. I've never done the classics before, but

I think I'd like to try it out. What do you think?" Some of the most memorable courses first-year students take are in areas that are completely foreign to them. Liberal arts colleges like Vassar encourage these students to go out on a limb and try something different.

"I think that's a great idea," Dean Long says. "Let's put it on your list.

Dean Long and Carla continue to horse-trade in this way, eventually arriving at a lineup of courses that both interest Carla and accommodate her schedule. "OK, Carla, now here's what I want you to do," Dean Long says, as she settles back in her chair. "I'm going to give you a PIN number. This will get you into the online registration system so that you can register for these courses. Take your time. Think about what we have just discussed and then enter the courses you finally decide to take next semester. But be patient. If you don't get everything you hoped for, just e-mail me, and we can discuss other options." Dean Long is making it eminently clear that Carla must ultimately decide for herself which courses to take. But like any good adviser, she is also saying that she continues to be available as a resource. "One last thing," Dean Long says. "How do you feel about the self-assessment form you filled out before coming to Vassar? Where would you place yourself now?"

"I would say I've moved up a bit, especially in self-confidence. But I guess I'm still a work in progress."

As I leave the room, I think to myself that this is the way advising *should* be. Unfortunately, advising at some colleges and universities does not measure up to Vassar's standards. According to the National Survey of Student Engagement, 24 percent of first-year students see their advisers only once per year. One in ten never sees his or her adviser.[8] In my opinion, first-year students should be meeting with their advisers at least two or three times per year if not more.

And what happens at too many advising sessions? Many first-year students reported that their advisers provided little or no information on academic-support options and academic rules and policies. Only half bother to discuss students' career interests or plans after college. The result of this lack of discussion and information is that too many first-year students later struggle to choose a major.[9]

There are additional concerns. At too many colleges and universities, first-year advisers are often adjuncts or new faculty who are unfamiliar with the curriculum or faculty who would rather be doing something else. The result can be misinformation (or no information at all!) that actually hinders a student's academic progress. In my opinion, first-year advisers should be drawn either from the full-time faculty, people like Professor Livingston or Dean Long, who are themselves teachers in the classroom and understand curricular requirements and who really *want* to work with new students, or from staff who are professionally trained to be academic advisers.

So what should parents do if they feel that their children are beginning to wander aimlessly? "I just don't know why I'm taking all these different courses." "I can't get focused." "What's the point of going to college anyway?" If parents hear statements like these from their children, they should ask them whether or not they are seeing their advisers on a regular basis and, if not, why. If the problem is the adviser, parents should encourage their children to seek out the appropriate dean and make a change. Bad advising is a key reason why students drop out of college and, as we shall see later in our discussion of first-year finance, leaving college without a degree after spending a small fortune on tuition can be disastrous.

What's the Rationale behind the First-Year Curriculum and What Are Its Challenges?

So, in this highly charged world where vocationalism sometimes trumps broad-based learning, what about all these liberal arts courses Carla is contemplating taking? Is History of the Ancient Greeks the best way to prepare her for the world of work in the twenty-first century? I would argue that it is. The liberal arts and sciences play a central and fundamental role not only in traditional liberal arts colleges like Vassar but also in comprehensive universities that operate vocational programs like engineering, nursing, or business. They do this by providing our children with two basic and universal skills that are at the core of any successful career, namely, intellectual flexibility and the ability to communicate effectively. The liberal arts also set the stage for further learning, necessary in an ever-changing world.

How is this done? Whether students plan to be lawyers, engineers, accountants, or physicians, most good institutions of higher education require them to complete a general education requirement—courses that expose them to the major areas of human knowledge. They also learn how to write and speak publicly, skills that will serve them well throughout their lives. Starting first year, college is when young people broaden themselves and sharpen their minds by being exposed to many different academic disciplines and then, later, by deepening their knowledge in a particular academic field or vocational discipline. By being in large part broadly educated, any job or profession could potentially be theirs just for the asking.

The words of John Cardinal Newman, the great British Roman Catholic leader and university reformer of the nineteenth century, make this point succinctly. Though inclusive language was not much used in the nineteenth century, what Cardinal Newman says applies to women as well:

> The man who has learned to think and to reason and to compare and to discriminate and to analyze, who has refined his taste, and formed his judgment, and sharpened his mental vision will not indeed at once be a lawyer ... or a statesman, or a physician, or a man of business ... or an engineer, or a chemist, or a geologist ... but he will be placed in that state of intellect in which he can take up any one of the [professions] I have referred to, with an ease, a grace, a versatility, and a success, to which another is a stranger.[10]

Returning, again, to the advising session I sat in on, I ask Dean Long—after the student had gone—to explain the rationale behind Vassar's first-year academic requirements, including the Freshman Writing Seminars, since parents often want to know why their children can't just take what they like. Dean Long tells me that far too many first-year students want to reproduce their high school schedule and thereby avoid trying courses or subject areas that are unfamiliar to them. Consequently, one of the goals of any undergraduate college or university is to encourage first-year students to try out disciplines they know little or nothing about, to experiment and expand their horizons. To achieve this goal, at least 25 percent of the courses Vassar students take must be outside their majors, ideally in each of the college's curricular divisions—specifically, the humanities, natural sciences (including mathematics), arts, and social sciences. To this end, every department has introductory courses to accommodate this requirement.

Remembering Nathan's and Phoebe's hope that college would be less restrictive than high school, I ask Dean Long whether first-year students at Vassar ever rebel against even these minimal requirements. "Most just trust that we know what we are doing. But sometimes we get pushback," she says. An advisee once tried to convince her that it would be OK to postpone Freshman Writing Seminar because he wasn't interested in any of the topics. She just said no, that he would do it like everyone else and that he might actually enjoy taking one of these courses. She tells me that, because the writing seminars deal with topics that would be of interest to practically anybody, this happens very rarely.

Every college has a different general education requirement, but the principle is the same: to give first- and second-year students curricular breadth before they focus in depth on a major or vocational discipline. But, increasingly, colleges are beginning to radically rethink the general education requirement. Because of the fact that, in the real world, knowledge is interconnected, some colleges have adopted first-year general education programs that feature interdisciplinary courses, often team taught by professors from different academic departments. Understanding how science is linked to politics, how politics is linked to art, and how art is related to the rest of the world gives students a foot up in our very complex and ever-changing society. Of course, all too often, parents and students alike view the general education requirement as something to be dispensed with as quickly as possible en route to students' majors, the assumption being it is their majors that will land them a job. So, what about the major?

Vassar encourages first-year students to be open about what they will eventually major in, letting them know that the glory of a liberal arts and sciences education in America is that while students (and their families) often think that economics or computer science is the only option for them, they might discover, after taking a variety of liberal arts courses, that they have a passion for anthropology, or for physics, or for music. Dean Long then says, repeating what I heard at Tufts orientation, that the same is true for first-year students who eventually want to go to medical school and think that the only option is to major in biology or chemistry. What premed students and their parents often don't realize is that medical schools want students who have taken a balanced course of study. And as long as they have taken the requisite science and math courses, they can major in practically any discipline that interests them, anthropology and music included.

Indeed, many engineering schools also encourage their students to be open-minded in the beginning, not only as to what engineering discipline they might study but also as to whether engineering—a very demanding discipline—is even their cup of tea. As a faculty member and administrator at Rensselaer Polytechnic Institute early in my career, I sometimes saw first-year engineering students, after taking some courses in the arts or humanities, decide that maybe their calling was to teach physics or calculus rather than become a civil engineer. Better to discover this early on rather than later.

How does Dean Long deal with moms and dads who have already planned out what their child will major in—or even their child's career? She suggests that it's sometimes the case that first-year students want to emulate their parents, but she often finds out that they really don't love what their parents love. She tells me about one of her former first-year advisees, whose father, a college professor, wanted her to major in a liberal arts discipline like psychology or sociology. But her passion was acting, and when she told him that she was contemplating a major in drama he was not pleased. So with a little encouragement from Dean Long she found a solution. Understanding that the course load might be heavier, she eventually decided to do a double major in sociology and drama. Everyone was happy. "I think a double major is often a good way to address this kind of issue," Dean Long says.

Very much related to the curriculum are two interconnected challenges, which are, to be precise, freedom of choice and time management. According to a recent study, 44.4 percent of first-year students reported frequently feeling overwhelmed by all they have to do.[11] So I switch gears and ask Dean Long how first-year students cope with the big change from high school, where everything is planned, organized, and monitored, to college, where students have lots of freedom.

She says that many students like Carla are highly motivated and organized and adjust very well. But for other first-year students, not having someone to tell them what to do can be a challenge. A high school student's schedule is invariable. Mom or dad might get them up early so that they can have breakfast and catch a ride to school. They then have classes all day long with a break for lunch in the school cafeteria. At 3 P.M. they return home or go to other scheduled events such as athletics, music lessons, volunteering; but dinner may be at a set time, after which there's homework to do, and then to bed. "At college, on the other hand, there is no set schedule," Dean Long says. "No one gets you up in the morning for breakfast. Classes are not spread evenly over the week. Indeed, some days you might not have *any* classes. In addition, you have to manage your social life, perhaps a campus job and extracurricular activities, including sports. In the evening there is no one to tell you when or where to eat, when to do your homework, and when to go to bed. Some freshmen find all this newfound freedom overwhelming. But they usually figure it out by second semester."

Dean Long shares with me the story of one of her first-year advisees who was struggling with time management issues. She was having one of those awful days first-year students sometimes have and when she came in to see Dean Long she seemed terribly distraught. She had had a Monday morning class but was exhausted from staying up until 3 A.M. the night before. Because she slept late she missed breakfast and so was starved by the time class started, and this was affecting her ability to concentrate. Moreover, she had put off doing the reading assignments until the last minute and so was unprepared for the class discussion. She was afraid that she would fail the course and wanted to know what she should do. After calming this student down, Dean Long suggested that if she couldn't get up for breakfast, she should buy some granola bars in the student snack bar to tide her over until lunch, buy a pocket calendar in the bookstore so that she could keep track of classes and assignments instead of trying to keep all of this information in her head, not wait until the day before to complete reading or writing assignments, build in time during the week for study and class preparation, and, finally, not stay up until 3 A.M. Monday morning when she had classes only a few hours later. "I gave her some very practical time management solutions," Dean Long says, "and now she is back on track."

Sometimes students think they can exploit this freedom and create for themselves a four-day weekend. Dean Long tells me about another one of her advisees who had managed to come up with a spring semester schedule that had no classes on Monday or Friday. But besides forgoing some really great courses that meet on Mondays and Fridays, this student wasn't really going to achieve his goal of a long, relaxed weekend. The five classes he was taking between Tuesday and Thursday were very demanding and therefore would require that he work on Monday and Friday anyway doing class preparation. "Many freshmen come to college thinking that the only work they do is in the classroom," Dean Long says, "when in fact most of the work they do is *outside* the classroom, and often on the weekend."

Sports provide an additional time management challenge. At Vassar over 25 percent of the first-year class plays on a National Collegiate Athletic Association (NCAA) Division III team. At many colleges, this percentage is even higher. Student athletes must devote an enormous amount of time to their sport, which is often in tension with their classes. But like other extracurricular activities, athletics can provide an important learning opportunity. By playing on a team, young people learn discipline and collegiality. Moreover, since in Division III at least they must be in good academic standing to play, coaches will bend over backward to make sure their sport does not interfere with students' studies. At both of the colleges where I served as president, first-year athletes were often required by their coach to be present at mandatory study halls, meaning that they often did better academically than nonathletes.

Of course, there will always be some tension when classes conflict with practices and games. Dean Long tells me that if a student athlete at Vassar wants to take an intro biology class that has afternoon labs, she will urge the student to check in with the coach. If the afternoon labs conflict with practice, she will then try to help the student find a lab section that meets in the morning or at a time when practice is not taking place. In other words, she works with the student, the coach, and the professor to come up with a reasonable solution to potential conflict. Dean Long suggests, however, that sometimes the problem is not clear-cut. Last spring, for example, she had a new student who requested that final exams be rescheduled so that he could participate in a weekend baseball tournament in Virginia. Now at Vassar, as at many colleges, moving exams is hardly ever done. So Dean Long checked with the coach. It turned out that the story wasn't quite correct. In fact, the tournament began the Saturday *after* the final exam.

Not only that, the coach had put in place a travel plan for all the athletes participating in the tournament. Some would travel to Virginia by bus on Friday. Alternative transportation was arranged for those who couldn't leave on Friday because of classes. So this student had not understood the situation accurately. Not only did he have the tournament date wrong, but the coach had already addressed the transportation issue. "The coaches get it," Dean Long says. "They make sure freshmen understand that academics come first. But then again, freshmen don't always listen!"

First-Year Class, Part Two: Active Learning, Writing Strategies, and Being Overwhelmed

Since my last visit, Professor Livingston has individually met with each member of the writing seminar, going over in detail two essays they have written. One is on a scientific subject of their choosing and the other a fictional story based on the science of the first essay. He is now collecting the edited essays and placing them in two piles in the center of the room, one pile for science essays and one pile for science fiction. To maintain anonymity, the student's names have been removed from the top of the papers.

One student sitting across the room from me has failed to bring in his essays and pleads ignorance about the assignment. But Professor Livingston points out that two days ago he e-mailed everyone clear instructions about what would take place this evening so there is no excuse for coming to class empty-handed.

Professor Livingston asks each student to pick up one essay from each pile and mark them, indicating where they feel the essay can be strengthened (for example, arguments that are unclear), what events in the story don't make sense, places where the narrative flow is disrupted or where stylistic features don't work, and any information that is lacking. In order to make it graphically clear why the students are engaged in this exercise he says, "You can't make an omelet without breaking eggs, so you won't become a better writer until your writing has faced criticism."

Students spend the rest of the evening discussing each other's essays while snacking from a table stacked high with assorted treats, including fresh apples and bananas, a neat concession to the fact that college students are always hungry. And they seem to be enjoying themselves. Tessa is laughing hysterically as she summarizes a particularly bizarre and implausible science fiction story about intergalactic travel. Brady, a kid wearing a Vassar soccer jersey and who I will later get to know in another context, is pouring praise on a science essay about chimpanzees. It's not that Professor Livingston is averse to lecturing. From time to time he will lecture the class on an especially difficult scientific concept as he is doing right now in response to a science essay in which the author misunderstood how the brain deals with placebos. But the focus of the seminar is on active participation and on writing about and discussing issues of importance.

The seminar is so involved that we fail to notice that it's 9:15 P.M. So Professor Livingston wraps things up. He asks the class what themes have surfaced from criticisms of each other's papers. Hands fly up. "Make clear in the first paragraph what the goal of the story is." "Put science into real life contexts." "Be sure to thoroughly edit your work." To this last comment, Professor Livingston declares, "Edit. Edit. And then edit some more! And use your computer. When you edit your papers, make a checklist of common errors, for example, using 'their' instead of 'there.' Then use the word finder in your computer to search out places where you repeatedly make these mistakes. Soon you won't need the list."

Professor Livingston and I leave Olmsted Hall together, and I ask him about the student who appeared in seminar without his essay. I speculate that not getting Professor Livingston's e-mail was just an excuse; that this student's real problem was that the assignment was overwhelming and he just couldn't get it done on time.

"You might be right," Professor Livingston replies. "Writing a lengthy paper can be a challenge for some freshmen. So much depends on where they went to high school, but maybe as many as 50 percent of the freshmen I teach never wrote anything over four hundred or five hundred words before they came to college." Professor Livingston points out that another possible reason this student couldn't get his essay in on time is that he might have been overwhelmed by the reading assignments, which are considerable for this course. "Reading is a challenge for many first-year students," he says "especially when they resist reading anything longer than one web page.[12] And forget about research. Their idea of research is to go to Wikipedia and nothing else." He says that many first-year students have no idea how to use powerful search instruments or even how to use the library, so he now takes an entire class period to show them how the library is organized and how to use it. "As I said," Professor Livingston concludes, "freshman year is a period of great change."

Needless to say, I am impressed with Professor Livingston and the seminar he is leading. But as with advising, not all first-year courses are of this high standard. In the first place, as noted previously, first-year teaching, especially at large universities, is often relegated to junior and adjunct faculty or to graduate assistants. I will never forget the admissions tour I took at a large eastern university with my youngest daughter. We were in the university's amazing gothic library and the tour guide, a sophomore, was bragging about the fact that most of his first-year teachers are graduate assistants. "They're really cool," he said, "and understand our generation," whereupon a mother standing next to me uttered under her breath (but loud enough for everyone to hear), "Why am I paying a small fortune to have my child taught by someone who is only a couple years older than she is?" Not all graduate assistants or adjunct faculty are bad teachers; but in my opinion first year is so important that its teachers should be drawn largely from the full-time faculty.

A second issue involves first-year courses themselves. Professor Livingston's method of teaching is what we call active learning—learning in which students are actively engaged rather than passively listening to a lecture in a room filled with two hundred or more students.[13] According to the National Survey of Student Engagement, almost 50 percent of first-year students taking their survey sometimes or never discussed or debated an issue of social, political, or philosophical importance and 26 percent never made a speech to a group, both hallmarks of active learning and both of which cannot take place in a large lecture class.[14] In his book, *Our Underachieving Colleges*, Derek Bok, former president of Harvard University, cites a study showing that, in the traditional lecture format, students can recall only 42 percent of the information imparted by the professor by the time the lecture ends and only 20 percent a week later. Bok goes on to say that students retain material longer when they acquire it through their own "mental effort," that is, when they are actively engaged in the learning process.[15] So, too, many educators who teach at large institutions, and those who teach at small ones as well (myself included), believe that first-year students *especially* need individual attention from their professors. Educators are beginning to question the virtue of the sometimes massive first-year lectures that most of us took back in the Dark Ages.

So, what should you do if your child ends up in a boring class of two hundred first-year students? As we saw at Tufts orientation, students will often shop around the first week of class to get a sense of what courses might work for them, a hit-or-miss proposition at best. Good advising, like that which Dean Long was doing with Carla, is still the best way for first-year students to make informed choices about what courses they should take—and which they should drop—and another reason why academic advising is so important.

Why Should You Encourage Your Child to Use the Writing Center?

Good writing is a powerful tool and it is central to an undergraduate education. If students can't write in a cogent and persuasive way, their futures will not be very bright. Virtually every line of work these days requires high-level communication skills, be it managing a bank, designing a bridge, or teaching elementary school students. This is why many colleges mandate writing (and speaking) across the curriculum, in the sciences as well as in the social sciences and humanities. If I learned one thing from my own college experience, it was how to write, and in every job I have held since graduating—as a young history professor, as a college president, and now as a school board member and foundation director—writing has been key. This is why most colleges have writing centers.

Fifteen upper-class peer consultants assemble precisely at 5 P.M. in a large, attractively appointed Writing Center lounge, located in the back of the Vassar Library. Sitting on hastily assembled chairs and couches, the group forms a large circle. Professor Lee Rumbarger, director of the Writing Center and assistant professor of English, is presiding. These peer consultants have been hand-selected to work here. They are all accomplished writers themselves.

Professor Rumbarger hands out a one-page summary of a study she wants the group to discuss this evening. It is written by Nancy Sommers and Laura Saltz, two Harvard researchers who followed 422 Harvard undergraduates through four years of college. One of their conclusions is that new students who admit they are novices at writing are more likely to learn new writing skills than students who think they are already accomplished writers.[16] As she holds it up, Professor Rumbarger asks whether the study rings true for the first-year students the peer consultants are currently working with.

A senior sitting directly across from me immediately responds, "In my sessions I see two extremes. On one extreme are first-year students who boast 'I was the best writer in my high school. Why do I need this?' On the other are students who seem so guilty about their novice status that they absolutely freeze when it comes to writing in class. At least the kids who admit they need help fare better in the long run." Emphatic nods are seen around the circle.

Eric, a sophomore, replies by saying that in his experience students who have an inferiority complex about their writing probably don't know what a paper should look like and therefore need models of good writing to help them. "But many Vassar faculty don't like models," Professor Rumbarger quickly counters. "They want their students to take risks and not get boxed into a particular writing style."

"But how do they take risks if they don't know what good writing looks like?" Eric asks. "I'm suggesting that we provide our freshmen with models of good writing but then encourage them to expand beyond these models."

A junior sitting across the room says that she's working with a first-year student who crams all his ideas into a paper even if the ideas are completely unrelated. "I think students need structure," she says. "I agree with Eric. They need models of good writing."

"So maybe we need to come up with some of our *own* models to show our students what Vassar professors expect of them," comments a senior who is wearing shorts even though it's beginning to snow outside.

"But the professors are sometimes part of the problem," a junior rejoins. "It's sometimes difficult to know what they consider good writing. Often they just give a grade. No comments, just a grade. But grades by themselves tell you absolutely nothing about what you need to do to improve your writing. Sometimes they make obscure comments. Sometimes you can't even *read* their writing! I work with a student who was in tears last week when her professor trashed her essay and then didn't give any concrete examples of how to improve."

The senior sitting across from me remarks that when a paper is that bad, the professor should write on the back "Come meet with me" rather than just making harsh comments and giving a bad grade.

"It's not the professor's fault," says Harper, a junior wearing a Vassar sweatshirt. "I encourage my students to develop a personal relationship with their professors. If they get harsh comments on a paper or a bad grade, they should immediately go talk to the professor. Get his opinion. Get to know him on a personal level. Vassar professors are *very* open to this. But professors shouldn't have to beg students to come and see them. Freshmen need to be more assertive. By the time they become sophomores they need to learn how to speak up. Isn't this part of what we are here to learn?"

I agree with Harper. According to one study, 42 percent of first-year students have not discussed course materials with their professors outside of class.[17] But professors expect (or should expect) their students to visit them during office hours or even more informally, where sometimes more learning takes place than in the classroom. I also agree that it's up to the student, not the professor, to initiate these conversations.

The discussion is warming up and ideas are flowing rapid fire around the circle. But the evening is getting late and a couple of the peer consultants have to leave. So Professor Rumbarger winds up the meeting. As the students leave, I pull up a chair next to the professor.

Considering the withering criticism high schools have come under regarding the writing skills of their graduates, I'm interested to know whether, in her opinion, high schools have done an adequate job preparing students for college writing. She tells me that the writing preparation students receive in high school varies widely and that at Vassar most first-year students are able, critical readers when they arrive and have a good sense of what makes an interesting paper. The problem is that many of them weren't invited in high school to use their writing to explore complex issues. "They can do simple summaries and descriptions," she says, "but many don't know how to make a coherent argument. So, while it would be wrong to suggest that the writing preparation freshmen receive in high school is defective, the challenge is how to get them creatively to use what they know and also to experiment with new ideas."

The image of high school students constantly texting and e-mailing each other leads me also to wonder whether the Internet isn't hurting writing. Many parents would argue that the Internet has been a liability for their children. But Professor Rumbarger disagrees:

> I don't think the Internet has been detrimental. Actually, because of this technology students are writing much more than ever. They are producing text on a regular basis. So we need to work *with* this technology, not against it. When they write papers, freshmen are often uninspired and dully mechanical, and this is not good. On the other hand, when they are texting each other they are often inspired and natural and this *is* good. So the trick is to get freshmen to write about things that *excite* them, like they often do when they are texting, and then build on this excitement.

So how does the Writing Center operate? When the school year starts, the peer consultants fan out to the various Freshman Writing Seminars and make a pitch for the Writing Center. These peer consultants aren't looking just for weak writers but for accomplished writers as well. One of the misperceptions parents often have is that Writing Centers exists only for students who have acute writing problems. Once word gets out that first-year students can drop in six days a week, the center starts getting customers. There is always a peer consultant staffing the reception desk, so when a student arrives and requests help, the peer consultant at the reception desk invites the student to join him or her on a comfortable couch in the lounge. Meanwhile, another peer consultant takes his or her place, so it's a rotating process. Once a consultant and student are comfortably seated, the initial consultation begins. Sometimes it's a one-time consultation, as when a first-year student needs the peer consultant to critique the first draft of a paper. Or the consultation might be ongoing, especially if a student has more fundamental writing issues. Students are encouraged to keep coming back even if they are pretty good writers because working with the peer consultants will only make them better.

Professor Rumbarger says that, when the first-year student initially arrives, the peer consultant fills out a brief form that asks some basic questions like what the client needs help with and when the paper is due. "Needless to say, we prefer not to see papers the day before they are due." When reviewing a paper, the peer consultant looks for big ticket items like sentence and paragraph structure, spelling mistakes, the presentation of ideas, and so forth. The peer consultant will then engage the student in conversation, asking who their audience is, what point they are trying to make, and what their conclusions are.

What does Professor Rumbarger want parents to know about writing? "Wherever your child goes to college" she says, "encourage them to make use of the writing or learning center whether or not they think they might need help. Here at Vassar, peer consultants can really make a difference in how a freshman writes. As everyone knows, a key to success in college as well as in life is being able to write well."

Professor Rumbarger is absolutely right. But unfortunately, only 11.7 percent of first-year students report frequently taking advantage of this kind of support program.[18]

First-Year Class, Part Three: More Writing Strategies, Texting in Class, and the Consequences of Disruptive Behavior

Professor Livingston starts the seminar off by engaging the class in a discussion of the writing process. "When do you write?" he asks. "What time of day?" He goes around the circle. Everyone is required to respond. There will be no wallflowers in Professor Livingston's seminar!

"I write in the morning and evenings."

"At really odd hours, usually between midnight and 2 A.M. But I'm also tired by then."

"No particular time, but no earlier than 10 A.M."

"At home in Nicaragua, I would always grab my books and coffeemaker, go out on the veranda where there is always a nice warm breeze and start writing," a young man with a pleasant Spanish accent says, to which Professor Livingston responds, "I think you're going to have a problem here. Just wait until Poughkeepsie gets its first blizzard!" Everyone laughs.

Professor Livingston next asks the class how they handle drafts or revisions.

"I do several drafts."

"I write the first draft in long hand, check for grammatical errors and sentence structure, and then call it a day."

"I jump around, maybe starting in the middle of the story, then go to the beginning, and then go to the end, revising all the time."

"I edit as I go but I don't do revisions."

Professor Livingston interrupts the student who made this last comment and asks the class how many also don't like doing revisions. Five hands go up. He is getting a pretty good picture of the class's writing habits. He stops the conversation and asks the class to grab a piece of paper. "Now write a paragraph about the one thing you would do to improve your writing based on what you and the others have been saying." He then quips with a big smile, "If you are happy with your writing style, just write yourself a congratulatory note!" Professor Livingston then asks members of the seminar to share what they have learned. The comments are interesting.

"Ask other people to revise and edit my work. By the time I have read and reread my essay, I need a fresh pair of eyes."

"Do an outline beforehand. I haven't done this before because I'm lazy."

"Start my essay well before it's due. I usually let things go and write my essay at the last minute and the result is obvious!"

"Turn off the Internet while I'm writing." The student who says this is the kid I have sat behind in several seminars who surreptitiously plays computer games during class discussions.

Professor Livingston breaks into the conversation. He asks the class how many of them are checking e-mails or otherwise using the Internet while they are writing. Almost everyone's hand goes up. Professor Livingston leaves his chair in the circle and walks up to the podium. What he shares with the class is enormously important.

"OK, I want you to listen to yourselves and do what I am about to tell you. The *only* effective way to change bad habits is to substitute new for old behavior. We know from studies that it will take about eighty days or three months to retrain our neural networks so that these new habits become permanent. You cannot backslide." He then notes that members of the class have mentioned several bad writing habits. Not revising their essays. Putting them off until the last minute. He says that they will have to decide whether they are going to change just one bad habit or all of them. He suggests trying to change all of them at once. "It will be harder but well worth the effort." He adds, "Most importantly, kick the habit of multitasking." As Professor Livingston says this he looks directly at the gamer. He says that data suggest that when you are trying to do two things at the same time you will degrade each task by 20 percent. If you are doing three things at the same time, it's 40 percent. And forget about doing four things at once. He suggests that they need to focus on just *one* task at a time. "So when you are writing, turn off your e-mail, Facebook, and phone."

The students take a break before discussing that night's assignment, one that raises an interesting question of identity that runs through much of the science and science fiction they have been reading and discussing during the semester. This conversation goes on till 9:15 P.M., past the end of class. To bring them back to reality as the class leaves, Professor Livingston barks out, "Don't forget your new life of writing. I'm going to be checking up on you!"

With the exception of the student who sometimes plays computer games during class, the young men and women I have been observing are model citizens. But all colleges have to deal with first-year students who turn up to class under the influence of alcohol or who are otherwise disruptive, sometimes e-mailing and texting during class or carrying on a conversation while the professor tries to lecture. So after the students have left, I ask Professor Livingston how he deals with aberrant behavior when it happens in his classroom.

In the beginning of this seminar, he says, there were two guys who weren't exactly disruptive but were starting out on the wrong foot. They always came to class together and while it was OK for them to chat before seminar began, they would often continue to talk while he was trying to get the seminar started. At one point he had to stop and ask them to end their private conversation because it was disrupting the class. They have been fine ever since. "One year I had a freshman woman whose texting during class got so bad that I had to call her into my office," Professor Livingston continues. "I was very direct with her. 'Your parents are paying a lot of money for you to be here. So if you are going to spend your time in seminar texting friends, save your parents' money and go to the University of Phoenix!' I didn't have to mention it again."

This is my last time observing Professor Livingston's class and I thank him for permitting me to sit in. As we get up to leave, he asks me what I thought of the seminar. I tell him that I have been very impressed not only by the caliber of the first-year students but also by the seminar itself, which has been an example for me of active learning at its best. Professor Livingston thanks me for my comments, then impresses me further. "I was serious about turning these freshmen into accomplished writers," he says. "They don't know this will happen yet, but in April of their senior year I will choose two essays that represent the best effort of each student, do some minor editing, and then have the essays bound as a proper book. Just before graduation in May three years from now, I will reconvene the class and present each member with the bound collection."

What a wonderful graduation present, I think to myself. And what a wonderful professor.

4

First-Year Finance

The high cost of a college education at both at private and public insti- tutions is a national concern at all levels of society. By most estimates, college costs have increased well above the annual rate of inflation. In the opinion of many, this rate of increase is unsustainable, raising questions about the viability of a college education for all but the very wealthy. But a subsidiary issue, and one that exacerbates the high cost of a college education, is that young people are often clueless when it comes to personal finance. We send them off to college without knowing what a budget is or how to balance a checkbook. Worse, we sometimes lead them to think that credit cards are an endless source of free money for them. The result is not only higher college bills but also a generation of college graduates who are incapable of managing their finances.

In this chapter, I address college costs, especially as they affect parents and their first-year students. How much debt is too much debt? What happens when crisis strikes and we are unable to pay the tuition bill? What do first-year students say about the financial pressures they are under and what suggestions do *they* have for managing college costs? Is it a good idea to take on a campus job? And finally, where exactly does all the hard-earned money we pay for tuition go?

On a bleak autumn day, I arrive on the campus of Washington College in Chestertown, Maryland, and look for Bunting Hall, the main administration building, where I am to meet Josh, a first-year student assigned to me by the college. I will be on the campus of this small liberal arts college for a few days to look into how new students and their parents are coping with the high cost of going to college, and Josh is serving as my host. A modish-looking kid wearing a brown fedora, he flashes a confident smile and introduces himself.

The plan is for Josh to take me to meet Jeani Narcum and Debbie Bergen—respectively, Washington College's director of financial aid and its accounts receivable manager—at the Office of Student Financial Aid. We cross the campus lawn, a broad expanse of green that fronts the college from its southern to northern extremities. Off in the distance I see a larger-than-life statue of George Washington, a gray eminence overseeing this bucolic campus. Washington contributed to the founding of the college in the eighteenth century and permitted it to use his name. We talk as we walk.

"I'm a townie, born and bred right here on the Eastern Shore," Josh says with a soft but distinctive Maryland drawl. "My dad is a waterman on the Chester River and my mom stays at home with my younger sister."

I ask Josh whether he is the first in his family to go to college. "I'm the first to graduate from *high school*," he responds with obvious pride. "Both mom and dad were high school dropouts."

"So are you here on scholarship?" I ask.

"You gotta be kidding," he says with a look of total disbelief. "No way could I have come here without financial help. My dad makes enough off crabbing just to get by." Josh tells me that even five months ago, going to college wasn't exactly in the cards for him. He didn't even bother to apply until one of his high school teachers told him that Washington College had a generous financial aid program. So he wondered what he could lose by trying. To his amazement, he was accepted the last week of August and got a pretty decent financial aid package as well, though not enough for room and board. So he's still living at home with his parents. But all in all Josh says that he has nothing to complain about. "If I hadn't gotten into Washington College, I'd probably be in the army right now."

Josh is among the 80 percent of all first-year students at Washington College receiving some sort of financial aid. And his story is typical. Paying for a college education is a big issue for most parents, and it isn't getting any cheaper. In 1975, the average cost (room, board, and tuition) of a private four-year college was a bit over $4,467. In 2014 it was $42,419.[1] Understanding that even in 1975 students received scholarships, an increase of this magnitude is still rather scary. The situation isn't much better at public universities. Because of state budget cutbacks, many publics are beginning to resemble their private counterparts as they also have had to increase tuition and fees at alarming rates.

We hang a left onto Martha Washington Square and enter the faux colonial building that houses the financial aid office, where Jeani Narcum and Debbie Bergen are waiting for me. As we part, Josh says, "I'll see you tomorrow, Dr. Martin. The financial aid office has arranged for us to chat so you can get a freshman's perspective on college costs."

What Are Some of the Financial Challenges Parents and Students Will Deal with First Year?

Twenty years ago, directors of financial aid were laureled heroes. Back then, doling out money was fun. Today, however, with the financial aid resources of most colleges and universities stretched to the limit, financial aid directors like Jeani Narcum are sometimes demonized as being too stingy, especially by parents who try to bargain up the amount of financial aid they feel their children deserve. And accounts receivable managers like Debbie Bergen, who actually collect the bills, are in an even less enviable position.

What are some of the ways Jeani Narcum sees financial stress play itself out with the first-year students and parents they work with? One scenario in which financial stress comes to the fore is when parents lose control of what they have budgeted by giving their college-bound children carte blanche access to credit cards or allow them to charge at the bookstore using their campus IDs. All of a sudden they get their child's first credit card statement or student account bill and can't understand why it's so much. They then phone people like Debbie Bergen to find out what's going on.

"Just this morning," Bergen says, "a father of a current freshman called me concerned about the quarterly student accounts bill he had just received. 'Why is there is an $800 charge from the bookstore?' he demanded to know. 'How can books cost $800? Are you trying to bankrupt us?'" She explains that this is the classic example of the left hand not knowing what the right hand is doing. This man's daughter had been using her student ID card to charge all sorts of things at the bookstore besides books, such as clothing, food, lattes, and you name it. And, of course, she hadn't bothered to tell her father.

"Most freshman parents understand tuition, room, and board because it's publicized," Jeani Narcum says. "But it's the *other* expenses that sometimes drive them nuts. Limitless charging privileges don't work for every student. Some parents need to give their kids a debit card instead." She adds that she has been begging the Student Affairs Office to do a seminar during orientation on simple budgeting as a requirement for all new students, an idea that many colleges have already implemented.

Debt is another factor that creates financial stress. Of the 350 freshmen who arrived at Washington College this fall, 291 of them—83 percent of the first-year class—were deemed to have some level of financial need. The college was able to meet 81 percent of this need through a combination of state, federal, and institutional resources that don't need to be paid back, but much of the balance was covered by debt in the form of loans, which do need to be paid back—and with interest.

Unfortunately, because of the economy, students are borrowing more than ever. In 2001, according to *The American Freshman: National Norms*, 44.8 percent of first-year college students nationally had taken out loans. In 2011, three years after the stock market tanked, 52.5 percent of all first-year students were borrowing, an increase of 7.7 percent.[2] This increase in debt has alarming implications. According to *New York Times* columnist Ron Lieber, between 2007 and 2009, 206,000 students graduated from college with more than $40,000 in student debt, a ninefold increase over 1998. Lieber sees these high debt levels as an "eerie echo" of the subprime mortgage crisis that, in part, caused the 2008 recession.[3] This fact is even more troubling because it is increasingly hard to declare bankruptcy on college loans.[4]

In light of these sobering data, I ask Narcum and Bergen how much debt they consider to be too much. In the past, this question would have seemed irrelevant—loans were a much smaller portion of the total financial package, and the default rate was incredibly low for private colleges and universities. For many years the student loan default rate at Washington College was only around 0.05 percent, and most students paid off their loans within six years of graduation. But can this low default rate be sustained if student debt levels increase? In 2001, 5.6 percent of entering first-year students who took the aforementioned *American Freshman* survey reported that they expected to borrow $10,000 or more for their first-year expenses. In 2011 this number had more than doubled to 13.3 percent.[5] Meanwhile the job market for graduates remains relatively flat.

The level of debt a student can or should take on will vary from family to family, of course, but it can be disastrous, especially in these very uncertain times, when students take on too much debt. "I know a student who graduated last year and who planned to work in the not-for-profit sector," Jeani Narcum says. "He was Washington College's 'Mr. Volunteer.' When he graduated he was $80,000 in debt. I was very concerned because this level of debt is uncomfortably high considering his career plans and I told him so. When I called him last week to find out how he was doing, he told me that because the nonprofit sector wasn't hiring, he had to take a job as a waiter. Even though his head is just above water financially, he still believes that he can keep up with his loan payments. I'm not sure about this, but what can I say? At some point you have to trust that these kids will figure it out for themselves."

It goes without saying that because college debt is increasing— 71 percent of college students in 2013 graduated with an average of $29,400 in debt[6]—we must give serious consideration to how we finance our children's higher education. Needless to say, most students should not plan to graduate with $80,000 of debt! Depending on one's financial situation, even $30,000 might be too much. So what are the options?

First, always try to get as much scholarship and institutional aid money as possible that does not have to be paid back. If your feel that the loan portion of the financial aid package is too high, encourage your child to revisit the financial aid office. People like Jeani Narcum are extremely resourceful and can often discover little known and often underused scholarships that don't need to be paid back. And if your student is thinking about going into a service profession such as teaching or social work or health care, they should enquire about federal education loans that can be wholly or partially excused if they are willing to teach or work in underserved urban or rural areas. Financial aid people will know about these possibilities as well.

Second, encourage your student to get a campus and summer job. It's surprising to me how many students who graduate with heavy debt never considered working while in college.

Third, think hard about whether it is imperative that your student go straight on to a four-year college after high school. There are other, lower cost alternatives worth considering. As a college president, I saw far too many first-year students who either were not ready for college (socially or academically) or didn't have the inclination to attend one. And this is OK. There is nothing wrong (indeed, everything right) with serving one's country in the military or through a service organization like AmeriCorps or by taking on an apprenticeship to learn a trade. All three can lead to further education down the road, if desired. Another great option for families who don't have the financial resources to pay for an expensive four-year college education is to encourage their children to enroll in an inexpensive community college for the first two years and then (again if they are interested) to complete the last two years at a four-year college or university. Many four-year colleges have articulation agreements with local community colleges (as Washington College does), making transfer almost seamless.[7]

Finally, and perhaps most important, it is widely agreed that getting a four-year baccalaureate degree is well worth it, even if your child incurs debt—that, ultimately, total life income will far surpass the income of someone who only graduated from high school. The problem is taking on debt and then *not* getting a degree![8] An incredible 47 percent of college students, including those who attend community college, never graduate.[9]

What happens when families are under financial duress and are having difficulty paying the tuition bill? Debbie Bergen first tries to make phone contact with the parents to find out if there are reasons why the bill hasn't been paid and to help work out a payment plan if this is the case. If they cannot be contacted in this way, multiple billing statements are sent out. Bergen says that she really wants to work out a way parents can make payments. But if they can't and all other financial resources have been exhausted, the student may be asked to leave.

Some people might feel that business office people like Debbie Bergen are being heartless when they try to collect on late tuition payments, or when first-year students are forced to drop out because of nonpayment. But the fact is, colleges have expenses, too, such as faculty and staff salaries, and therefore must collect tuitions in a timely manner in order to pay their own bills. One of the hardest things I had to do each semester as a college president was review with the business office the list of tuition payment defaults and then sometimes notify otherwise deserving students that they couldn't return next semester unless they and their families could pay the bill. Nobody enjoys doing this.

I ask Jeani Narcum and Debbie Bergen what they think colleges without enormous financial resources can do to make education more affordable so that students aren't saddled with so much debt. Narcum admits that this is a difficult question. Each year, she says, Washington College gives out approximately $15 million in institutional grants. Of this, $2.5 million comes from the college's modest endowment. The rest is the result of tuition discounting. This year, 40.2 percent of the college's first-year tuition was turned back into financial aid. "We're lucky," she says. "Some colleges are discounting at 60 percent or even more. But this is how we keep college affordable."

Narcum is talking about the "sticker price" of a college education (what it advertises as its tuition) versus what parents and students actually end up paying. The American public is correctly alarmed by the steep increases in tuition we have seen over the past couple of decades. But much of this increase is given back in the form of financial aid. Indeed, two-thirds of all first-year students are not paying the advertised sticker price. While discounting has helped to make college more affordable, the discount rate cannot keep going up forever. It's simple mathematics: at some point the return on tuition will not be adequate to support the college's operation.

Do Jeani Narcum and Debbie Bergen have any advice for first-year students and their parents? "Yes," Bergen says.

For parents: read the communications we send you and then call us if you don't understand them. Too many parents don't take advantage of the help we can offer. For freshmen: read your college e-mails for goodness sake! You are the generation that is constantly twittering and texting each other. I recently sent an e-mail and a follow-up letter to a freshman reminding him that he needed to complete his Stafford Loan application on time or risk a fine. He responded to neither, missed the deadline, and to his father's chagrin was fined $100. As it turned out, this student's campus mailbox and e-mail account were full of unopened mail. Not reading your mail and e-mail can become very costly.

Narcum offers her own advice: "We must remember that this is the first time most new students and their parents have had to pay a tuition bill and they become confused when filling out financial aid and loan forms. It's like trying to figure out your own income tax without an accountant. No wonder there is so much frustration! Don't get rattled. And as Debbie said, use us. This is what we are here for."

Sadly, not all colleges and universities can claim Jeani Narcum's and Debbie Bergen's level of competence and service. Some colleges are simply misleading in what kind of financial aid is available to incoming students, overstating the availability of institutional scholarships in their literature but ending up packaging too much debt.[10] Some financial aid directors (really a small number) don't know what the external scholarship possibilities are or are too lazy to find out. Others are not particularly "user friendly," out of touch with the students they counsel. Of course, financial aid offices cannot be blamed when first-year students refuse to use their services, as is the case 62 percent of the time. But it is equally disconcerting that almost 11 percent of first-year students feel dissatisfied with the financial aid office.[11] In my opinion, all colleges and universities, as part of their retention efforts, should be actively tracking the financial aid status of their first-year students because lack of proper funding is one of the leading causes of attrition.

If your first-year student is struggling financially, what can you do? Of course, the best time to negotiate a financial aid package is before your child accepts admission.[12] But if this didn't happen, ask your child to revisit the financial aid office in search of additional scholarship money. If this doesn't work, you should try to renegotiate your financial aid package at the beginning of your child's sophomore year, especially if your financial situation has changed for the worse.

What Does a First-Year Student Say about the Financial Challenges He Is Facing?

Josh and I regroup. We talk about how he is dealing with the $42,992 that Washington College charges its students for tuition and fees. Like most students with financial need, Josh is not paying full freight. He tells me that he received a $21,000 outright scholarship from the college, and the federal government then chipped in with a $4,000 Educational Opportunity Grant and with $5,350 for a Pell Grant. In addition, he earns $1,500 for a Work Study job and $3,500 working in the dining hall, leaving a difference of $7,642 per year. Taking into account about $3,000 he can make over the summer, Josh will graduate with about $18,500 of debt, much of it covered by a low-interest Stafford Loan.

Josh plans to major in music, his passion, but since music is not always equated with high-paying employment right after graduation he worries about how he will pay off his debt. "Maybe I should major in accounting and become an investment banker with Goldman Sachs," he says as an afterthought and with some sarcasm.

A raging controversy in higher education is whether it makes sense to major in a liberal arts discipline especially if students are incurring debt in the process. What can someone do with a major in music or anthropology or art history in this cutthroat work environment, we wonder? It could very well be that Josh will have to forgo his love of music and major in a more vocational discipline like accounting so that he can find a higher-paying job and pay off his college loans as quickly as possible. But there are other options worth considering, such as doing a dual major that pairs a liberal arts discipline like music with a more vocational one. My son-in-law, for example, double-majored in music and business at New York University and now owns a company that provides background music for corporate ads. Interning can also help chart a viable postcollege career path. The point is, students shouldn't consider a major they otherwise have no interest in pursuing *only* because it will garner a large salary. This is a recipe for almost certain unhappiness down the road. But they must plan ahead and explore their career options. Graduating from college with high debt and no clue about a career plan is foolhardy. So, in addition to considering a double major or doing an internship, first-year students should visit the career-planning office early on. Students needn't decide right away what their first jobs will be; but by checking out career possibilities sooner rather than later, they will be in a much better position to be productively employed down the road.

To help address his financial concerns, Josh has not one but two campus jobs. He has a Work Study job at the Global Information System Lab at the college making three-dimensional buildings on the computer. He also works in the dining hall. All total, Josh works about fifteen hours per week. While work doesn't interfere with his studies, Josh laments that he doesn't always have the luxury of a free weekend to party. "On the other hand, I'm not spending lots of money on beer every weekend like some of my friends are," he says. Josh tells me that so far his grades are mostly As and Bs.

Josh offers some additional suggestions for keeping college costs down. For instance, because of his family's tight financial situation, his parents have required him since he was ten to create a personal budget and then stick with it. "Money doesn't grow on trees, and so you might as well learn this early on because from now on you're going to have to live within your means and a budget helps you do this." Josh also collects coupons, something his mother taught him to do. "You'd be amazed at how many local businesses offer coupons as well as student discounts. I bet I've already saved almost $1,000. Oh yes, and get your books secondhand. They're the same as new books, but they're a heck of a lot cheaper!"

Should a First-Year Student Take on a Campus Job?

As tuitions continue to increase and financial aid budgets hold steady or, indeed, diminish over time, more and more students like Josh will have to pitch in to help pay for their education. Consequently, I want to get the perspective of Natalie Story, who oversees Washington College's Federal Work Study program, on the advisability of first-year students taking on campus jobs. Does working negatively affect academics? What are the benefits of working? What's the maximum number of hours a first-year student should work?

"This fall, ninety-five out of 350 freshmen are on Federal Work Study," Story says, "but if you want to know what percentage of the freshman class is doing *any* kind of work, I would give a ballpark estimate of about 40 percent."[13] So is taking on a campus job a good or a bad thing for first-year students to do? Story says that for the most it's a good thing. "Of course, not all parents will agree with this position," she says. "Some will say things like 'I don't want my daughter stressed with work.' Or, 'She is playing field hockey and that will take up all of her free time.' Or, 'Working will be too much for her.' Frankly, anybody working six to ten hours per week isn't going to suffer academically. Just the opposite."

Story tells me that there are several benefits to a campus job. First-year students who do this become connected to the college at many different levels and as a consequence tend to be happier alums once they graduate. Also, as long as they don't work too many hours, new students tend not to drop out of college after the first year. It's harder to leave a college when you have established multiple relationships, inside and outside the classroom. "But there are more personal benefits," she continues. "A campus job helps freshmen learn new skills. It builds their resume. It teaches them time management skills. By balancing academics with a campus job, freshmen tend to use their time more efficiently." Besides the fact that work is character building, it also makes first-year students appreciate their education—sensing that their education isn't just a free gift from their family but something they *also* worked hard to obtain.

And how much work is too much? "I would say no more than twenty hours a week max. If they were working twenty hours in high school they can probably manage twenty hours in college.[14] If they never worked before, then I would say six to ten hours might be better." Story's observation is supported by hard data showing that students who work between one and twenty hours per week perform a little better in the classroom than students who do not work at all. However first-year students who work more than twenty hours per week do less well.[15]

"I believe strongly that college is more than just the classroom," Story says. "Extracurricular activities like sports or clubs or volunteer work are also part of a liberal arts education. Same thing with a campus job. Not only do freshmen get a lot of practical experience, but when they graduate they become much more attractive job candidates."

So, Where Does All Your Hard-Earned Tuition Money Go? A President Talks Candidly about College Cost

I don't think the issue of college cost will go away any time soon. For the time being at least, tuition will continue to increase in both the private and public sectors, though hopefully at a more modest rate than in the past. I know this from personal experience. For each of the twenty years I was a college president, tuition at virtually every independent college and university in America, including my own, increased well above the rate of inflation, outraging the American public who wanted to know why this was the case, what college presidents like me were doing about it, and what all the money was being used for in the first place. Because the buck stops at the president's door, I decide to drop in on Baird Tipson, twenty-sixth president of Washington College, to hear what he had to say about this national issue.

We sit in the kitchen of the president's residence, the Hynson-Ringgold House, an early eighteenth-century sprawling brick affair facing the Chester River. It has a "Washington Slept Here" feel to it, and indeed, maybe he did. President Tipson has just returned from a grueling day with his senior staff trying to figure out how to shave another 5 percent off the budget. On behalf of college parents everywhere, I ask him to explain what their tuition dollars are used for.

President Tipson says that because colleges are labor intensive, a large percentage of the tuition goes to pay faculty and staff salaries. But colleges also have to pay for health care insurance, for computers and computer networks, for books and periodicals, for scientific equipment, for heating and ventilation, and increasingly, because of reductions in federal and state support, for financial aid. Public universities have the same expenses, but, of course, their lower tuitions are partly subsidized by the state.

Stating what every college president in the country intuitively knows, I point out that tuitions can't keep going up over the rate of inflation forever. At some point only a small group of wealthy people will be able to afford a college education. "I worry about that as well," President Tipson replies. "How can we make education more affordable?" he asks. "How can we bring tuition increases under control? Aren't there costs we can cut?" Answering his own questions, he points out that colleges like his can't very well cut costs by reducing faculty and staff salaries, which make up a major portion of his budget. Compared to what other professionals with similar training earn, faculty and staff compensation is relatively low. In fact, over the past decade most colleges have had trouble keeping salaries at the rate of inflation, and in some years they have actually lost ground. "So we can't—and we won't—balance our budgets on the backs of our faculty and staff." Nor can colleges cut health insurance or energy costs. President Tipson points out what every employer knows—that both of these costs have been rising much faster than the rate of inflation and that they are beyond a college's control. He says that there's nothing more frustrating to him than finally getting next year's budget balanced in May, only to have it thrown out of whack in September when health insurance rates go up at a double digit rate. "Of course, we can trim the budget around the edges, just as I was doing earlier today with my senior staff, but doing this can become counterproductive" he says. "So until health insurance and energy costs are brought under control, or until someone drops a large amount of endowment on us, we must pass some of these increases on to families in the form of tuition hikes."

I point out to President Tipson that what he just told me is of little consolation to parents who have to pay more and more each year. According to Sallie Mae, rising tuition continues to be a major economic concern for today's parents.[16] "Yes, I know. I know," President Tipson sighs. "I think all of us in higher education are *painfully* aware of the sacrifices parents have to make so that their children get a good education." He tells of a first-year parent who pulled him aside at Fall Family Weekend. "Why is tuition so expensive?" this father asked in exasperation. "It seems out of line with everything else I have to pay for." President Tipson responded that this parent was right, that college *is* a major expense. But then again, this father's expectation is that the college education his son receives will fundamentally change his son's life. And this simply cannot be done on the cheap.

What President Tipson doesn't mention (but I will) is the fact that after taking into account increased discounting, grants, and tax benefits, the real cost of a college education has not varied much over the last ten years.[17]

President Tipson suggests that in the future it could be that advancements in technology will make it cheaper to operate a liberal arts college like his, but it's hard to imagine that technology will ever be a silver bullet. We agree that technology can never, for instance, replace real professors having face-to-face contact in and outside the classroom with small numbers of students. So can a college president cut costs by making faculty teach more classes? President Tipson shakes his head. "There is an erroneous notion out there that faculty who teach four courses per semester work only twelve hours a week. As a former faculty member, I can tell you that a typical faculty member puts in fifty to sixty hours or more a week." The time a faculty member spends in front of a class of students is just the tip of the iceberg. Preparing for classes and labs, grading papers, and meeting with students takes up countless hours, in addition to which faculty members share in the operation of a college by serving on important faculty committees like the one that determines whether a faculty member will gain tenure or be promoted. "Just as important, we want members of our faculty to be actively contributing to their disciplines by doing their own research," he continues. "The employers where many of our graduates will seek jobs, and the graduate schools others hope to attend, expect them to understand the very latest developments in their chosen field, not the knowledge of ten or twenty years ago. To stay current in a field one needs to be involved in the trial and error of contributing to it. Active research keeps teaching alive and current."

I empathize with the dilemma President Tipson has expressed here. Quality education *is* expensive. And with health care insurance and energy costs sometimes out of control and state and federal funding declining relative to the cost of living, there are no simple solutions to containing college costs. Perhaps we need to scale back on building new facilities like the ones I see rising on this and many other campuses. Do we need state-of-the-art performing arts centers or fancy dining facilities? But then again, the very people who complain about tuition increases expect colleges and universities to provide their children with these amenities, perhaps explaining why over the past decade colleges are spending a larger share of their budgets on recreational facilities and a smaller share on instruction.[18]

As I well know, the issue of college cost is sometimes a catch-22 for college presidents, and it's on presidents' minds more than parents might think.

5

Living on Campus

One of higher education's great debates is whether online courses will eventually replace the need for residential colleges. The arguments for online colleges are compelling, especially to parents who, as we have just seen, must bear the ever-increasing costs of a college education. If our children can get a college degree from the comfort of their room, thus reducing tuition and eliminating altogether the cost of room and board, why have residential colleges at all?[1]

While current educational technologies like massive open online courses might reduce college cost and even increase learning, college isn't just about academics.[2] Residential colleges are also places where young people begin to learn how to become responsible citizens, where they live in diverse residential communities, learn how to manage their financial resources, gain leadership skills in student government and on athletic teams, develop a sense of moral and ethical responsibility, and prepare for positions of responsibility in a democratic society. This is difficult to do if they never leave the comfort of their homes. So what happens outside the classroom to help prepare students for their futures? Indeed, what is life like in the residence halls and during the weekend? And what happens to students when they get into trouble?

To get a sense of what life is like in a residence hall, I check into Dimmitt, a former women's residence at Morningside College, a regional comprehensive college in the suburbs of Sioux City, Iowa. The building, which was built in the 1930s, is a U-shaped pile of red brick with two wings that were added sometime in the late 1950s or early 1960s. Today, a large portion of the first-year class lives here, with men on one side and women on the other. The interior is what one might expect a largely first-year residence hall to be: narrow hallways with small rooms lined up on each side. Each room holds two single beds, two battered desks, a dresser, and not much else. This, my home for the next week, brings back a flood of memories, some of them even pleasant.

Sheri Hineman, the residence hall director, drops by my room to greet me. She gives me two keys, one for my room and one for the front door. She then points out the bathroom across the hall, a rather basic, Clorox-smelling affair. I thank Hineman for her help and then I crawl into one of the two beds in my Spartan room. A boom box down the hall is blaring hip-hop music. I sleep fitfully until a blessed quiet descends at 3 A.M.

How to Deal with Separation Anxiety and Why Parents Need to Chill

I'm up at 6:30 sharp and decide to head out to the Olsen Student Center, a modern dining hall just off the main campus, to grab some breakfast and maybe meet some first-year students. I'm alone in the early morning dusk as I walk up an extremely steep hill toward Olsen. As I enter the dining hall I am greeted warmly by Connie, an exceptionally friendly Sodexo food service employee. I look around the expansive and altogether pleasant dining room. Not one student is to be seen. What was I thinking? The kids all went to bed around three this morning and are still sound asleep.

After my solo breakfast, I visit the office of Shari Benson, director of new students. Many colleges employ a person like Benson whose primary responsibility is to keep an eye on first-year students. My objective in meeting with her is to explore in a bit more depth what takes place right after parents say good-bye to their kids and the end of orientation.

Shari Benson conjures up the image of a sympathetic parent the moment you meet her. Indeed, she is so familiar to Morningside students that she is known around campus as "Morningside's Mom" and has been known to bring home-baked cookies to her meetings with new students.

For most parents, having a child leave for college is a big deal, one of those seismic moments in life. It's not the same thing as when they went off to summer camp for a couple weeks because they eventually returned. Rather, going off to college often means leaving home *for good* because the beginning of college generally signals the beginning of independence from family and home.

Benson and I compare notes on the pregnant moment when parents are gently asked to leave campus. At Morningside College this happens the very first day of orientation, right after the 4 P.M. question-and-answer session for parents. In my experience, parents sometimes just don't want to leave and linger on and on and on. But she tells me that, at Morningside, parents really do leave when they are asked to. Of course, there are lots of tears. But then, once parents have gone, homesickness eventually begins to set in for some first-year students. This usually happens sometime between the end of orientation and the beginning of classes. So right after orientation ends, the RAs have lots of activities going on in the residence halls to keep the new students involved. Then soon after orientation, Benson meets with each new student individually and encourages them to attend the college's activities fair at the beginning of fall semester and sign up with at least one club or organization. She also suggests that they not go home Labor Day, thus cutting the metaphorical umbilical cord and establishing that campus is now their home.

Most students survive these first moments of independence after their parents say good-bye to them. But there is a safety net for those who waver. Resident assistants and professors teaching first-year courses are instructed to call Benson if they spot a homesick or depressed student, and she then arranges a follow-up meeting. Indeed, most colleges, concerned about premature attrition, watch closely for signs of depression like unexplained absences from class or students who rarely leave their residence hall.

When I first became a college president in the mid-eighties, first-year parents tended to be reserved and unassertive. We only heard from them when there was a really serious problem, like their child getting into trouble with the police. But starting in the mid-nineties, a key topic of senior staff meetings was the high volume of postorientation phone calls we were receiving from parents concerned about rather minor issues like a broken refrigerator or a roommate problem that could—and should—be resolved by the students themselves. Enter the helicopter parent—moms and dads who "hover" above their children, refusing to let go and, in the process, assuring that they will never grow up.[3] The advent of the helicopter parent began, I think, when tuitions started to spike and parents saw college as a commodity, like a new automobile, rather than a privilege. Consequently, if they felt the product was shoddy or defective they would complain, more often than not, directly to the president.

I ask Benson how involved parents of first-year students get here at Morningside. "How much time do we have?" she responds with a hearty laugh. "Let's just stay with the homesickness issue because this often generates a tremendous amount of parental concern. For example, a mom called me soon after orientation this fall to say that her son was super homesick. But after talking with her for awhile, it became apparent to me that it was mom who was super homesick, not her son! When I met the son as a follow-up to his mother's call, he was bubbling over with enthusiasm. 'How's it going?' I asked. 'Great,' he answered. 'Have you been home?' 'No.' 'Do you miss your family?' 'Not really.'"

And it's not just homesickness issues. Parents sometimes feel that their child cannot survive without them and therefore become overly protective, feeling they must constantly be in contact with their child. So how often should parents and children be on the phone with each other? "Not ten times per day!" Benson responds, adding that going home every weekend is not a good sign either. According to a recent study, 23.5 percent of first-year students report frequently going home on weekends.[4] The excuse some first-year students use for spending every weekend at home is that there's nothing to do on campus. "There's *plenty* to do on the weekends!" Benson exclaims. "Just look at the Morningside website."

OK. So your child has settled in. Things seem to be going pretty well. He's not coming home every weekend, and you aren't speaking to him ten times per day. When he does call, he reports enjoying his new life as a college student. And then, all of a sudden, you get wind of the fact that not everything is so great. You discover that he is having roommate problems. Or he didn't make the football team. Or he got a D on his first physics test. He's ready to give up. What now? In my experience, poor initial grades are often caused by too much partying and too little study.[5] The result is one of those grim family conversations over the holidays when parents begin to question whether the return on their investment is worth it. Perhaps your child should throw in the towel and come home? "No," Benson says. "Parents act positively when they encourage their student to have a good time but to make academics their priority," she continues, repeating what Dean Long told me at Vassar. "When academics are not going well, parents are not helpful when they tell their student to just give up. In this situation, tough love is what's needed! They need to tell their student to maybe reduce their academic load if it's overwhelming and stick it out." Parents should also encourage their children to meet with their academic advisers.

Shari Benson's parting words: "Trust that you raised your freshman well. Now is the time for your child to be independent and to grow up." She pauses and smiles. "If you think about it, we parents grow up as well. By the time my kids graduated from college, I was a new person. It's not just a one-way street!"

Everything You Wanted to Know about Residence Hall Life but Were Afraid to Ask: Roommates, Noise, and Coeducational Dorms

Often, the trauma of the first week of college is followed by. . . . silence! Some parents, who just three or four weeks ago were saying emotional good-byes, have yet to hear from their children and are wondering what happened to them. The following letter was shared with me by a first-year parent whose daughter had not written or called for at least a month after orientation:[6]

Dear Mom and Dad,

This letter may come as a pretty big shock to you. I think you better sit down to read it. I'm very sorry I haven't written or called, and I hope you haven't been worrying about me. Actually, my leg is much better now . . . you know, the leg I broke when I jumped out the window during the dormitory fire, after the campus riots. But this fellow who works in the garage across the street from our dorm was so nice; he let me move right into his apartment with him. And now I think I'm in love. And don't worry, we've decided not to get married until after the baby is born next year. Will that be all right with you, Mommy and Daddy?

P.S. I didn't really break my leg, and there was no dormitory fire or campus riot. I'm not in love . . . yet. And I'm not going to have a baby. But I'm flunking math and getting a D in history, and I just thought you ought to know how much worse things could be.

For the majority of parents, what goes on after their children have been dropped off for orientation—especially what goes on in the residence halls—is a big mystery and so they often imagine the worst, egged on by their sometimes evasive children. Do roommates really get along? Is it true that residence halls are defined by binge drinking, random sex, and loud noise? And what about men and women living together in the same building?

The person most knowledgeable about what goes on in the residence halls is the director of residence life. At Morningside College, this person is the aforementioned Sheri Hineman. She not only is the resident director of Dimmitt, the college's largest residence hall, but also oversees residential life for the entire college.

So how is your child's roommate selected? The procedure followed by Morningside and managed by Hineman is fairly typical for many colleges. Well before they arrive for orientation, all new students fill out a questionnaire that asks all sorts of questions about their living preferences, like when they get up in the morning and go to bed at night or what their study habits are. This questionnaire is then used to assign rooms based on these preferences. For example, Hineman will often put athletes together because they have early morning practice.

However, because roommate assignments sometimes cause anxiety (as we saw with Phoebe as she was leaving for Tufts), the process can get complicated. Hineman tells me that at Morningside about 10 percent of the first-year class doesn't want to be assigned a stranger as a roommate and requests to live with someone they already know, like a friend from high school. She usually turns these requests down. Why? Because living with a stranger is an important part of your children's education. It provides an opportunity for them to learn how to deal with people who come from a completely different social or religious background, or who have different tastes, or who subscribe to a different political philosophy. In other words, by living with someone they don't know, your children are being prepared to live in an increasingly diverse and multicultural society. This doesn't always happen when they room with friends or (as 25 percent of prospective college students do) use online roommate matching services like Facebook's roomsync.com to find a mirror image of themselves.

Parents complicate the process when they become overly involved. It still amazes me the number of phone calls I received when I was a college president from parents trying to engineer their children's roommates. Sheri Hineman faces this problem as well. "I had a freshman return his roommate questionnaire during summer registration," she tells me, "only to discover that his mother had completed and mailed in the same questionnaire several weeks before. Needless to say, her son was mortified."

Not that questionnaires guarantee a perfect match. According to a recent study, almost 50 percent of first-year students report having difficulty living together.[7] Why does this happen? Well, as you perhaps know, teenagers are not always considerate. Hineman gives an example: "Two freshmen roommates last year here in Dimmitt were soccer players. During practice, one of the roommates collided with another player, causing a minor concussion. After being checked out at the hospital, she was able to return to campus. But when she tried to enter her room that evening, her roommate told her to get lost because she was with her boyfriend. The roommate with the concussion ended up sleeping outside in her car." I later learn that the offender was talked to and when she still refused to apologize was removed from the room. Bad roommate situations happen and when they do they can usually be remedied. But in the first instance colleges want students, not their parents, to seek a solution; after graduation, it will be up to them to deal with annoying neighbors or problematic colleagues.

Sheri Hineman and I turn to a different subject concerning residence hall living, which is to say, the sometimes challenging environment in which first-year students live. Here I can speak with some authority, not so much because I was a college president (most college presidents live in stately homes often at some distance from the undergraduate residence halls) but because I have been living in a typical first-year residence hall for several days and nights.

There are many reasons why first-year residence halls sometimes resemble bedlam, especially in the early fall before midterm exams have taken place. As I am witnessing, most of my male teenage hall mates have an enormous amount of testosterone-driven energy and many of them haven't yet learned how to study. According to a recent study, 36.8 percent of first-year students report having difficulty developing effective study skills, probably as a result of the chaos that surrounds their living situation.[8] So what do our students do when the boom box is at high pitch and there is a floor hockey game going on down the hallway? There are a number of options for quiet study—the library, of course, but also the various public lounges and even the laundry room, where the white noise of washing machines and dryers helps block out the more unpleasant sounds emanating from the hallways. For serious students or, even more so, for students who come to college with a learning disability and require a quiet place to study, colleges like Morningside usually have "quiet dorms." To get into one of these, however, requires a request from the student (again, not from the parent).

Alcohol can also be a disruptive factor. Knowing that all colleges prohibit underage drinking in residence halls (or, for that matter, anywhere else on campus) but also understanding that teenagers will drink anyway, Hineman and I discuss what the drinking situation is like in the residence halls at Morningside and how the college deals with the negative behavior that often results from alcohol abuse.

"Many freshmen have tried alcohol before they arrive at college, some more than others," she says. "And the drinking scene varies from year to year. We don't have statistics, but my gut tells me that 50 percent of our freshmen drink, some of them at the level of binging." Hineman tells me that the college respects the privacy of first-year students and that the RAs don't go looking for alcohol violations. But if there is an obvious problem or the drinking is flagrant, the RAs will write the student up and then pass the offender's name on to the student dean who oversees alcohol-related violations. At Morningside College, this person is Associate Dean Andrew Pflipsen. If the offending students do any damage as a result of drinking, like pushing out window screens or punching holes in a wall, they will get a bill from the college. "Actually, since I've been here," Hineman says, "illegal alcohol consumption has gone down. Getting a sixty dollar fine might be part of the reason, but it also might be because we are doing more education around alcohol abuse. For example, we have an organization here called CHA CHA, the acronym for Choosing Healthy Alternatives, Curbing Harmful Actions, that offers campus-wide programs around wellness. We also have wellness floors that promote healthy living alternatives, including not smoking."

What Hineman says about a reduction in alcohol consumption at Morningside seems to ring true. So far I have not seen any evidence of systemic alcohol abuse like beer cans strewn around the hallways or discharged fire extinguishers. Yet on most college campuses, teenage drinking is a big problem, often resulting in the student involved ending up in the dean's office—or worse.

One of the hot topics concerning residence hall life is whether it's a good idea for men and women to live together in the same residence hall. When I went to college, men and women lived in separate residence halls, but starting in the late '70s, living arrangements began to change rather dramatically—from men and women living in the same residence hall but on separate floors to men and women living on the same floor and even sharing bathrooms. Morningside's situation is kind of a compromise between single-gender and fully integrated residence halls. Here in Dimmitt, men and women live on opposite sides of the building but they can visit each other's rooms until 1 A.M. during the week and 2 A.M. on weekends. Whatever the living arrangements are, most parents (especially the dads with daughters reading this book) probably conjure up all sorts of sinister images when it comes to coeducational living. Truth be told, most first-year men and women living in the same residence hall treat each other as brothers and sisters. If they are doing sinister things, it's probably somewhere else! Also, according to a recent study commissioned by the Association of College and University Housing Officers, first-year students living in a coed residence hall feel slightly more secure than those living in a single-gender residence hall.[9]

I think it is fairly obvious that Morningside College has their act together as far as residence hall living is concerned. But what if your child lands on a campus where this is not the case? What do they do, for example, if they are in an impossible living situation like the concussed soccer player discussed above? Your student—not you—should bring their concern to the appropriate college administrator and, if necessary, work up the college's chain of command. They should go first to the residence hall director (a person like Sheri Hineman), but if nothing happens, the next person up the chain of command (and the person most residence life directors reports to) is probably the dean of students.[10] If there is a legitimate complaint (and not all complaints are legitimate), this person should be able to work out an equitable solution. Parents should resist the urge to override their student and ignore the chain of command. As President Bacow said at Tufts's orientation, the college really wants your student, not you, to deal with matters that affect their lives. And of course, except in the most extreme circumstances, most presidents and board chairs will not get involved in a residence hall dispute.

To What Degree Should Your Child Become Involved in Social and Extracurricular Activities?

On a beautiful fall morning, I meet with Andrew Pflipsen, associate dean of students. While many larger institutions have separate deans, each with responsibilities for either social programming or discipline (at Tufts University and Vassar College, for instance), Dean Pflipsen must wear both hats at Morningside College. In a sense, he deals with first-year students at both ends of the spectrum: those who are leaders and model citizens as well as those who get into trouble. Wearing two or even three hats is typical for administrators working at smaller colleges like Morningside.

A big question on the minds of many is whether first-year students should become involved in out-of-classroom activities such as clubs and athletic teams and to what degree they should, to put it bluntly, enjoy the party scene. My own view is that not taking advantage of all that a college has to offer can result in a truncated and often disappointing college experience. Belonging to a club or socializing with classmates is an integral part of your children's college education. The statistics bear this out: 63.4 percent of first-year students report participating in a club or group, many of them devoted to social outreach and community service.[11] Moreover, evidence suggests that involvement in a club or in student government or on an athletic team complements academic work in beneficial ways.[12]

Dean Pflipsen agrees. "Our philosophy here at Morningside," he tells me, "is to develop students holistically and to provide them with opportunities for leadership. And yes, I, too, think there is a positive correlation between extracurricular activity and academic success. What I know for sure is that first-year students who get involved are most likely to stay in college and graduate."

One concern I share with Dean Pflipsen is that more first-year women than men tend to become involved with the student newspaper, or student government, or a club. I'm not sure why this is. First-year men often say they *plan* to join a club or write for the student newspaper and then never show up. But as Dean Pflipsen points out, fully 67 percent of Morningside's first-year men are involved in intramural or intercollegiate athletics, a figure that is comparable to other colleges, and sports take a lot of time.

Partying is another social activity parents worry about. Parents may wonder whether their children are attending a suitcase college— that is, one at which the majority of students go home on the weekends, resulting in there being nothing to do on campus then—or, at the opposite extreme, a party school, where students are dissipating themselves in profligate debauchery. Of course, most colleges are neither extreme. Monday morning through Friday afternoon is for classes and study, but even during the week colleges like Morningside might sponsor an occasional evening study break. For example, Dean Pflipsen tells me about a midweek program called Salsabrosa Night, when students can take a break from study and learn how to salsa. Weekends are for further study but also for fun. Consequently, most students remain on campus during the weekend. During homecoming weekend ten days earlier, for example, the college was popping with all sorts of activities. Dean Pflipsen then cautions that the coming weekend might be a bit different since there is a big football game in Sioux Falls, South Dakota, and lots of students will go home Friday night and then drive up to the game Saturday morning with their families. So not every weekend will be an entertainment spectacle.

Weekend festivities also take place off campus, especially in upperclass off-campus residences like fraternities and sororities. And since underage alcohol consumption is not permitted on campus, this is where most of the drinking takes place. Indeed, when we think about fraternities and sororities (which are often called Greeks because of their use of Greek symbols for their names), most of us probably have in mind the motion picture *Animal House* where, during the weekend, students drank themselves into complete oblivion. But not all Greeks are this way.

"Our Greeks are very different from most colleges," Dean Pflipsen says. "We have two fraternities and one sorority and they are excellent. They have broken the stereotype of what so many Greeks have become in this country because all three have a purpose beyond being just a place to party and drink. They are heavily involved in community service."

Dean Pflipsen's comment reminds me of what Greeks should be, namely, places where, besides having a good time, students can learn leadership skills and engage in altruistic activities like community service rather than dissipating themselves by constantly drinking and partying. But I see little evidence of this happening, at least at the national level, and I advise students who are contemplating joining a social fraternity or sorority to know beforehand what they are getting themselves into and, in any case, to wait until sophomore year when they have a better handle on their studies. Of course, many colleges—and Vassar is a good example—do not have Greeks.

As Dean Pflipsen and I are talking, I notice a somber-looking kid in the reception area accompanied by equally somber-looking parents. My guess is that he is in trouble for some childish indiscretion. I take my cue and make a diplomatic exit.

What about Your Child's Spiritual Life?

An interesting paradox on most college campuses is that, while first-year students don't attend church or synagogue in large numbers, issues of religion and spirituality are, nevertheless, matters of great interest to them. And so most colleges and universities—even public ones—employ a chaplain or group of chaplains, and often the chaplaincy is an important center of college life, even for students who are not committed to organized religion. Morningside College was founded by Iowa Methodists in 1894, and while most of its students

are not members of the United Methodist Church (Roman Catholics have the largest church representation), the college has a robust
chaplaincy program presided over by Kathy Martin (no relation), an
ordained United Methodist minister. New students immediately feel
comfortable in her presence because she comes across not as a fire-
and-brimstone preacher but as a person who is really interested in
their intellectual and spiritual development.

I ask Martin what percentage of the first-year class is involved in
a church or religious organization. At most nondenominational colleges, such as Vassar or Washington College, for example, the percentage will be relatively low. "We are in the Bible Belt of the Midwest," she says as we sit in her sunny office on the second floor of
Lewis Hall, "so it shouldn't surprise you that 30–50 percent of our
freshmen were actively involved in a church back home. Sometimes
freshmen come to Morningside and are not involved first semester,
but by second semester they will start exploring again. During the
first week of college, I often take interested freshmen on a tour of the
area churches and synagogues so that they can find a church home."
She tells me that every week first-year students get an e-mail from
her with a menu of activities that are sponsored by her office. This
week, for example, besides some worship opportunities and Bible
study, there will be a lecture by Stephen Carter, a well-known law
professor at Yale University who has written extensively on civility;
an opportunity to travel to Cedar Rapids during fall break to help with
flood recovery; and a hunger walk in Sioux City sponsored by Church
World Service. "What I want these students to know," she says "is that
they are spiritual persons and that the spiritual part needs to grow
just like the intellectual and social parts."

Chaplains like Kathy Martin also deal with a wide range of personal issues. "I often see freshmen who are experiencing difficult
family situations," she says, "for example, parents getting a divorce.
I saw a freshman a few weeks ago who came to me after his parents
separated. This young man felt that perhaps he had caused them to
break up and he was contemplating dropping out of college to be with
his mother and little brother. He was looking for encouragement and
support. I told him that he was most certainly *not* the cause of the
break-up and I encouraged him to do the right thing by staying in
college." She believes that encouragement and help in these kinds of

difficult situations make spiritual growth and learning possible. This, of course, can be done by others as well. But most college chaplains see themselves as companions and a resource for students who are seeking to find themselves.

What Is Your Child *Really* Up To?

I once spotted a mother hiding in the bushes outside her daughter's room peeking into the street-level window. I recognized this mother from orientation two weeks before and asked her what she was doing. "I've just got to know what Carrie's up to!" she exclaimed, displaying not a little embarrassment at having been caught in the act by the college president. This is an extreme example of parental concern, but every parent, if he or she is being completely honest, would like to take a surreptitious peak into his or her child's life, just to make sure everything is OK. I understand. I was a first-year college parent myself. But now I'm experiencing this parental fantasy by living in a first-year residence hall

Back at Dimmitt Hall—which I have only recently been told is called the Jungle—I've been having difficulty contacting Barry and his roommate Elliott, who were assigned to me as dorm buddies. My e-mails and phone calls, however, have gone unanswered. Finally, I just walk down the hall and pull Barry out of his room. Elliott is nowhere to be seen, so I invite Hank, who is also in Barry's room, to meet with me in my single room across from the Clorox-scented bathroom and the now dormant boom box. They happily comply.

Come spring, Hank and Barry will be pitchers on the Morningside College baseball team and even though Barry is a Cornhusker from Lincoln, Nebraska, and Hank is a Cyclone from Ames, Iowa, they seem to be best friends. Indeed, they plan to room together next semester. They report that they enjoy being on their own, but they both miss home-cooked food! "And not having to do laundry," Barry adds.

"OK guys, fess up. Have either of you been homesick since arriving at college?" I ask, thinking back to my conversation with Shari Benson about first-year separation anxiety. Barry and Hank look at each other sheepishly, then Hank admits, "I was at first, but it went away when I made friends." There is an awkward pause. "OK, OK," he blurts out on further reflection. "I've got to admit I was *really* homesick twice. The first time was during orientation. I wasn't sure Morningside College was the right place for me. The second time was a few weeks ago when I had a fender bender. I had to drive my car back to Ames to get it fixed and then went to see my mom and my little brother. She and dad just separated and I began thinking that maybe I should stay at home and take care of them. But I came back. It was really hard." I can see a tear welling up in Hank's eye, and I wonder whether he is the first-year student Kathy Martin, the college chaplain, mentioned to me. Morningside is a very close community.

I ask Barry why he is splitting with Elliott, his current roommate, next year.

"Oh, Elliott and I get along fine," Barry says. "It's just that he's a swimmer and has to get up at 5:30 in the morning and so we figured it would be better if we both had roommates who shared the same wake-up times. But I know of other difficult roommate situations, like the two guys upstairs. One parties every night and comes back very early in the morning. The other stays in the room all the time playing Halo on his computer and feels like he's been abandoned. They just aren't compatible."

Thinking of Andrew Pflipsen's description of the robust social scene at Morningside, I ask Hank and Barry whether there is enough to do on campus socially.

"Oh, yeah. Most of us socialize *really* well here," Barry says.

"Where besides the Jungle?" I ask, having survived the midnight flag football games and noisy parties outside my door at the beginning of the week.

Hank and Barry look at each other again, waiting to see who will answer first. "Do you *really* want to know?" Hank asks.

"Absolutely," I say. "Don't worry, I won't snitch on you."

"Well, the seniors on the baseball team have an off-campus place where we and the women's softball team hang out," Barry says, confirming what Dean Pflipsen told me about off-campus parties.

"Yeah, they got plenty of booze and hopping parties going on Fridays and Saturdays," Hank adds.

"But football games are also big," Barry says, not wanting to reveal too much more about the baseball house soirées, "especially this weekend when we play the University of Sioux Falls. They're the number two team in the Midwest and we're number four or five."

"Lots of freshmen will be there," Hank adds. "You oughta go."

"What about fraternities?" I ask. "Do you plan to join one?" At both of my colleges this would be a silly question. Half the student bodies joined fraternities or sororities. But, as Dean Pflipsen pointed out, the Greek scene at Morningside is not a big deal, at least not socially.

"Not me," Barry says. "If I were at the University of Nebraska I might join one. But the baseball team is our fraternity. Most of the freshmen guys gravitate toward a team." Hank is nodding his head in agreement.

I get back to Hank's comment about partying at the baseball house. "So do a lot of your classmates drink?"

"Yes sir," Barry says. "Over 90 percent drink," Hank agrees. "Of course Hank and I don't drink," Barry immediately adds with a devilish grin.

"Of course not," I say. But my bet is that Hank's estimate is inflated. New students often think that this level of drinking is taking place when in fact it isn't. According to the National College Health Assessment performed in 2014 by the American College Health Association, while college students perceive that 94.9 percent of their classmates used alcohol within thirty days of the survey, in fact 66.8 percent actually did, and 20.1 percent abstained altogether.[13]

"If you are quiet, you won't get caught," Barry continues. "Most Morningside freshmen are smart and keep a low profile."

Hank then touches on an issue that is very much under discussion at the highest levels of university administration. "Most freshmen drink to make a point," he says. "We're told that we can't drink. So because we are told we can't drink, we drink anyway. If the legal drinking age was eighteen, I would go to a bar every once in a while and maybe have a couple of beers rather than figuring I have to down a six-pack or two at a party." Barry is nodding in agreement.

Some college presidents would agree with Hank and Barry for the exact reasons these two guys are articulating—to be precise, that if the drinking age was lowered to eighteen, dangerous drinking might diminish considerably. The big question, of course, is whether highway deaths would then increase, as those opposed to lowering the drinking age argue.

"Of course drinking often leads to date rape," I say remembering the "In the Sack" presentation I witnessed at Tufts's orientation.

"Date rape is not that big an issue here," Hank immediately tells me, "though girls drink as much as the guys do. But when we see a girl drunk, we make sure that she gets back to her residence hall."

"Yeah, just last week I saw a freshman girl who was smashed trying to find her residence hall," Barry says. "I was concerned both about her safety and that she was going to get in trouble with the police. So I got her back to her room and got her to eat some bread and drink water."

"What about the dating scene at Morningside?" I ask.

"We don't really date," says Hank. "We mostly hang out with the girls' softball team over at the baseball house we were just talking about." I stand corrected: hanging out, not dating is what this generation does.

"And how did you do on midterms?" All this week, first-year students have been taking their midterm exams, the moment of truth for many of them.

"I bombed a sociology test. But otherwise I think I'm doing OK," Hank replies.

"I'm not doing as well as I wanted to," Barry says. "I'm just going to have to work harder next semester."

The boom box down the hall starts thumping again. "How do you guys study with all this noise?" The weekend is approaching.

"I try to study between 6:30 and 8:00 in the evening," Hank says. "But it's sometimes tough to sleep."

"You just get used to it," Barry adds. "Well, sort of used to it. I have to admit I was pissed the other night when someone put the boom box in the bathroom and turned the volume way up at 4 A.M. That was going too far."

"So what about enforcing the 10 P.M. to 9 A.M. quite hours?" I ask.

"I wouldn't argue against that," Barry replies, to my surprise.

What Happens If Your Child Gets into Trouble?

Midway through my presidency at Randolph-Macon, for reasons I will mention in a moment, I decided that at literally the first event of orientation that year, just after the new students and their families had arrived on campus, I would personally meet with them in Blackwell Auditorium, a facility large enough to accommodate everyone. The students sat directly in front of me, their families in the back. I spoke with force that day because I wanted everyone, families and new students alike, to hear what I had to say. Looking straight at the new students and with all the conviction I could muster I told them that starting *right now* they should focus on being students and avoid all things that might divert them from this task. I said that some students think that college is a time to cast off family values and that while rebellion is a natural thing, some go to the extreme and their days are not spent being college students but being something quite different. I stressed that there are consequences to bad behavior.

I then told them about what had happened the year before. Just after orientation had ended, a large number of first-year students who had bought drugs from a returning older student were arrested by the Virginia State Police in a sting operation. The entire community was in total shock, and dealing with this nightmare was one of the hardest things I had to do as a college president. In the end, five first-year students, who had been recruited by the ring leader to sell drugs at the local high school, went to jail. The others were charged with possession of marijuana, a misdemeanor in Virginia. At least one student ended up serving six months in prison. All were suspended from college. Whether or not they felt grown up, the justice system considered them adults.

What happened at Randolph-Macon unfortunately happens on too many college campuses across America. According to the National Institute of Drug Abuse's "Monitoring the Future" survey in 2012, about 23 percent of high school seniors have tried marijuana in the previous year (6.5 percent use it daily).[14] These figures correspond to a similar survey recently done by the American College Health Association showing that, in 2014, 21.7 percent of college men and 16.3 percent of women used marijuana within thirty days of the survey.[15] Most colleges have zero tolerance for drug use and when students are caught either using or distributing drugs, they are automatically turned over to the police and suspended from college. The first year of college is supposed to be the beginning of a new life. But for some, this new life ends almost before it begins. I wanted these new students and their parents in Blackwell Auditorium that day to know what had happened the year before, and I wanted it to not happen again.

Because of my own experience as a college president with negative student behavior, especially concerning drinking and drugs, I return to Andrew Pflipsen's office, this time to talk about the dark side of his job: dealing with first-year students who manage to get into trouble. What happens when students screw up? How are their indiscretions adjudicated? What are the penalties and consequences for bad behavior? Deans of students like Andrew Pflipsen see almost everything, from violations of residence hall rules, to the illegal consumption of alcohol, to, on rare occasions, the possession and distribution of drugs.

Alcohol is the drug of choice on most college campuses, and it is the main reason why many students get in trouble and end up in the dean's office. Dean Pflipsen shares with me a typical first-year drinking incident:

> I had a freshman this year who was hanging around with upperclassmen. One night, at an off-campus party, he consumed multiple alcohol beverages. I still can't figure out how he managed to get back to campus, but campus security found him passed out on the sidewalk in front of Olsen. The Emergency Medical Service was called and when this kid regained consciousness, he refused to go to the hospital. The EMS people determined that his situation was not a matter of life or death and so called my office. Campus Security then got him back into his residence hall and put him to bed.

As we saw at Tufts's orientation, many colleges have a "three strikes and you're out" policy with underage alcohol consumption. In the incident described by Dean Pflipsen, the offending student ended up in his office the next morning. After a stern lecture, he was then given the option of either paying a sixty dollar fine or, if he agreed to take an alcohol awareness course, to have the financial penalty reduced to twenty dollars. Dean Pflipsen tells me that if this student is again caught consuming alcohol, the penalty will be more severe. A third violation could result in suspension for a semester or more.

Why are colleges so strict about underage drinking? Besides the fact that underage drinking is against the law, alcohol abuse can lead to serious violence, such as date rape. We also know that drinking impairs academic achievement. According to a study by the National

Bureau of Economic Research, all college students, but in particular high-achieving students, experience significant reductions in academic performance when they drink.[16]

Most minor offenses such as getting caught drinking underage are dealt with informally through the dean's office, as we have just seen. If the infraction is serious enough, however, the college's judicial board gets involved. So, how does a judicial board operate?

Many parents incorrectly believe that colleges adjudicate bad behavior the same way the courts do. But while the two systems have some similarities, they are in fact very different. When a Morningside student is accused of breaking a significant college rule, like discharging a fire extinguisher in a residence hall or getting into a fight (both often alcohol related), a judicial hearing officer is appointed by the vice president for Student Life (usually a member of the administration) who then investigates the incident. Within two days, the accused student learns the specifics of the violation after which the officer hears testimony and assigns sanctions. If either the officer or the accused student feels that the violation should go before a larger group, the case is then referred to a judicial hearing board, a group made up of two full-time students appointed by student government, two faculty members, and two members of the administration. The accused student has the right to be accompanied at the closed hearing by a student advocate but only the judicial hearing board can hear testimony from the accused student and from witnesses. When testimony is completed, the board decides by majority vote whether college rules have been violated and, if so, what the sanctions should be. If there is new evidence, or if the juridical process has in some way been compromised, an appeal can be made within three days of the board's decision to the vice president of Academic Affairs. This vice president can overturn the decision of the judicial hearing board, return the case to the board for further consideration, or reduce the sanction. But their decision is final.

With variations, most college judicial boards operate in similar ways. The problem, of course, is that if one's child gets into trouble one's tendency is to insist that the family lawyer be present at the hearing. While the involvement of a lawyer might be appropriate if a student runs afoul of the law for a serious crime like selling drugs at the local high school, lawyers (as well as parents) are usually barred from internal college judicial hearings because minor infractions do not stay on a student's permanent record. Most sanctions involve being fined or losing a privilege, like being banned from playing on an athletic team or serving in student government or living in a college residence hall. The worst that can happen for more serious infractions, such as plagiarism or lying to a college official, is getting kicked out of college for a defined period of time. Though it is painful, this kind of tough love is often a necessary wake-up call for a student who has made a bad decision. These hoped-for transformations cannot happen when parents make excuses for their children or try to protect them from the consequences of bad behavior.

What Does Your Child Do on the Weekend?

I wake up Saturday and the Jungle is dead. No midnight flag football games in the hallway, no boom box blasting away. Around 10 A.M. I walk up the hill toward Olsen for brunch. But something isn't right. The campus is unnaturally quiet. Indeed, there is hardly any sign of life at all.

Etched on the sidewalk in front of Olson in faded chalk is a list of last weekend's homecoming activities I've failed to notice until now. They included a performance by an area comedy team called Mission Improbable, followed by an annual event called A Taste of Morningside, in which area restaurants provided dinner for students and reuning alumni on the tennis courts across from Dimmitt. Finally there was an all-college dance from 9 P.M. to 1 A.M. But today— nothing. And then I remember Dean Pflipsen's prediction that this weekend might be quiet since there is a major off-campus football game this afternoon—most students will have gone home last night to visit with their families before driving up to South Dakota where today's game will take place.

I have a pretty good idea what most people would say if they were visiting Morningside on this particular weekend: this is a suitcase college! But Morningside really isn't and, in any case, not every week- end is like homecoming at most colleges. So after a leisurely brunch, I hitch a ride with two faculty members and make the eighty-six-mile drive to Sioux Falls. When we arrive at the University of Sioux Falls' football stadium, I see what seems to be the entire Morningside College undergraduate student body, all 1,180 of them, tailgating with their families in a marked-off area next to the stadium. The game has been billed by my Jungle hall mates as THE game of the year, since Sioux Falls is rated number two in the National Association of Intercollegiate Athletics League, and Morningside really wants to beat them as they did three years ago.

A mob of people are now entering the stadium. I grab a seat in the stands on the Morningside College side and find myself sitting next to Didi Simmons and her parents, Champ and Jill Peterson. Didi's son Billie ("See him over there? He's number twenty!") is a first-year starter for the Morningside Mustangs and a resident in the Jungle. The crowd on both sides of the stadium is huge. I ask Champ, a retired high school football coach, how many people he thinks are in the stadium. "Six thousand easy," he says. I'm incredulous. Most small-college football stadiums boast maybe five or six hundred spectators, a thousand at best. This place is more like what you would expect of a major Division I university football team back East. A huge screen above one of the goalposts comes alive, and everyone is suddenly on their feet. Cartoon bombs burst on the screen as the University of Sioux Falls Cougars come running onto the field. Now it's Morningside's turn. Three thousand fans are hollering at the top of their lungs. "Go get 'em, Billie," Champ Peterson yells as his grandson's name is announced. Didi is now on her feet, jumping up and down and pointing. "Look! Look! There's Chaps." She turns to me, "You know, Chaps is Billie's best friend." It's none other than Chaps Wilcke, my next-door hall mate, who had jokingly asked me the other evening if I could mention him in my book. I promised I would, never realizing I would have such a great opportunity for doing so. Go, Chaps! The roar of the crowd abruptly dissipates as "The Star-Spangled Banner" is sung by a Sioux Falls cheerleader. And then the game begins.

I'll spare you the gory details. The Sioux Falls Cougars dominate the game from beginning to end, creaming the Morningside Mustangs 28–3. Where their quarterback consistently connects with a series of Hail Mary passes, ours consistently throws the football directly into the hands of the nearest Cougar linebacker. But no matter. This is weekend entertainment at its best for the students and families of both colleges. Champ Peterson turns to me as the game winds down and says, "I wish the results were different. But can you imagine wanting to be anywhere else?" I half-heartedly agree. It was great fun sharing this event with my first-year friends and their families—until the temperature dropped thirty degrees! But then again, this is South Dakota.

Back in the Jungle, snug and warm in my bed after making the return drive from Sioux Falls, I am awakened at 2 A.M. by the fire alarm and a resolute knock on my door. When I open it, a stern-looking RA instructs me to follow her down the stairs and out of Dimmitt. Not the most pleasant experience but absolutely necessary. Everyone has been drilled to respond to a fire and nobody is allowed to stay in Dimmitt. Just what any caring parent would hope for—not a fire but a well-planned evacuation. Or so I foolishly thought. The alarm turns out to be a prank. My hall mates have returned and the Jungle is back in action.

6

Health and Safety

There's an old saying that bad things happen in threes. While I was president of Randolph-Macon College, three crises descended on the college in less than a year. On October 19, 2002, the so-called Beltway snipers landed in Ashland, Virginia. John Allen Muhammad and his sidekick Lee Boyd Malvo had been driving around communities just off Route 95 randomly shooting people. They arrived at the Ponderosa Restaurant on England Street in Ashland, just a half mile from campus, and from the trunk of their car shot Jeffrey Hopper as he emerged from the restaurant. Hopper survived but ten other people spread between Maryland, Washington, DC, and Virginia didn't. Needless to say, the good citizens of Ashland including the entire college community were terrified.

Muhammad and Malvo were eventually caught, but later that winter Ashland was hit by the so-called President's Day Blizzard that shut down the entire East Coast. The following September, Hurricane Isabel made its appearance, killing thirty-two people in Virginia alone and causing $2.3 billion in damage, one of the costliest hurricanes in Virginia history. So I wasn't surprised to receive the following e-mail from an understanding first-year parent with a good sense of humor: "Ironically, our vision of a 'safe' community was shattered with the snipers. It's apparent that nowhere is really safe anymore. Combined with the blizzard and the hurricane we fear locusts for next year!"

Once they leave home for college, concern number one for most parents is the safety of their children. The literature we daily read about date rape, concussions, and the H1N1 virus that killed a large number of teenagers a few years ago (including college students)— not to mention occasional campus shootings—cause many parents to fear that college is some kind of black hole from which their children might never emerge—or emerge severely damaged. So what's the truth? Are you sending your children into harm's way? What are the available support services they can count on if they get sick or become depressed? What safety nets are available when they do stupid things like drink too much or wander alone downtown and get lost? In short, how can you know whether your children are learning in a safe environment?

What Should Your Child Do When He or She Gets Sick?

Children, of course, occasionally get sick, but when they're away at college, you aren't around to take care of them. But don't worry: virtually every college in America has some sort of health center. The problem is that parents are often unaware of what is available for their children on campus and panic when they get a call in the middle of the night with a health concern. So let's see how Washington College in Chestertown, Maryland, deals with student health issues.

One early morning, a group of students, some of them looking like death warmed over, is entering the Student Health and Counseling Services on the ground floor of the Queen Anne's House residence hall. They register with an administrative assistant who finds out from them whether they need medical attention or counseling. On a large bulletin board in the reception area are various tips on good health, including a poster with statistics suggesting that, contrary to popular opinion, you don't have to binge drink in order to be cool.

Dawn Nordoff, clinical director of health services, greets me with a smile, looking more like a professor than the nurse practitioner she is. She employs another full-time and two part-time nurse practitioners. She also contracts with four area physicians who are available to students a couple hours or so every day, five days a week. Serious medical cases are referred to the Chester River Hospital Center, which is adjacent to campus. This setup is typical of many colleges—a small health care facility linked to a nearby hospital—though many larger institutions like Tufts have their own in-house physicians.

Nordoff describes her typical day at health services. She normally arrives at about 8:30 A.M., along with one of the physicians, and begins seeing all of the students who became ill during the night. If the illness is serious enough, the RA or an officer from Public Safety won't have waited until morning but will have sent the student directly to the nearby hospital emergency department. She also fields phone calls from concerned parents, follows up on diagnostic tests, and notifies students of the results. Depending on the seriousness of a given situation and the need to arrange for referrals to specialists or contacting parents, sometimes these activities take up most of her morning. Nordoff's afternoons are filled with campus and community meetings, mostly committees that she serves on like the Emergency Operations Group, which exists to address campus-wide concerns like a flu outbreak. I ask her whether she ever has time to practice nursing. "Well, probably not today," she responds. "But normally I can see about fifteen students each day. The hands-on aspect of seeing patients of course is my favorite activity, but everything I do here is part of practicing nursing."

What are the most common health issues that Dawn Nordoff and her colleagues deal with? Asthma, gastrointestinal upset, anxiety, upper respiratory infections, and seasonal flu are the most common ailments, and a handful of students come in just for a little bit of mothering. "We do that too," she says. What about more serious health issues? "Virtually every health issue you can imagine walks through those doors. I remember receiving a phone call from a freshman who couldn't get out of bed one morning. The student was burning up with fever. I knew this student had recently traveled to a country where malaria is prevalent." The doctor confirmed that it was, indeed, a case of malaria.

Increasingly, first-year students are coming to college with serious eating disorders like bulimia and anorexia and their parents are sometimes beside themselves about what to do. I ask Nordoff for her view on this subject. "Thank you for that question!" she exclaims.

> I want all freshman parents to hear this: if your daughter or son has a serious eating disorder like anorexia or bulimia, please have them tell us *before* they arrive on campus. We really need to know about these condi-

tions so that we can deal with them. We want to work with these students to put a plan in place that will allow them to be successful here. If we aren't aware of a problem then we can't help. I think some freshmen want to start out with a clean slate and so keep their health problems secret. But this can be a *big* mistake.

Nordoff gives me an example: a recent first-year woman who arrived at orientation thin as a rail was always exercising in the fitness center. Within the first two weeks of college she was in the health services office complaining of nausea and depression. When Nordoff suggested that this student seek psychological counseling, she refused. Nordoff was so concerned that, with the student's permission, she contacted the mother. But even after she expressed concern, the mother would not admit that her daughter had an eating disorder. It took several more contacts with the student and her mother before the mother confided that just before orientation her daughter had been in the hospital for depression and anorexia. Nordoff feels that, had the daughter or her family informed the college of her health issue prior to arrival at orientation, the health services office could have been of more assistance sooner. This first-year student had a very difficult start to her college career.

Some parents reading this might wonder whether informing the health center of a child's medical condition could result in their child not being accepted or invited to leave college after arriving on campus. The answer is no. First of all, it's against the law for a college to discriminate against a student because of a medical or psychological condition. Medical histories shared with a health center are privileged information and unless those histories suggest someone might do harm to the community or to themselves, they are never shared with the college administration—including the admissions office. I can remember as a college president being concerned about the mental stability of a particular first-year student. He was being seen by a staff psychologist in the counseling center after publicly telling his classmates that he intended to torch a residence hall. I wanted to know the details of this student's state of mind. I was told, however, that even as president I could not have access to the student's mental health history but that I would be informed if it was felt that the student might do harm.

Eating disorders are part of a larger student issue—eating in general. As Julie Lampie pointed out at the Tufts orientation, what students eat is very much a health concern on America's college campuses, especially in light of the growing incidents of student obesity. According to the American College Health Association, 40.6 percent of college men and 31.3 percent of college women are either obese or overweight.[1] I am wondering whether, in Dawn's opinion, college students, especially those that are free from home and family, eat healthy meals.

"Well, maybe," she says slowly. "But their idea of eating healthy is not always mine. Freshmen who tell me that they are vegetarians or vegans sometimes raise a red flag. It makes me want to know more about what they are *really* eating. Being a vegetarian or a vegan is fine, of course. But what I often see are students not eating meat and then not replacing meat with another form of protein. So even though they say they eat healthy, they often don't." Nordoff tells me that when students with a weight problem come to Health and Counseling Services they are put in contact with a local dietician and encouraged to exercise at the fitness center. But obesity is an ongoing challenge. She tells me that it's especially hard to see students this unhealthy at such a young age, especially students who have had gastric bypass surgery which can lead to additional health problems.

Smoking is also a big and increasing health concern on American college campuses. In a recent survey, 14.2 percent of first-year students reported smoking, and the evidence I have seen at my own colleges and the colleges included in this book—that is, cigarette butts all over the place—visually supports what students themselves say.[2] Nordoff says that when she came to Washington College, smoking was permitted everywhere, including in the classroom. She personally lobbied the college administration not to permit smoking in the residence halls and won that battle. But students, women foremost among them, still smoke just outside the front doors of their residence halls. First-year students who come to the health services office are automatically asked whether they smoke. Those who say they do are encouraged to attend Kicking Butts, a tobacco cessation program sponsored by the college. Many colleges run similar programs. Students who wish to quit are then offered free nicotine patches, education, and prescription medications to assist them. Studies show that the longer a student smokes, the more difficult it is to quit, so places like Washington College feel that it's important to get as much information as possible to first-year students about the dangers of tobacco use and the resources available on campus to help them quit.

Returning to the topic of parents of students, how does Dawn Nordoff handle those inevitable calls she gets from first-year parents, worried about any one of the student health concerns we have been discussing? According to the law, she can only release information to parents if the student gives permission. If it's a truly serious problem, she will contact the parent or an emergency contact given to the college by the student. "If I am very concerned about a student I am seeing," Nordoff says, "I generally will say to the student, 'I think we need to talk to mom or dad. Which one do you want me to call?' Only twice has a student refused to allow me to make that call."

Nordoff's general advice for first-year parents: "First, if you know your student has a health problem please have them share this information with us *before* they come to college. And, second, let go. Before they come to college, students need some practice handling their own problems, including managing their health care, because once they are here they have to accept that responsibility."

What Do First-Year Students Say about Health, including Eating, Smoking, Sex, and Depression?

Dawn Nordoff has arranged for me to meet three first-year students who have agreed to speak in confidence about campus health concerns from their perspective, and I have chosen to do this over lunch—not only because healthy eating is a hot topic with college students and their parents but also because I want to see the Hodson Hall Commons, Washington College's magnificent new dining facility.

College dining has changed radically since I was a college student. Back then, you simply went through a cafeteria line and ate whatever was served up, usually some kind of mystery meat with overcooked vegetables. But the current college generation, habitués of suburban malls with their various food courts, require a variety of eating options, from fast foods like pizza and hamburgers, to vegetarian selections and salad bars, to what most of us would recognize as a proper meal. Hodson Hall Commons has all of this and more. It is really a two-story mini-mall with a variety of food courts on the first floor, all built around a circular core that features a small entertainment and performance space. On the second floor is a more formal dining area. Adjacent to these dining areas are meeting and recreation rooms.

I spot Tico, Michelle, and Sukie, three first-year students, waiting for me in Coyote Jack's Grill.

"How's the food?" I ask as I join them at the table after going through the food line and heaping my plate with healthy selections. "The food's not that bad," Tico says. "I'm a fast food freak so I appreciate all the burgers and fries I can eat. The pizza isn't bad either," he says as he bites into an enormous slice of pepperoni pizza.

Michelle feels differently. "I guess if I ate like Tico, this place would be veritable paradise. But I hate the food here. You either eat like a vegan or you eat fatty junk foods like Tico is doing right now. There are usually four vegan options and then a variety of junk foods. The food is boring and unhealthy. Almost *everyone* feels the way I do. I tried to petition the Student Senate to get more nutritional food but nothing happened. Maybe things will change with this new facility. But I'm not holding my breath."

Sukie is vigorously shaking her head in disagreement. "How can you say that, Michelle? Everyone *doesn't* feel the way you do. The food is definitely healthy. Just look around. The problem is that most Washington College students are like Tico. They want French fries, ice cream, and cookies. The bigger problem for me is not the *lack* of healthy food but the *amount* of it. Once you swipe your card you can eat all you want. I've put on at least ten pounds since I arrived here in August."

So it goes. I have never met a group of college students who are of one mind on campus food! But as I look around this new facility, I find myself agreeing with Sukie. There are plenty of healthy food options, several of them on my plate. The problem is that, given their druthers and without mom's supervision, too many new students quickly slink into eating fatty food.

"On the way over here I noticed lots of cigarette butts," I say, seeing that this conversation about food has ended in a hopeless impasse. "Do you or your friends smoke? Do you see smoking as a health problem on campus?"

Tico says, "I don't smoke and neither do most of my friends. But the thing that blew me away when I arrived here at orientation last August were the number of freshmen who do. Smoking is everywhere. I think many freshmen do it because they weren't allowed to in high school. I'm an athlete so I've never smoked. But when I tell my friends who smoke not to do it because they might get lung cancer they just say, 'Fuck off, Tico. Mind you own business.' Also, many of the people I see smoking cigarettes smoke weed as well. So I think this is done mostly for social reasons."

Michelle agrees with Tico. "There is lots of smoking here, especially outside the freshman dorms. Why? I think most freshman started smoking when they started drinking. Smoking and drinking seem to go together." As she digs into a healthy-looking salad, Michelle continues, "I once asked a friend why he smoked. He told me 'People who don't smoke can never understand people who do. It just gives me a buzz. Relaxes me. My friends smoke as well and I want to be like them.' I agree with Tico. I think my classmates smoke because of peer pressure."

"Well," Sukie adds, "it's also addictive. I started smoking in high school and couldn't stop. My parents were *very* concerned. But last week, during the Great American Smokeout, I attended a bonfire sponsored by a club here called Kicking Butts. We roasted marshmallows and were given 'quit kits' with nicotine patches. At the end we were encouraged to throw our cigarette packs into the bonfire. I haven't had a smoke since!"

"Drinking can also be addictive," I say. "What are your observations on this subject?"

Sukie responds that "drinking is a big issue on *all* college campuses. More freshmen drink than don't. The problem is that they don't know when to stop."

Tico interrupts: "I think the problem also is that many freshmen never drank before they came to college so they don't know what their limit is. Also, they are free from mom and dad and figure there is no one now to say 'no.' But they need to stop for three minutes and think about what they are doing."

"Some of my classmates came from homes where there was little adult supervision and were drinking by middle school. When they got here they went ballistic," Michelle says. "Also, the law that says you can't drink until you are twenty-one is a joke. It only makes things worse. Freshmen are always going to want what they can't have." Michelle is repeating what Hank said at Morningside College about rebellious teenagers who drink *precisely* because they are told not to.

I carefully delve into a sensitive issue that is on the minds of students and especially their parents, namely, sex. "OK guys. I want you to be very candid with me now. And I promise to protect identities. But is sexually transmitted disease an issue here?"

Sukie says, "Our generation doesn't publicly talk about sex that much. But when we do, it's not so much about sexually transmitted disease but rather about getting pregnant. So those of us who are sexually active—and I'm not saying I am—take advantage of the reproductive counseling that is given here. Also, we can get Plan B free of charge in health services and our boyfriends can get condoms for free as well." Plan B is a pill, now on the market, that, if taken at least seventy-two hours after sexual intercourse prevents pregnancy.

"What about AIDS?" I ask, knowing that for these kid's Generation X parents, AIDS was *the* number one health concern when they were in college.

"AIDS isn't big an issue anymore," Michelle says. "All through high school we have been warned about AIDS. So most of my girlfriends practiced safe sex. Washington College is also good about providing information about STDs. At orientation we were told that if we do sex to do protected sex. Every residence hall bathroom has baskets of condoms."

Sukie disagrees. "Well, I think we *should* be concerned about AIDS. Lots of women are on the pill, but some have the attitude that if you just pick your partners carefully you can enjoy unprotected sex. I'm concerned by the number of freshmen women I know who are sexually active with multiple partners." According to a 2014 study by the American College Health Association, an alarming 28.7 percent of college men and 25 percent of women report having had sex with two or more partners within the last twelve-month period.[3]

I bring up the subject of mental health, and ask my friends whether any of their classmates have been struggling with depression or homesickness since coming to college.

Michelle doesn't hesitate to respond. "My roommate is definitely struggling," she says shaking her head.

When we arrived at college in August, Abigail was having a really difficult time adjusting. She is very close to her family and even though they live only a couple hours away, she was extremely homesick. She was crying all the time—in our room, at dinner, after class. As a result, her parents were on campus a lot, and this just made matters worse. She started crying all over again once they left. It was getting so bad that I suggested she go to the counseling service. "Only sickos go there," she told me, kind of angry that I would even make the suggestion. "Hello Abigail, you *are* sick," I thought to myself. But I later realized that Abigail was probably afraid that by going to counseling other freshmen might think that she was mental. Fortunately things worked out. She joined crew with me and then quickly bonded with our teammates. She finally stopped crying, thank God!

Tico jumps in: "I know a freshman on the soccer team who seemed so homesick at the beginning of the semester he sometimes couldn't make it to practice. I'm not sure what was wrong with him. Rumor is that he had suicidal tendencies in high school. All I know is that he ended up in the counseling center. I never saw him again."

The table falls silent. Everyone is now checking their watches. Afternoon classes are about to begin, so as we get up to leave, I ask the group if they have any advice for first-year parents.

"Yes," Sukie says. "Parents have to understand that freshmen live in the equivalent of a small city where there are all sorts of health issues. But they *really* need to chill. Living or not living healthy is a choice each one of us has to make for ourselves, whether it's getting enough sleep, eating well, or dealing with stress. When we do get sick *we* need to deal with it. Parents need to take off the training wheels."

Sometimes parent need to listen to their own children!

What Should Your Child Do When She or He Becomes Homesick or Depressed?

Depression and homesickness are on the increase among college students, especially those in the first year. According to a survey involving thousands of first-year students published in *The American Freshman: National Norms Fall* in 2009 and then again in 2014, the percentage reporting above-average emotional health dropped from 55.3 percent in 2009 to 50.7 percent in 2014.[4] The same year (2014), 15.7 percent of first-year students reported frequently feeling depressed, with slightly less feeling lonely or homesick.[5] Stress over the economy as well as the fear many have that they might do less well in life than their parents probably has a lot to do with this. So what can parents do when their children become homesick or depressed? How does homesickness in college manifest itself? To answer these and other questions and to get a professional perspective on first-year mental health, I head back over to the Counseling Center and meet with Ann O'Connor, a part-time counselor who has been at the college for over a decade.

Ann O'Connor's accent betrays her British roots. A native of Gloustershire, England, she earned her license in the United States to become a certified social worker, after which she was hired by Washington College in 1999 as a part-time counselor. The combination of positions she holds today must give her an interesting perspective on life, to say the least: for part of the week she counsels college students who are just beginning their adult lives, and then, for the rest of the week, she works at a local hospice providing bereavement support for hospice families before and after the death of a loved one.

I ask O'Connor to describe a typical day on campus. She tells me that she arrives at the Counseling Center at 8:30 A.M., about the same time Dawn Nordoff does, and is available to students until about 4:30 P.M. or later on Mondays and Wednesdays. She sees all kinds of students, including those who are homesick or have a significant mood disorder such as anxiety and depression. According to the American College Health Association, the most common causes for visits to the counseling center are anxiety (14.3 percent), depression (12 percent), and panic attacks (6.7 percent).[6] A typical counseling session generally lasts about fifty minutes and involves a wide variety of issues. She says that staff at the Counseling Center have their own strengths and that students are matched with counselors who will best serve them.

We talk first about homesickness, which makes up a relatively small number of the cases she and her colleagues deal with—in large part because students who get homesick or who are depressed often don't seek professional help.[7] O'Connor tells me homesickness in first-year students manifests itself in various ways. Frequent calls home complaining about classes, roommates, or college life in general are one sign. Isolating themselves and falling behind in class are two others. What O'Connor says supports what Dean Long told me about the factors leading to first-year attrition at Vassar.

Parents are often the first to know when students are homesick or depressed, so I ask O'Connor how they can help out. She suggests they can do so by listening to their children, proposing that they become involved in a student club or other activities available on campus, or remarking on the possibilities of college weekends and opportunities to meet and connect with other students. She cautions that while parents should be supportive, they should also be careful not to encourage too many trips home. By avoiding the effort to connect with classmates, college adjustment will only become harder. In her opinion, involvement with activities on campus is the key to student satisfaction.

She tells me that parents can also be helpful by being aware of how their children are progressing academically. "Frankly," she says "it is difficult for me to understand why parents who pay a small fortune for tuition don't get permission from their children to access their grades. Low grades are a good indication of some problem going on, and I would think parents might want to know about this because the sooner we can address academic underachievement the better for the student."

Several parents I interviewed in preparation for this book asked me what they can do to assure their child's success in college. O'Connor shares some of her thoughts on this subject. She proposes that parents can help their children with practical matters, such as teaching them how to budget, to use a credit card wisely, to balance a checkbook, to take care of personal health and hygiene, to be careful to do their laundry regularly, and to be respectful of a roommate and his or her space. Parents can also help by discussing with their kids the academic challenges they might face, encouraging them to search for and use the many academic resources available in the Counseling Center. She suggests that we need to talk with them about making wise choices, especially in developing friendships and mixing in groups, and discussing with them the temptations that will cross their paths. She points out that listening in conversation is always a good parental gift.

"One last thing," she says as a student arrives for an appointment. "Allow your child to make mistakes. A good number of freshmen do.

Let them learn from these mistakes. Encourage them to do better and support them in making the right decisions. Avoid making comparisons either to themselves or their siblings. And don't try to fill your own aspirations through your child."

Before leaving this conversation with Ann O'Connor, I would like to address a complaint I sometimes hear from parents of first-year students, namely, that their children have a difficult time gaining accessing to the counseling center at their college. One mother recently told me that it took two weeks before her son could see someone at the counseling center at his Midwestern college. All college counseling centers want to see their clients as soon as possible, within twenty-four hours, it is hoped, if not sooner. But when they are understaffed, especially at larger universities, they will often have to do triage in order to determine who needs to be seen immediately (for example, a student expressing suicidal tendencies) and who can wait a bit longer for an appointment (a student who needs counseling on proper diet). If, however, your student is deeply depressed and can't get an appointment to see someone in the counseling center you should immediately get them help in the community and then report the incident to the dean of students. No college wants to delay helping a student who is in serious need.

Is Your Child Safe? The Inside Story on Drinking, Date Rape, and Campus Shooters

In the basement of Wicomico Hall, a 1960s era dormitory, I meet Jerry Roderick, director of Washington College's Department of Public Safety. The office is situated a few steps down into an area that looks more like a renovated basement family room than a modern campus police station. Roderick tells me later that sometimes during a Northeaster, this place is called the Pond because it floods so easily. He is a slim, fit, and about as low key and informal as you can get in his profession. Indeed, he seems the antithesis of the officious, close-minded police officer many of us imagine people in his position to be.

When I appear for our meeting, he is sitting in his office with a concerned-looking senior discussing an incident that happened the previous night involving some townies and Washington College students getting into a shoving match. The senior is the student government's liaison with Public Safety. Roderick invites me to sit in on the conversation.

Like most four-year colleges and universities in the United States, Washington College has an open campus, meaning that anyone who wants to can walk onto its property unimpeded. In this case, eight townies, probably bored high school students with nothing better to do, strayed on campus at about 10:30 P.M. and tried to crash a party that was taking place in one of the residence halls. When they were denied entry, there was some pushing and shoving, which only escalated when a first-year woman was verbally insulted by one of the invaders. At first the college students thought that they could handle the situation by themselves, but when the jostling intensified someone called Public Safety. Both Public Safety and the Chestertown police were on the scene within minutes, but by the time they arrived the townies had taken off. One college student suffered a minor bruise on his face from a random punch, but otherwise nobody was seriously injured. The student government rep wants to know what Public Safety is going to do about this unfortunate incident, especially since it seems to him to be just another example of rampant crime in Chestertown.

Roderick listens to the senior and then makes the suggestion that when students see a suspicious group of people coming on campus they need to call Public Safety immediately, before the situation escalates. Had this been done, he tells the senior, Public Safety might have prevented a fight and caught the intruders. Meanwhile, the incident is under investigation. He also points out that crime is not rampant in Chestertown, that in fact theft and vagrancy are down by 30 percent over previous years. The meeting ends and Roderick promises to keep the senior updated on the investigation.

In my experience, parents have mixed feelings about campus law enforcement. On the one hand, they appreciate having a trained campus police force around to protect the safety of their children. On the other, they worry about their children getting caught by these same people doing something illegal like drinking underage or smoking marijuana. So any good campus police force must walk a fine line between preserving the openness and safety of a college campus and enforcing the law when students break the rules.

Roderick and his department first make contact with new students soon after they arrive at orientation. At this point, of course, they are on information overload, so he tries to make his message clear and simple. He tells them that Public Safety exists to protect them and that if they follow the rules and obey the law they won't have any problems with his officers. "Most of our freshmen are incredibly mature and responsible," he says, "but a few almost immediately get into trouble. For them it's as though college is one big party and they are already on spring break. Consequently, we sometimes witness some unbelievably bad behavior."

Roderick reiterates that immaturity is a big factor, especially with first-year males. "When you walk through one of their residence halls and see the number of penises drawn on their doors," he says "you understand what I mean." Some first-year students also have a difficult time with community rules and expectations. What they think is acceptable behavior, upper-class students find appalling. For example, the college recently built two new residence halls, each accommodating a hundred students of which twenty are first year. Within six weeks of the buildings being occupied, the elevators had to be locked down because of the damage done to them by the first-year occupants, several of whom had been drinking. The upperclassmen, who really appreciated finally having elevators, were not happy about this. They had been complaining all semester long about the senseless and sometimes malicious behavior of their first-year hall mates. "This is just one example of the huge difference between adolescent first-year students and mature seniors," he says. "When they catch first-year students doing stupid things like this I tell my officers, 'Just remember, we haven't graduated them yet. We still have time to work on them!'"

Of course, as my recent lunch partners noted, much of this bad behavior is alcohol related and caused in large part by peer pressure. Before they arrived on campus, many of these first-year students probably drank only a couple beers or no alcohol at all. But when they meet upperclassmen who introduce them to high-energy drinks laced with vodka, they start drinking as well, followed by foolish and sometimes risky behavior. "But as the semester progresses, these incidents taper down," he says "because the reality of a very demand-ing academic program begins to set in. Midterm grades are out. And all of a sudden, mom and dad are on the telephone having a serious conversation with Johnny who just got three Ds and an F."

What happens at Washington College when a first-year student is caught drinking or using drugs? If Roderick's officers catch a first-year student (or any student for that matter) with illegal drugs, the student is immediately turned over to the Chestertown Police, which means that they will automatically be charged with possession. He then files an internal report with the campus judicial board, which means the student may be suspended. Washington College's no-tolerance policy on drugs is similar to Morningside College's and is standard for most colleges and universities.

Roderick tells me that it's a bit different with alcohol. In the first couple of weeks after orientation, his officers take the educational approach when they see an underage student using alcohol. They make sure the offending student understands campus policy and state law. After the second week, however, his officers go into an enforcement mode. First-year students caught drinking receive a citation with a monetary penalty. A copy of the citation is sent over to Student Affairs, where they will keep track of future offenses. At three citations, the student must complete mandatory alcohol counseling and evaluation. Beyond this, students face judicial action, including possible suspension. There are many strategies on how to deal with this growing problem, but Washington College's "education first, enforcement second" policy is quite common.

As we have already seen, underage drinking is a big issue on most college campuses. And first-year students are often the worst offend-ers. Estimates vary, but according to recent studies, 46.5 percent of first-year students report drinking beer and 54.1 percent drinking wine or liquor either frequently or occasionally since entering col-lege, and of these students, 33.6 percent reported having binged in the past two weeks—40.9 percent for men and 29.8 percent for women. Binge drinking is defined as more than five drinks in one sitting over a two-hour period for men and four drinks over the same period of time for women.[8]

While these figures are instructive, many believe that irrespon-sible drinking is pervasive in the first year. I am remembering, for example, my conversation with Hank and Barry at Morningside who told me that 90 percent of their first-year classmates drink. Unfortunately, naive and easily influenced first-year students often follow what they think is the norm and begin to drink excessively themselves. It is for this reason that many colleges are posting statistics in the student newspaper and on campus bulletin boards, as I recently saw at the Health and Counseling Services office there, showing that perception does not always match reality and that in fact many students choose not to drink at all.

Irresponsible drinking is often related to aggressive sexual behavior, and so we discuss how Washington College deals with date rape. Roderick tells me that date rape is not a significant issue at Washington College, but that nationally it's probably a bigger problem than most think. As we both know, only a small number of rape victims will report what happened to them. Larger numbers probably go to friends. Still, when a date rape victim steps forward most colleges will spend a lot of time providing the victim with support and legal advice.

Roderick tells me of an off-campus party several years ago where a first-year women had been drinking all evening. She started flirting with a junior who took her to his residence. They went back to his room back on campus where they started to hug and kiss. When the junior started to put the moves on her, she told him that she didn't want to go any further. He then raped her.

"She reported this to the Health Services and to Public Safety," he says. "Both families threatened to lawyer up. It became a classic 'he said, she said' case. Charges were filed at the college through the sexual assault and grievance process. It was a very difficult campus hearing. In the end he was found responsible." Here was a first-year woman, he laments, who went through the awful experience of date rape, had to relive the experience in a contentious campus hearing process, and really never completely recovered after the hearing was over. He tells me that she eventually dropped out of college.

Roderick's observation that date rape is underreported on most college campuses is borne out by my own experience. In a survey done several years ago of Randolph-Macon College women by the Pan-Hellenic Council (a group of sorority presidents), respondents were asked: "Have you ever reported an incident of date rape to a college authority?" Only 1.7 percent of those who said they had knowledge of a date rape bothered to report it. Part of the problem, of course, is that many victims of date rape are either too ashamed or too scared to report what happened to the authorities. In some cases, the victim doesn't even realize she was raped. Education around this issue, for men as well as for women, is extremely important.

Roderick and I discuss what safety strategies are in place to make sure that students—men as well as women—are safe. Like most colleges and universities, Washington College has an emergency broadcasting system with loudspeakers and twenty-two surveillance cameras that are monitored by his officers. In addition, the college has an alert system that can notify students via e-mail, text, and landlines of emergencies as they arise. But it's the college's nine full-time and two part-time officers that are the backbone of campus security.

Though Washington College's security system is impressive, when the Beltway snipers come to mind, I wonder out loud whether these precautions would be enough to head off the kind of tragic incident that happened at Virginia Tech not so long ago.

The shootings at Virginia Tech in 2007, which killed thirty-two people, have more than any single factor led a lot of people to think that college campuses are not safe. In fact, though, college campuses are among the safest places on earth to be—if students use common sense. Statistics on incidents of violent crime committed on college campuses are insignificant compared to incidents of crime committed elsewhere, and according to a recent survey, 78.7 percent of first-year students report feeling perfectly safe on campus.[9]

"Everyone thinks that Virginia Tech was a landmark event, and in some ways it was," Roderick says, "but my FBI father told me long ago of being on the University of Texas campus in 1966 when Charles Whitman, a deranged student, shot fourteen people to death from a perch in the campus bell tower. Virginia Tech is not a new phenomenon. Unfortunately, tragedies like this occasionally happen, in shopping malls, in post offices, and even in schools. God knows how many school shootings there have been since Columbine in 1999. But because of the media attention Virginia Tech has received, many parents think this is a new phenomenon and that college campuses are very dangerous."

Roderick tells me that even before Virginia Tech, Washington College's officers were trained to respond to a campus shooter. If such a person were to appear, the college would simultaneously lock down the campus and operationalize the campus alert system, and then (because Public Safety officers are not armed), call in the Chestertown and Maryland State Police, both of whom are only seconds away.

Many small colleges, including the two where I was president, do not arm their officers, and so I ask Roderick whether, in light of Virginia Tech, he thinks this still advisable. "I think guns can become a liability in a tightly crowded situation like we have on most small college campuses," he responds. "Using a gun runs the risk of inadvertently shooting an innocent bystander. On the other hand, not having a gun forces my officers to 'work smart,' to stop and think about how they are going to handle the situation. Again, for us this would mean immediately calling in the Chestertown and Maryland State Police who are especially trained to deal with a situation like this. Still, I get calls from parents wanting to know whether Washington College has a SWAT team."

I believe Roderick is right in his thinking about the use of guns on small college campuses. When universities like Tufts have a police force especially trained to deal with hostage takeovers or shooters, being armed makes sense. But the campus police at most colleges are not trained for extreme events like these and so it's almost always better to pull in law enforcement officers, like the state police, who are. The idea that students should be fully armed, a movement that is gaining traction in some circles, is simply mind-boggling to me and other college and university presidents.[10]

Jerry Roderick and I have covered a lot of territory. We've talked about many of the safety concerns that are on the minds of most prospective college students and their parents. What advice would he give parents if they were here in this room with us? "Before their children leave for college," he says "parents should have a frank conversation about what they and their children expect the college experience to be. If there is a big disconnect, they should talk about it. They should talk about alcohol and drug use and about personal and community safety."

He then shares his philosophy of what it means to be a college community. First-year students need to think of their residence hall as their home. At home they keep the doors locked, not blocked open as too often happens in the residence halls. At home, they don't bring strangers into the house. At home they look out for their parents and their siblings. "And you know what?" he says, "Most kids respond positively to this conversation. Most are responsible people when they come to college. They do look out for themselves and for their classmates. They call Public Safety if help is needed."

What Do First-Year Students Say about Campus Safety?

At a coffeehouse in downtown Chestertown, I meet with four Washington College students who are in their first year, all of whom are in some way involved with campus safety issues. Courtney and Connie participate in Safe Ride, a student organization that provides rides for classmates who get stranded downtown on weekends, and Susan and Tony work as dispatchers for Public Safety.

I ask Courtney how Safe Ride works. She illustrates by telling me of a recent incident in which she fielded a call from a first-year classmate attending an off-campus party that had been busted by the Chestertown Police because of the town's noise ordinance. The student, slurring her words because she had too much to drink, told Courtney that she was at a house downtown but didn't know where it was located. She wanted to know whether someone could pick her up and drive her back to campus. Courtney knew where the party was because another student had called Safe Ride earlier. "So Connie and I ran over to the van and drove downtown to the party where we found this girl standing on the front porch of the house," Courtney says. "She was really spaced. Couldn't walk a straight line as she approached the van. We thought she was going to throw up. Everyone at the party was laughing at her, which was ridiculous. They should have been showing a bit more concern. Anyway, we delivered her to the residence hall and called the RA."

"But Public Safety officers get involved in more serious incidents," Tony, the student dispatcher, quickly adds. "For example, just the other night a freshman woman was walking alone through the graveyard just off campus going to a party on High Street when she saw a suspicious person approaching her. She called Public Safety, and I answered the call. I radioed one of our officers who responded within seconds and so did the Chestertown Police."

"Never walk by yourself, men included," Connie states the obvious. "Make sure your keys are out. Be aware of your surroundings."

Susan agrees. "I feel very safe here. But be aware of your surroundings. Don't trust people you just met."

Listening to these students you might think that Chestertown is a dangerous place. Quite the contrary. Chestertown is a quaint colonial town with many of its original eighteenth-century houses still lining the Chester River and a downtown that attracts tourists as well as students with small shops, restaurants, art galleries, and a fine old hotel. But as I learned from John King, director of public safety at Tufts, vigilance is needed even in seemingly safe environments.

"So any advice for new first-year students?" I ask the group.

"Yeah, don't get fake IDs," Susan immediately responds. "It's not worth getting caught. Believe me!"

Susan is reflecting on the fact that many first-year students come to college with fake automobile licenses saying that they are over twenty-one. I remember a conversation I had at Tufts orientation with a junior resident assistant. She told me that first year she had a fake New Jersey driver's license and used it to enter a well-known downtown Boston nightclub where lots of college students hang out. Unfortunately for her, the Massachusetts State Police were doing a sting operation that night at the front door and she ended up in tears calling her parents from the precinct. This was her first offense, and she wasn't charged. But she learned a lesson. Susan's advice is worth heeding.

"Also," Tony adds, "If you see a fellow student in trouble, call Public Safety even though you might have been drinking illegally yourself. We have an amnesty policy here that says that unless gross negligence is involved, a call for help from a friend who might also be under the influence will not get the caller in trouble. Without the amnesty clause, a student might have second thoughts about calling Public Safety for help worried that they will also end up in the dean's office. The college's main concerned in these matters is always student safety."

A Walk around Campus Late on a Busy Weekend
Evening with a Campus Safety Officer

Jerry Roderick has arranged for me to accompany Sergeant Burton Brown of the Washington College Public Safety Office on his rounds so that I can witness firsthand how they deal with the party scene on a busy weekend night. It takes great confidence for Jerry—and Sergeant Brown for that matter—to accommodate me, considering that it's Halloween and first-year students will be out in force. Who knows what might happen!

I'm excited because I will finally see what the "Orange Fence Party"—advertised on signs around campus with the tag line "What goes on inside stays inside"—is really all about. This event has been billed by the first-year students I have met as something between an old-fashioned mixer and a drunken orgy that no college official, including Public Safety officers, are permitted to attend. I doubt this is true, but I'll soon find out.

Sergeant Brown finally arrives. He is a big bear of a man, maybe six feet two, with a round face and a neck as thick as a telephone pole. He looks more like a tackle on the Baltimore Ravens than a member of the Department of Public Safety. He takes my measure, probably asking himself why anyone besides a Public Safety officer would want to spend a perfectly good Friday evening watching first-year students party until two or three in the morning. I introduce myself, and we establish some ground rules. Brown will do his rounds in the normal way, and I will tag along. In the unlikely event that something dangerous happens, like a fistfight, I will back off and not get involved. Otherwise I will be privy to everything he and his officers do.

Brown is unarmed. He only carries a nightstick and a can of mace. But he is so physically imposing that he could probably take on a whole army of intruders by himself. I ask him what he would do if confronted by someone with a gun. "See this radio I'm carrying?" he says. A faint voice can be heard coming from it, saying, "Copy that, Tom. We have the guys you mentioned in sight walking up Washington Avenue toward campus. We'll check them out for you. 10–4." He continues: "Hear those voices? One of them is a Chestertown Police officer checking out a group of townies walking up Washington Avenue towards the campus. The other is one of my officers over at the Orange Fence Party. All of us, the local police and my officers, are constantly in radio contact with each other. In the unlikely event I see someone who is armed, all I need to do is call for help, and the Chestertown Police will be here within seconds. And they *are* armed!"

We see a gaggle of first-year women dressed up in cat costumes blithely skipping across the grass as they head for the Orange Fence Party. They are giggling hilariously. Brown and I follow the women. They are very happy to see him. "Hey Burton, what's up?" one of them shouts. "How do you like our costumes?" He gives the girls two thumbs up, "Out of sight."

"So does everyone know you?"

"Most students do. Maybe not all the freshmen yet. But they will by the end of second semester. That's a big part of my job. Getting to know the freshmen. Making them feel safe."

We approach the Orange Fence Party. It is located in a courtyard surrounded by three fraternity houses. An orange plastic fence is wrapped around the perimeter with an entrance on one side and an exit on the other. Manning the entrance is a big hulk of a man wearing a tan shirt with "Public Safety" emblazoned on his chest and looking like a nightclub bouncer. Standing next to him is Sara Feyerherm, the associate vice president for Student Affairs, who will have ultimate say over this evening's activities. She greets me, but it's hard to hear what she is saying. Music is blasting from three huge speakers as students line dance to "Shake Your Booty."

Brown suggests that we walk through the area. "Hold on," I shout to him over the blaring music. "I was told by some first-year students that neither Public Safety nor anyone else from the administration can walk into the area." He shouts back, "Really? Just watch me." With me in tow, he defiantly walks into the courtyard. Some students acknowledge his presence. Most ignore him and just go on dancing.

I join Brown at the beer station. "How does that work?" I ask, pointing to a long table that sports several brands of low-carb beer. The music has temporarily stopped so we can now hear each other.

"If you are twenty-one or older you can bring three cans of beer into the party," he says. "The adult 'bartender' behind the table then keeps track of which cans are yours. You can retrieve from him one of your beers every half hour or so until you've consumed all three. But when it's gone, it's gone, and you can't bring in any more. Of course, first-year students aren't allowed to drink."

Unless we believe that total abstinence can or should be enforced at college parties, I think this is an excellent way to educate students around responsible drinking. It shows students who are over twenty-one that responsible social drinking does not require the consumption of large amounts of alcohol.

Brown and I leave through the back entrance to the roped-off courtyard. Two more burly bouncers guard the exit. "Who are those guys?" I ask him. "They are supervisors at the local minimum-security prison who work for us on busy nights like this," he replies. "I sometimes joke with the students that if they get into trouble, they might end up dealing with these guys rather than with me. So, better behave."

Around 10:30 P.M., Brown and I walk toward some first-year residence halls. Small groups of costumed students continue to saunter toward the Orange Fence Party. We soon come upon a young woman dressed up in a fairy outfit who looks genuinely scared and disoriented. We are in a poorly lit area in the back of one of the residence halls, and she is alone. "I don't know where I am," she says, obviously panicked. "I'm trying to get to the party but I'm a freshman and I don't know my way around yet." Brown speaks into the microphone on his lapel. "Is there an officer near the back of Sassafras Residence Hall? I need an escort," he says. In less than fifteen seconds, Officer Gene Davis wheels up on his bicycle.

As we enter the courtyard of Sassafras Residence Hall, Brown spots a student dressed like a Catholic priest. He sports a clerical collar, a huge silver cross dangling from his neck, and in his right hand he holds a large red cup, which, as soon as he sees Brown, he hides behind his back. Brown asks, "Are you a Washington College student?" Sheepishly, the student responds, "I'm a freshman." But Brown seems suspicious of this. "Let me see your college ID," he says. The student now looks sullen. "Don't have it with me," he replies.

At this point two other security officers, Tom Knox and James Shaw, both also on bikes, have assembled near Brown. They have been listening in on the conversation over their two-way radios. Shaw asks the student for his name and his residence hall. The dispatcher back at Public Safety checks the information and confirms that this kid is who he says he is. I recognize the dispatcher's voice. It's Tony, the first-year student who works for Public Safety.

"OK," Brown says, "Give me the cup." The student reluctantly hands him the red cup. It's half full of beer. Brown pours it into the bushes. "I'm going to give you a citation," he says, "and I don't want to see you drinking again. You're underage."

Officer Knox pulls out a pad and writes the young man up as though he were getting a speeding ticket. The kid sheepishly apologizes and thanks Brown for being lenient. "Just get your act together, young man," Brown says, as though he were talking to his son. And then picking up on the theme of the costume (and with a sparkle in his eyes) he makes the sign of the cross. "Go and sin no more." Everyone laughs and the crisis is over.

The radio crackles again. Two officers on the top floor of Sassafras are heard dealing with a student who has just passed out in his room. Brown and the two other officers take off, entering Sassafras through different doors and steaming up opposite staircases. Out of breath, I follow one of them. Down the hall, we see a cluster of students standing around a first-year student on the floor. He has passed out, not because he was drinking, but because he slipped on a wet floor after taking a shower and banged his head against a mirror, breaking it into pieces and creating a bloody head wound just above his right eye. An officer administers first aid as Brown calls for a squad car to take the student to the hospital emergency room for stitches.

It's now 11:30 P.M. Brown and I resume our patrol, heading back toward the Orange Fence Party. "I've noticed, Sargent Burton," I say as we walk at a brisk pace, "that you don't check everyone who has a red cup." Three students pass, all holding cups. "Our policy here," he says, "is to assume that students are not drinking underage. Some, of course, are, but many are drinking soda pop. If we checked everyone, we wouldn't be able to focus on much more important safety issues like the kid who just sliced his head open in Sassafras."

"Then why did you stop the kid in the priest's costume?"

He tells me something I kind of knew. "You might have noticed that when we approached him, he tried to hide the cup. When a student does this it's almost always a sign that he or she is underage. Whenever this happens, we will confront the student. Also, while I don't know all the first-year students yet, I know most of the upperclassmen and how old they are. I didn't know this kid so I assumed that he was underage."

It's almost midnight. The Orange Fence Party has reached a feverish pitch. We stand at a distance and just watch the action. I ask Brown whether a student has ever accosted him. "These kids just aren't that way," he says. "Most of them are polite, and if they get into trouble and I have to deal with them they will be cooperative. Only one time has a student been abusive. He was a freshman who had been drinking too much. Alcohol often brings out the worst characteristics. When I started to write him up he used the N word and took a swing at me. This kind of behavior is forbidden at Washington College and I turned him in to the dean's office. Next morning he was at Public Safety with his father profusely apologizing for his behavior. He went through J board and got the book thrown at him. He learned an important lesson."

By 2 A.M. a light rain begins to fall and the Orange Fence Party starts winding down. It's been a relatively uneventful night and Brown starts to relax. As they leave the party, more students come up to him and ask what he thinks of their costumes.

Clearly, Washington College students are fortunate to have people like Burton Brown and his fellow officers watching out for them. Jerry Roderick has set up a campus safety operation at Washington College that is appropriate for a college community, with safety officers who understand that their priority is community safety. Unfortunately, not all college and university safety officers are this way. We recently witnessed the spectacle at the University of California, Davis, where a university police officer was caught on video spraying mace on a group of otherwise peaceful student and faculty demonstrators. This is inappropriate on any college campus. If your child is being treated like a criminal rather than a student, she should express her concerns to the powers that be. It is often the dean of students to whom campus security report. Parents should also know about the Clery Act, which requires all colleges and universities to file annual crime statistics on their campuses. You can find out ahead of time what the crime rate is, if it exists, on any college campus in America.

7

Athletics and Physical Fitness

Intercollegiate athletics is big in American culture as witnessed by the high-profile NCAA Division I college football and basketball programs that almost define their respective institutions. But even at nonscholarship Division III institutions where sports are still played at a truly amateur level, significant numbers of first-year students will try out for some kind of team.[1]

Some parents fantasize that their student athletes will one day end up playing professional ball, and so they push them to excel in Little League, in middle and high school, and finally in college, preferably at a Division I institution. But if so, they are missing the point. Extremely few students who go to Division I universities make the team. Of those who do, even fewer become professional athletes. And forget about Division III. For 98 percent of all student athletes, at all NCAA divisions, the point of joining a college athletic team should to be better prepared for life in general, not to become a professional athlete.[2] Arthur Wellesley, the first Duke of Wellington, Eton College graduate, and one of the leading military and political figures of the nineteenth century, was alleged to have said that the Battle of Waterloo was won on the playing fields of Eton. Even if he didn't really say this, the idea resonates: playing on a team—any team—teaches students how to work successfully together toward a common goal or cause, a lesson as valuable in life as being able to write clearly or think critically.

Of course, not every child wishes to be (or can be) an athlete. But even for them, physical activity is important. As Plato said in the fourth century BCE, body and mind are symbiotically related. In an era when over 30 percent of the college population is obese, playing an intramural sport or just working out at the gym goes hand in hand with good physical health and academic success.[3]

In this chapter, I take a look at first-year students involved in intercollegiate athletics, physical activity, or both. What happens to first-year athletes when parents drop them off at preorientation practice? What are the views of coaches and athletic directors on the place of intercollegiate athletics in children's lives? What do some first-year athletes themselves say about playing at the college level? And why should the fitness center be a destination for first-year students?

What Happens Before and During the First Game?

For those who have aspiring first-year athletes, the home-to-college transition process usually begins a week or so before orientation. Parents drive them to campus, drop them off at their residence halls, and then almost immediately go back for home, invited to return a week or so later to rejoin them for the first day of orientation. Consequently, sending a first-year athlete off to college is initially a rather lonely thing to do, even more so if parents live at a distance from campus and have to leave their son or daughter at the airport, as I had to do. Parents are then left wondering: What's happening to them as they compete for a place on the team? What's the coach like? Did they perform well? Of course, parents get the full story when they finally rejoin their children at orientation. But that one week, when parents and children are sometimes almost completely out of touch, can seem like an eternity.

Want to know what you are missing? Join me and some first-year men's soccer players for fall preorientation practice back at Vassar College. And stick around for what happens as the season gets under way.

On a bright, sunny, and hot—over 90-degree—August day, I wander to the Prentiss Athletics Field on the far western side of Vassar College's ample campus to watch the first practice of the men's soccer team. The team is assembled on the practice field. The upper-class students are informally chatting with each other. They exude sublime confidence. I can tell who the first-year students are because they don't yet have numbers on their practice jerseys. They are subdued. Walking toward them from the field house I spot Andy Jennings, head soccer coach, and his assistant, Tony Flores. Coach Jennings, who everyone just calls Coach, wears a pair of long shorts and a vintage-style tennis hat. He looks like he just came back from a Caribbean cruise. An Englishman by birth, Jennings has an enviable win-loss record during Vassar's relatively short history as a coeducational college—123 wins, seventy-nine losses, and twenty-seven ties—resulting in two Eastern Collegiate Athletic Conference regional championships.

Coach Jennings calls the team from the sidelines to join him and Flores at midfield. About thirty young men (over a third of them first-year students) trot out onto the field and gather around for a perfunctory speech: he is not deciding on positions quite yet but, instead, will be focusing on team development. Any questions? Complete silence. The team is then sent out on the field to do some basic soccer exercises directed by Flores. Jennings walks from group to group carefully examining each player but saying nothing.

The temperature continues to rise and sweat pours down the players' faces. Jennings orders the team to the sideline for Gatorade and water. "OK guys, listen up," he says. "Some of you freshmen haven't e-mailed back the registration forms you received from the athletic office before orientation. Get them filled in *tonight* and e-mail them back because if you don't do this, you can't play." I'm again thinking about how this "connected" generation is sometimes not connected at all!

Jennings takes over practice. The first game is in a week, and so he has little time to get the team in shape. The exercises are now more sophisticated, resembling actual soccer. "We're not as big as some of the competition," he yells out as four groups form up to play practice games against each other, "but if we use our brains, we can beat them. So play smart."

As the athletes move up and down the field, Jennings does not yell disparaging remarks but encouragement, especially to the first-year team members. The point now is to get these kids to enjoy themselves and to know that the coaches are there for them. Critical comments will come soon enough. Jeremiah, a first-year student, suddenly breaks away and shoots at the goal. "Good! Good! I like it! I like it!"

Jennings yells as Jeremiah runs. But he misses the goal by a long shot. "Except for that," he immediately says. "That was crap." Jeremiah looks totally dejected, and Jennings notices. "The *net* was crap, Jeremiah, not you!" Jeremiah and his teammates laugh.

As play continues, Flores pulls some of the first-year students over to the sideline where one of the trainers, holding a laptop computer, shares each student's time for the mile he ran just before practice. He later tells me that the athletic department keeps track of each new student's vital statistics—not only running times, but also things like blood pressure and heart rate—to make sure that each athlete is in maximum good health.

As the practice ends and the team leaves the field, Jennings reminds the team that they must verbalize and communicate with each other. "Interact not react" are his parting words.

We'll soon see how this strategy works.

A week later, on a clear, blustery day at Weinberg Field, hip-hop music blares. Loud music seems to be the standard fare at intercollegiate athletic contests. The bleachers are practically empty for this first home game against nonleague opponent Manhattanville College. Soon the starters for both teams assemble midfield as they are introduced by the announcer. Three first-year students are included in the Vassar starting lineup. The announcer reminds the onlookers that Vassar adheres to good sportsmanship, that there will be no ethnic or homophobic comments, and that we are not permitted to drink alcohol in the area of the field. Everyone stands for the national anthem.

Soccer can sometimes be a slow-moving and uneventful sport, and, as play begins, I fear this will be one of those games. Vassar dominates in the opening minutes but then nothing happens. I notice that team members are talking to each other on the field just as Coach Jennings instructed them to do at practice last week, but Manhattanville begins to dominate the game. A kick on the Vassar goal is miraculously saved by Ryan Grimme, a six-foot-seven first-year student from Gahanna, Ohio. Then another attempt at goal. The game continues to go back and forth without a score. Jennings is sometimes yelling out orders from the sidelines but mostly just watching, hands on hips. There are now six (!) first-year team members on the field.

At halftime I follow the Vassar team to a knoll on the far end of the field to listen in. Vassar hasn't been playing particularly well, and the team knows it. But Jennings is a teacher, and good teachers always keep their cool. "We're not looking competent," he says calmly. "You've got to keep looking and asking yourselves, 'Can I get the ball? Can I get the ball?' We're not doing a great job getting the ball and holding it. And we're not looking for the channels going down the middle." He pauses. "Did you hear me, Miles?" Miles, a first-year forward from Trinidad, has been dreamily gazing at the girls in the stands. The buzzer sounds, and the original starting lineup returns to the field.

Back and forth. Back and forth. Vassar just can't seem to get past midfield. Everyone is tired, exhausted. A Vassar defender is shamefully fouled near the home bench by a Manhattanville player. When the referee doesn't call the infraction, a parent sitting behind me goes ballistic, standing and shouting unprintable epithets. Some other Vassar parents, embarrassed by her and for her, urge her to sit down and shut up.

Suddenly, with just two and a half minutes left of play, a Manhattanville forward breaks out from nowhere and angles a clean pass to his teammate positioned just outside Vassar's goal box. BANG. His shot sails into the left corner of the net, past Ryan Grimme's outstretched hands. The Vassar crowd groans. I look over at Jennings. He is not about to give up and urges the team on with only a few seconds left. But to no avail. The final buzzer sounds.

What Is the Philosophy of College Athletics and What Is Your Role as a Parent?

For a person who manages the crazy world of a college's athletic program, Dr. Sharon Beverly, Vassar's athletics director, looks calm and relaxed as we sit in her office at the Athletics and Fitness Center. A former college athlete herself, she exudes the demeanor of a no-nonsense coach. In 2002 she was hired by Andy Jennings, then Vassar's athletics director, as his associate director. She became athletics director one year later when Jennings decided to go back to coaching soccer full time.

What is Vassar's philosophy of intercollegiate athletics? Like all the colleges in the elite Liberty League, Beverly says, Vassar has a student-centered intercollegiate athletics program where academics are at the core. "Our coaches are teachers foremost," she says, "and because they play such an important role in the lives of these students beyond coaching them, we structure contracts that take the pressure off just winning." She pauses and then quickly adds, "Of course winning is important, but there are many other factors that define a successful coach beyond a win-loss record."

In light of the bad press intercollegiate athletics sometimes gets—including scandals involving illegal contributions to players by alumni and low graduation rates—Beverly and I discuss the benefits of playing intercollegiate sports, especially at the Division III level. She lists four. First, intercollegiate athletics teaches students how, in this very competitive world, to compete. Second, being on a team made up of students from extremely diverse backgrounds teaches important lessons about interpersonal relations and conflict resolution. Third, being an athlete is not only about winning but also about losing, and in life we all must also deal with disappointment. And finally, being an athlete is all about time management. Athletes quickly learn how to balance practice and games with academics. "But intercollegiate athletics provide an even deeper resource for freshmen," she continues. "Freshmen are faced with many choices they will have to make on their own. Being on a team means that they will have a built-in support system that can help them make good choices. This support system isn't just the coaches, but teammates as well."

What about the parents of first-year athletes? While most parents are great, some promote their children in unhelpful ways, she says. Everything they didn't accomplish in life they now live vicariously through their child. "These parents need to let go!" she says. She then rattles off the kinds of comments she gets from these parents: "'Coach is putting too much pressure on my daughter. You need to step in.' 'Coach played so and so, who wasn't at practice all week. My son *was* at practice, so why is he sitting on the bench. It's not fair.'" She tells these parents to have their children first speak directly to the captain or to the coach if they aren't happy, not to her.

But sometimes it's the athletes who come in to see Beverly because they are not playing. 'I'm more talented than X. Can't you make the coach play me?' And she always says, "Have you spoken to coach about this?" The answer is almost always no. "We want them to mature as adults while at college," she says "and *they*, not me nor their parents, need to take responsibility for their lives."

We discuss parents who act inappropriately at games. I'm thinking of the bad behavior by the parent I recently witnessed at the Manhattanville game. "Intercollegiate athletics is really about 18–23-years-olds playing and enjoying a sport. It's not about the parent! Also, we are trying to teach sportsmanship," she says. "How can we do this when parents behave badly at games, frequently because they have had too much to drink?"

I wonder out loud whether all of this pressure on athletes from parents and from society in general sometimes leads to premature burnout. Beverly nods. She says that a big reason for burnout is that everything is so structured these days. When she was a kid growing up in New York City, sports was a casual activity. She and her friends used the street in her Queens neighborhood to play stickball. No coaches. No parents. Just kids. They figured out how to come together as a team, set the rules of play, and work out disagreements on their own. "But some of the athletes I see today are so programmed that they need coaches to tell them what to do. They lack critical leadership development and don't know how to enjoy unstructured play and have fun. And so, having played in this overly structured environment since the time they could walk, these kids are burnt out by the time they get to college." She often sees first-year students who are outstanding athletes that decide to skip sports in college because their lives in high school have been so orchestrated.

What advice does Beverly have for parents with kids who want to play an intercollegiate sport? "If you have a student who excels in sports at high school and if you know this will be a big part of their collegiate experience," she says "be sure that both of you look into the program thoroughly. Look at the retention and graduation rates of the team. Ask whether the coach has any NCAA violations. And then attend a game and watch the coach in action."

What If Your Child Isn't an Athlete?

Not all of our children can or want to play intercollegiate sports. Some are burned out from playing a sport since grade school. Others simply don't have skills or inclination to be on an intercollegiate team. But everyone needs to be involved at some level of physical activity lest they become couch potatoes. As noted elsewhere above, good health and good academics go hand in hand!

So, what are some of the strategies used to get first-year students involved in exercise? What facilities and programs are available to first-year students? And what are some of the ancillary benefits to hanging out at the gym?

With these questions in mind I march over to Vassar's impressive Athletics and Fitness Center. Three walls of this facility are composed of massive, two-story-high picture windows that frame a picturesque sloping back lawn, the fairway of the ninth hole of the Vassar Golf Course. A line of StairMasters, exercise bikes, and treadmills face these windows, and several racks of weights fill the room. The center is packed with students, several of whom are just standing around casually chatting. As I climb the stairs to the second-floor office area and conference room, I spy a huge varsity basketball court and, above it, an indoor running track. Vassar certainly isn't lacking for modern indoor athletic facilities.

In the conference room I meet Roman Czula (pronounced *zoola*), who directs the Fitness Center. A short, wiry gentleman without an ounce of fat, Czula is like Professor Livingston, something of an icon at Vassar. I estimate that he is in his midsixties not from his youthful appearance but from what he's told me about his background: he was born in a displaced person's camp in Lintz, Austria, at the end of World War II.

Czula came to Vassar in 1975, six years after the college had opened its hallowed halls to men. For most of its history, Vassar had been a prominent women's college, a member of the so-called Seven Sisters that included Radcliffe, Wellesley, and Smith. So when it became coeducational in 1969, its athletic program for men was virtually nonexistent. When Czula attended his first meeting of the Department of Athletics and Physical Education, there were three female professors of physical education, a modern dance instructor, and a ballet teacher. He ended up marrying the ballet teacher one year later! Czula has been at Vassar ever since, coaching men's basketball, soccer, and tennis, chairing the physical education department between 1982 and 2004, and helping Vassar develop an intercollegiate athletic program that today, as I am witnessing, successfully competes at the intercollegiate level. In 1991, he was given the assignment of developing Vassar's now enormously successful Life Fitness Center Program, and just this year took on the additional assignment of overseeing intramural sports.

Because most good colleges and universities really care about the physical well-being of their students, I want to know about fitness activities available to all first-year students, not just those involved in intercollegiate athletes. Czula tells me that about 25–30 percent of the entering class makes use of the center on a regular basis, the average for first-year students nationally. "We make a special point of getting the word out, especially during orientation, when we sponsor a program called Just Move It," he says. "This program is very popular and is probably a major reason why freshmen end up using the fitness center in fairly high numbers." There are many other programs as well and, indeed, while waiting to meet with Czula, I noticed a list of activities on the center's bulletin board. In any given week you can do meditation with a Tibetan Buddhist to reduce stress. If you want to run faster or jump higher, my friend Tony Flores, the assistant soccer coach, has designed a program to "improve your speed and explosiveness." But there are also tai chi, yoga, aqua fitness, life fitness, and Pilates classes, Reiki treatments (whatever they are), springboard diving, swing dancing, self-defense for men and women, karate, strength training, badminton, roller hockey, fencing, and something called "Mindfulness Based Stress Reduction."

I am curious to know what Czula thinks draws busy first-year students to physical activity. Besides the noncredit courses offered at the center, students come to work out or just shoot hoops. "Another draw might surprise you," he says. "The fitness center is also a great place for first-year students to socialize and make new friends." Having seen the large number of students standing around downstairs kibitzing with each other, I'm not surprised. And like most colleges, Vassar has a robust intramural program, everything from flag football, to pickup basketball, to volleyball, tennis, and squash.

My bet is that there are other equally important reasons why this facility is full to the brim beyond what Czula just told me. As I saw at both Tufts and Washington College, the current generation of college students is extremely health conscious, despite the statistics that an estimated one in three Americans is grossly overweight. Have college fitness centers like the one here at Vassar become an antidote to bad eating habits? Yes, Czula says. An underlying motivation for some new students coming here is to fight the war on calories so that they don't put on the infamous freshman 15. "Our job is to get these kids *moving*," he says. "And part of what we do here is help students feel comfortable about working out."

Another important role fitness centers play is to relieve stress. During the last week of classes and the exam period at the end of each semester, the center sponsors free stress-buster classes, such as a body percussion dance class that enables first-year students to "stomp their cares away," a very popular program, Czula says.

Knowing from national statistics that college students are not getting the exercise they need, I ask Czula what he is doing to encourage more first-year Vassar students to use the fitness center.[4] Czula admits that this is a challenge. He says that during Just Move It, the program he does at orientation, he invites inactive first-year students, especially those who might be embarrassed about coming to the center, to drop by his office for a confidential chat. He also does everything he can to advertise as widely as possible the programs he has available here at the center. "By being nonjudgmental about exercise," he says "I have had some success. But at the end of the day we can't make these students get exercise."

When Your Kid Isn't a Starter

I head to the field house before Thursday soccer practice and catch up with assistant coach Tony Flores in the locker room. This fall, 35 percent of the Vassar men's soccer team are first-year athletes. Do first years present special challenges? "There are a lot more things you have to keep in mind with first-year athletes compared to their upper-class teammates," Flores says as he laces up his cleats. "For one thing, this is the first time away from home and so we want to make sure they are settled in and comfortable and that they are making friends."

Eight weeks into the semester, does he see any first-year teammates with academic or social issues? Are any of them homesick?

Flores sees little homesickness but he is less certain about academics. "It won't be until after they take midterms in a couple of weeks that we'll hear from Dean Long," he says. "Then we'll know if there are any problems." If there are, he and Coach Jennings will talk to some of the first-year team members about how well they are adjusting to college.

I ask Flores whether any of the first-year athletes are talking about quitting the team. I've noticed quite a few first-year starters, but most new members of the team are still sitting on the bench. As far as he knows, no one is talking about leaving. "These guys are very competitive and they have a great attitude," he says. "They are willing to learn, to take criticism, and they usually listen to us." In fact, he knows of only one kid who quit the team. This happened last year, and he left not because of soccer but because he felt Vassar was too small. "This is why we encourage our recruits to visit campus and stay overnight so they know what they're getting into," he says.

Though there seem to be fewer players at practice than normal today, the team (and especially the new students) is looking much more confident than when I saw them the first day of practice. I sense a feeling of real excitement. They now have four victories under their belts and the next day they play their first league game against Saint Lawrence University. As Coach Jennings waits for everyone to assemble, I ask him why so many members of the team are missing. This is the problem with Thursdays, he says, because there are lots of afternoon labs and classes, which make it especially difficult when there is a big game the next day. "But, hey, academics come first!" he exclaims.

After doing some calisthenics with the team, Jennings calls the guys in to form a big circle around him. He says that this will be a short practice because of the next day's game. He also diplomatically says that his rationale for who will start tomorrow is not about particular people but about balance in light of Saint Lawrence's 4.3.3 offense. He then names that game's starters and asks them to put on the black jerseys that are piled up on the sidelines midfield. Four first-year students are chosen: Adam McCabe at midfield, Rex Smith and Ian Robinson at forward, and Ryan Grimme at goal. As the first team takes to the field, Coach names the guys who will practice against them. Those left out, including six first-year students, are looking pretty glum. One of these students is Brady, my classmate in Freshman Writing Seminar. As the two teams run out on the field, Coach Jennings unexpectedly walks over to me. "Did you see the faces of the freshmen who aren't starting?" And then pointing out how unrealistic these guys sometimes are he says, "They *all* feel they should be starters."

What Do First-Year Student Athletes Say about Sports and Academics?

The following week, before a big game against Hobart College, I catch up with Ryan Grimme, the goalie, and Adam McCabe, a first-year student from Tallahassee, Florida. I ask Adam what challenges he and his first-year teammates have faced handling academics. His biggest challenge, he says, has been time management. While he wasn't totally surprised by the amount of work he'd have in college (he attended a pretty tough prep school in Florida), he just wasn't prepared for the level of work at Vassar.

Ryan agrees: "The biggest challenge for me has been how much academic work I have to do outside of soccer. I think I spend about 90 percent of my free time on homework."

I ask him what a typical day is like. "I'm usually up at 7:30 A.M., attend a German language drill from 8:30 to 9:00, take my environmental politics class from 9:00 to 10:15, eat brunch from 10:15 to 11:00, and attend German class from 11:00 to noon. Then political science from noon to 1:15, after which I work in the gym doing laundry from 1:30 to 4:00. Over to soccer practice from 4:30 to 6:00, a quick dinner at 6:30, and then homework from 7:00 until midnight. Finally to bed."

My head is reeling. "So how do you have a life?" I ask. There doesn't seem to be any down time in Ryan's schedule.

"Well, you just take your opportunities," Ryan says. "When there is no weekend game, the men's and women's soccer teams usually hang out together." He tells me that sometimes he parties at the town houses where some of the senior soccer players live. I think of Barry and Hank, the two first-year baseball players at Morningside College, and their similar social life as student athletes.

Adam jumps in and says that he lives in Main Hall, which has a large common room where he and his friends can study. "I guess studying is part of an athlete's social life at Vassar," Adam says. "I wanted to join the UNICEF group here and the Hip Hop Club, but with my job at the Vassar nursery school and soccer practice, there just aren't enough hours in the day."

How are classes going? Ryan tells me that he is doing surprisingly well. He says with great pride that he got an 89 on a political science test. "But unlike high school, where I was able to get good grades with very little study," he says, "I had to work my ass off for that 89!"

Adam, by way of contrast, is ambivalent about his grades. He says that he really has no idea how well he is doing. For example, he recently wrote a paper but hasn't gotten the grade back yet and midterms are still a week off. He says that because you are always being tested in high school, you can pretty well gauge how you are doing. "But here at Vassar, freshmen are living in the land of the unknown. Having no feedback grade-wise I really don't know what to expect." Adam is expressing a key difference between college and high school.

"The lesson I am learning," Ryan adds, "is that you need to keep up with your work because if you fall behind, you're screwed."

Do Adam and Ryan ever wish they had played soccer at a Division I university? Ryan says that if he had wanted to play soccer professionally he probably would have been better off at a place like Ohio State. But since his aim is to become a lawyer, he feels he has a far better chance at getting into a good law school from Vassar than he would from some large university. So he's quite happy to be here playing Division III. Adam agrees with Ryan. In high school he aspired to play in Division I, and he probably could have done this at any number of universities in Florida since his high school soccer team was in the playoffs for the Florida State championships. But for him, the choice of college came down to which could best help him achieve his career dreams since, like Ryan, he's not planning to play soccer professionally. "I think I'm better off here at Vassar."

Both Ryan and Adam have made wise decisions. According to the NCAA, only 2 percent of high school athletes are awarded athletic scholarships at Division I and II institutions, and of this 2 percent, an even smaller percentage goes on to play professional sports: 1.7 percent in football and 1.2 percent in men's basketball.[5]

I ask Ryan and Adam whether they plan to play a second sport at Vassar.

"Maybe basketball," Ryan says, stating the obvious, considering his height. "But I really look forward to a break when the soccer season is over and I can just be a regular college student." Even if Ryan decides not to play varsity basketball, he can still play the sport at the intramural level over at the fitness center.

Adam reveals that, because he had to drop a required class this semester, he will have to retake it spring semester. Consequently, there is no way can he can play another sport. He also wants to study abroad in the spring of his junior year and playing a second sport might make this impossible. Adam is talking about a common problem student athletes face who either want to play a second sport or play a sport in the fall like football for which practice is also held in the spring. In either case, the possibility of studying abroad is pretty much eliminated.

And how do Adam and Ryan feel about their coaches? "On top of being our coach, Andy is always trying to be our friend," Ryan says. "He doesn't like us calling him Coach. He wants us to call him Andy. Also, he doesn't yell at us like some coaches do."

Adam agrees: "Andy's style is very different from what I was used to in Florida. He's very English and calm, whereas many American coaches get very emotional. The first time I met Andy was at practice last August, so I didn't know what to expect. But I am very pleased with what I found."

A Coach's Perspective on First-Year Student Athletes

Andy Jennings and I meet in the conference room of Vassar's sprawling Athletic and Fitness Center. He has just returned from recruiting in southern Massachusetts. Since first-year enrollments at most colleges involve relatively large numbers of student athletes, people like Jennings not only coach one or sometimes two sports, but they have also become an essential part of a college's admissions effort.

Jennings proudly points out that during his tenure as athletic director between 1996 and 2004, the college's $30 million master plan for athletics was completed, including the building we are now sitting in. Vassar also joined the Liberty League, made up of prestigious colleges like Union, Saint Lawrence, Hobart, Hamilton, Rensselaer Polytechnic Institute, and the University of Rochester. He has a lot to be proud of. But being an athletic director is not easy. Between endless budget meetings, difficult personnel decisions, and weekends away attending games, many athletic directors I have known yearn to be coaches again. And this is exactly what happened to Jennings. After taking a sabbatical leave, he returned to Vassar in 2004, happy once again to be the men's soccer coach. He has been successful. In 2009, he was named the Liberty League's Coach of the Year.

What does Jennings think of the season so far? With over 30 percent first-year athletes, the team this year is a truly young one and so everything being equal, it's doing as well as can be expected. He points out that the team is coming off a good season last year but lost several great seniors, especially one in particular who was a role model for the entire team. He says that without these guys, it's hard to know how well the team will finally do. He pauses and then adds, "I love to win. I judge myself by the success of the team. So we'll just have to see."

Considering the young team, is he coaching differently than the year before? "No," he says, "but of course, there is a difference. Both technically and tactically this young team is not yet in touch with what I want them to do. It's hard to cram everything into new kids in a couple of weeks of practice before the season begins. It takes time."

Jennings normally likes to give his teams as much freedom as possible when they are on the field. "I'm not a Vince Lombardi type who yells and screams and insists that the team do it only *my* way," he says. "As long as they can be taught in a team environment, these kids need to be given an opportunity to learn by their mistakes." He also believes that the older players can teach their new teammates. But with only three seniors, he just doesn't have a lot of older players to rely on. "So I suppose that even though I hate micromanaging I need to be more of a force as a coach this year because of the relatively young age of the team."

I have enjoyed watching Jennings coach, probably because he so clearly sees himself as a teacher. "And I believe varsity sports are the equivalent of upper-level courses in the major rather than introductory courses students take freshmen and sophomore year," he says. "Like an upper-level course, I deal with very complex issues. Varsity athletics is an emotional, physical, psychological, and social experience."

I ask a rhetorical question: "But don't these kids sometimes also place their sport above studies, especially first-year students who don't yet understand how academically demanding college can be?" I know from my many years of involvement with the National Collegiate Athletic Association that this is often the case. Jennings is adamant in his response. He says that these kids are students first and he is proud of the fact that every year his team has been named an all-Academic team with the National Soccer Coaches Association. The priorities at Vassar are simple: "Academics *always* trump soccer," he says. "So does family and religion. If you need to skip a practice or a game to celebrate Rosh Hashanah, you do it, and I will be supportive." But sometimes things aren't as they seem. He tells me about a first-year athlete he coached several years ago who said he had to skip practice because of a paper that was due. When Jennings asked him what he had done the previous weekend, the student replied, "I partied." "Partying *doesn't* trump practice!"

Do partying and alcohol create problems for Jennings as a coach? He tells me that Vassar has a forty-eight-hour rule for players who are over twenty-one, which is to say that they cannot drink forty-eight hours before the game. He quickly adds that first-year athletes who are under twenty-one are told that they must abide by the laws of the state and not consume alcohol. Jennings pauses, then articulates a feeling that is shared by a growing number of educators, college presidents included. "Frankly, I have a problem with the law that says you must be twenty-one in order to drink. Because of it, we aren't teaching kids how to respect alcohol. We teach them how to be good citizens. We prepare them for the responsibilities of family and parenthood. But then we leave them on their own when it comes to alcohol." To illustrate his point, Jennings tells me of an incident several years ago. He took the team to Barcelona where, like most of Europe, students can drink when they are eighteen. When they first arrived, some of the team went to a bar and drank too much. But then they realized that within the context of Spanish teenage culture they were making absolute asses of themselves. Once they had returned to America, a team member commented that because of this embarrassing incident, he thought the guys had learned a life lesson: they had gone to Spain as immature boys, saw what fools they had made of themselves and returned home more grown up.

Alcohol isn't the only health issue athletes—indeed all students—face. Recently, the newspapers have featured a rash of health-related incidents involving student athletes who get dehydrated or suffer concussions. Jennings tells me that he is particularly concerned about hot days, especially with young, macho first-year athletes who are out to prove themselves and who don't want to seem weak. "I always tell them not to be intimidated by the coaches," he says. "If you need water, go get it. Do what you need to do!" Concussions are a similar concern. First-year athletes especially don't want to say that they are injured. They will fight to stay on the field even if they aren't 100 percent, but Jennings won't let this happen. He has required that one of his juniors sit out the season this fall because of a concussion he got last year. "It's *never* worth sacrificing health just to get field time!"

What about new recruits who end up warming the bench most of the season? Does this cause discord with parents? I am thinking about Brady, my friend from Freshman Writing Seminar, who has been played very little so far. Not playing is a big disappointment to many first-year students and their parents. "And frankly," Jennings says, "it's disappointing to me as well because I know that these kids really want to get field time." He points out that unless they are standouts, first-year athletes expect to sit on the bench. But if they don't play later, they probably will leave the team. So, in the recruiting process, he tries to get prospective students to understand that not all of them will play first year. "I don't get many complaints from freshman parents," he continues. "I'm always straight up with them. I tell them that we want to win and so I will play the kids who I think will give us the best chance of doing this. I'll also tell prospective freshman who in my opinion are not very good soccer players—and I do this in front of their parents—that it is not automatic that they will get on the team and that if they really want to play, intramural soccer might be a better alternative."

Not all coaches are like Andy Jennings. Even in division III, there are a few coaches who care about one thing only—winning—and will do anything to achieve this objective. Jennings (like most good coaches) believes in winning as well, but he also understands that athletics is part of a college's educational mission and that mission should not include winning at any cost. So what does a student do when she or he inherits a coach or an athletic program that seems out of sync with the college's otherwise high ideals?

I'm going to limit my comments here to student athletes (like those in Division III or the Ivy League) who are not on athletic scholarships because scholarship athletes have other issues they must deal with that would require a book of its own! But if the time demand on your student athlete is such that they cannot keep up with academic work, or if they are being told by the coach that they cannot take a junior year abroad because doing so will compromise the team, or if they are being encouraged to violate NCAA rules (by taking steroids, for example), then they should talk to the athletic director. Likewise, if the coach is not providing the team with adequate refreshment breaks during practice, especially when it is very hot, they should talk to the coach first and then, if this doesn't work, to the athletic director. And what if your child isn't getting field time? Who plays is really at the discretion of the coach and unless there is obvious bias, there isn't much your student can do about it. Of course, there is always the option of intramurals or a club sport like rugby. But as we will now see, for many first-year student athletes, not getting field time is truly disappointing.

Reflections of a First-Year Bench Sitter

Brady enters the side door of the Retreat, Vassar's snack bar, where I'm eating a pizza. Soccer season ended several weeks earlier: eight wins, seven losses, and one tie. Not enough to get the team into the Liberty League playoffs, but still a winning season. I wave Brady over to my table. Since sharing soccer *and* Freshman Writing Seminar, we've become friends. "Hope you're getting your reading done," I joke, recalling a sideline conversation during practice when Brady had to pull an all-nighter because he was behind in his work for the seminar. Brady laughs as he takes a seat. He admits that his life has gotten a whole lot simpler since the season ended and that he has no problem getting the reading done now.

So what is life after soccer like? Brady tells me that he can now be more like a normal first-year student, if indeed there is such a thing. But he admits that he still does a lot of weight lifting in the fitness center to stay in shape. "I also go to captain's practices maybe a couple of times each week," Brady adds. "They're not mandatory but strongly encouraged." I know very well what "captain's practices" are, but I ask Brady to give me the Vassar version. "We just play soccer for the fun of it," he responds and then adds, "Coaches can't be present."

I am of a mixed mind concerning so-called captain's practices. They are a way student athletes get around NCAA Division III regulations forbidding postseason practice and play. By having informal practices without coaches present, team members aren't *technically* violating the rules. At the same time, because teammates are expected by their peers to participate—and Brady is a good example of this—these unofficial off-season practices can pull them away from being involved in nonathletic activities. But I wonder: Should students be prohibited from being involved in a healthy activity? Better captain's practice, in my opinion, than being holed up in a residence hall room playing Halo on the computer.

I bring up a subject that I recently discussed with Coach Jennings. I point out that he and some of his first-year teammates have sat on the bench most of the season. Has this been frustrating? Brady is honest. He has been playing soccer since grade school, and his perennial dream has been eventually to play soccer at the professional level. He was one of two soccer captains his senior year in high school, and so as a starter played on a regular basis. At Vassar this fall he played a total of maybe thirty minutes in three games. "So yes, it has been very frustrating to sit on the bench," Brady says shaking his head. He continues: "To get playing time, you need to make a positive impression on the coaches from the beginning. I didn't have a lot of confidence this August when I came to Vassar and for me playing well is having confidence. Maybe I didn't have confidence because four freshmen were cut from the team and so I was nervous that I might be cut as well. Also, I had physical issues. A pulled groin muscle limited playing time and kept me off the travel roster."

Brady is being hard on himself. The fact is that most first-year athletes sit on the bench. As Coach Jennings just said (and as Megan told me at Tufts's orientation), you pay your dues and then by the time you are a sophomore or a junior you are usually playing on a regular basis. One of the reasons Ryan and Adam got so much playing time this year is that, besides being very good, Vassar had only three returning seniors.

I ask Brady whether he plans to play soccer next fall and whether just being on the team is enough to keep him interested. "The team is almost like a fraternity," he says. "I still hang out with them. So this season it was OK just being on the team. But next year I'm pretty certain that I will be playing on a more regular basis."

As Brady says this, I remember an off-the-cuff observation made by Baird Tipson, Washington College's president, about student athletes who so identify with their sport that they can't imagine *not* being on a team. He suggested that more and more young athletes are pressured to choose one sport early in their lives and then to concentrate on that sport year-round. They join clubs with semiprofessional coaches and often compete during the nontraditional seasons. They are under enormous pressure from their parents, who imagine them winning an athletic scholarship or even going on to play their sport professionally. They are completely defined by their sport. If they turn out not to be as good as they and their parents had imagined it can easily precipitate a crisis, a ticking time bomb for far too many first-year student athletes. I sincerely hope that Brady, if he is still sitting on the bench next year, won't be that ticking time bomb President Tipson expressed concern about.

8

First Gens

My first introduction to first-generation college students happened in 1969. I was fresh out of graduate school and had gotten a job working for the city of New York helping to create a program that encouraged underserved students, mostly Latinos and African Americans, to apply for admission to four-year colleges and universities. Virtually all of these kids were the first in their families to go to college. My job was to convince the admissions directors of mostly private colleges and universities around the country to take a chance on these so-called first gens even though their SAT scores and high school grades were well below kids whose parents had college degrees. The program successfully placed a number of deserving first gens into good colleges and universities. Later that year, however, the City University of New York adopted a program that guaranteed admission to most New York City high school graduates at one of their senior or community colleges and the Education Incentive Program quickly became redundant.

But over the year I worked for the Education Incentive Program I learned about the uphill struggle first gens faced as they confronted a world that, up until then, had been largely out of reach for most of them. Not only did they often come to college from understaffed and underfunded public high schools but many had also been tracked into vocational courses and therefore had not received adequate precollege preparation. On top of this, their parents had little knowledge of what universities are and how they operate and therefore could not be as supportive as parents who themselves had attended college. Some of the first gens I worked with were successful. Many, unfortunately, didn't make it.

It might seem counterintuitive, but between 1971 and 2014, the percentage of first-year first-generation college students as a percentage of all full-time first-year students attending four-year colleges declined from 38.5 percent in 1971 to 18.7 percent in 2014. The reason for this decline is in large part attributable to that fact that over this period of time more Americans generally were going to college, as well as the fact that first gens were tending to favor two-year as opposed to four-year colleges and universities immediately after high school. If, however, we believe in the role higher education can play in opening the door to opportunity, we must do much more as a nation to encourage qualified first-generation students to consider getting a four-year college degree.[1]

This chapter features many of the first-year issues already discussed, but it focuses on challenges that are particular to first gens: What's it like to be a first gen at a university where many if not most of the students have parents who attended college? What are the unique challenges first gens face as they enter college? What are the particular obstacles faced by first gens who happen to be African American or Latino?

First Gens Talk about Going to College: Parental Support, Challenges, and Fitting In

The reception area of Queens College's Academic Advising Center is a rambling affair located on the second floor of Kiely Hall, the college's main administration building. Queens College is a division of the City University of New York, an urban public university that serves 270,000 degree-credit students at twenty-three colleges and institutions across New York City. Over 20 percent of its students are the first in their families to go to college, and almost all of them come to college with substantial financial need. On the afternoon I visit, Kiely Hall is a hub of throbbing activity as students prepare to meet with a counselor. A young woman dressed in a sari walks into the center and joins one of the queues. Another student, a bearded Sikh wearing a black turban, explains to the receptionist that he needs to change two of his courses. Between students entering and exiting the advisers' offices, using the Internet stations, and just chatting with each other in the reception area, this room is a miniversion of New York's Grand Central Terminal. Laura Silverman, director of advising, waves to me from her office at the end of the reception area. Considering the remarkable busyness she must coordinate, she looks uncommonly relaxed.

Twenty years ago Laura Silverman was a first gen herself. Because her parents' education ended in high school, she says that she didn't really know what going to college involved. In her mind at least it was a place you went for one reason only—to prepare for a good job. And so she applied to and was accepted by the Fashion Institute of Technology in Manhattan for a two-year applied associates degree in advertising and communication. As Silverman began her first year at the institute, she was required to take general education courses in the arts and sciences, and these led her to see that there was more to life than—as she puts it—designing a package. Taking these courses at the Fashion Institute of Technology began to challenge her notion of what college is all about. And so she decided to transfer to a senior college and get a proper bachelor's degree. Her parents were skeptical.

At the State University of New York at New Paltz, Silverman majored in communications, a theory-based subject that required extensive reading and class discussion. It was in a senior-year communications class, reading the thought-provoking theories of Noam Chomsky and Andrew Bell, that a light went on. With the help of a favorite professor, she began to see a panorama, a wider world out there that was bigger than the world she then knew. She also saw that she had an ability to write and so she had decided to minor in journalism. She went on to get a master's degree in media studies at Queens College. "Here I was motivated by a faculty that was rigorous, challenging, and absolutely first class," she tells me.

It seems the people at Queens were equally impressed with her. Starting out as a graduate assistant in the dean of students office, she progressed through the ranks, eventually becoming assistant director of the Office of Honors and Scholarships and then assistant and finally director of academic advising. She is a perfect match for the job she now holds. She daily works with first-generation students who share her background, young men and women who come from families that know very little about what college is about beyond being the ticket to a job.

I am so intrigued by Silverman's story that I fail to notice that outside her office three first-year students, all the first in their families to go to college, have gathered, patiently waiting to meet with us. Silverman invites them in and asks them to join us around the conference table. Because it was hard to get volunteers to meet with me, she and I agreed beforehand that she would remain during the conversation just to make sure the students feel comfortable. Unlike the first-year students at Tufts and Vassar, most of whom come from college-educated families and were actually anxious to meet with me, these first gens are not sure they want to share their intimate stories with a total stranger.

Silverman asks the students to identify themselves and then tell me a bit about their backgrounds. She assures them that their identities will be protected.

The first to speak is Molly, the only child of an Irish-American mother living in Rockaway, Queens. A high school dropout, Molly's mother separated from her father when she was an infant and then remarried. Her stepfather legally adopted her, but five years ago moved out of the house. Even though he works for the Metropolitan Transit Authority and makes good money, he no longer supports either Molly or her mother. So, at age eighteen, Molly is financially independent. She lives with a boyfriend off campus.

Next to Molly is Imran, a Pakistani American. His parents, with whom he lives, came to America from the Punjab. Though Imran is American born, he didn't speak English until he started elementary school in the Fresh Meadows section of Queens. His father washes dishes at a Korean restaurant in lower Manhattan and his mother stays at home with Imran's four younger siblings. Both parents have only the rudiments of a formal education.

Chang, a Chinese national, was born in Shandong province south of Beijing, where his parents still live. His father works for a company that makes signs and his mother is employed by a clothes factory, making sweatshirts for export to North America. Neither have a college education. A couple years ago, Chang moved to the Bronx to live with his uncle, an apartment superintendent and handyman. Chang still struggles with English and it is probably for this reason that he is very quiet. He now resides in Queens College's new residence hall.

I thank the students for the introductions, tell them what I am writing about, and encourage them to be as candid with me as possible. To get the ball rolling I start out with a noncontroversial question: What are they thinking about majoring in?

Silence. Molly finally ventures an answer. When she came to Queens a few months ago she was thinking that she would go into either speech pathology or speech therapy. But now, after taking some of the general education requirements, she's thinking about majoring in psychology. "All I know is that I want to work in some kind of therapeutic profession or as a high school guidance counselor," Molly says. "My plan is to go on to graduate school."

"What about you, Imran?" He hesitates. "I'm not sure—I'm thinking now about physical education and, if I do this, I plan to go on for a master's here at Queens. Eventually I want to teach physical education at the high school level."

Encouraged by Imran's response, Chang joins right in. Considering that he has been living in the United States for only a couple years, his English is impressive. "I'm going to major in physics and then, after I become a U.S. citizen, go to Cal Tech to do a master's in aerospace engineering." The ice has been broken.

I am interested to know if being the first in their families to go to college has been a problem. Yes, says Imran. His parents really didn't want him to go to college. He says that in Punjabi culture, men go to work right after high school, and this is what his parents wanted him to do. Fortunately, he was eventually able to convince them that in America you need a college degree to get a good job. So do Imran's parents support his plan to teach physical education? "I don't think they really know what physical education is," Imran responds, "so I don't bother to discuss these things with them."

Molly chimes in. Her mother is neither supportive nor not supportive—she never went to college and so she has no idea what college is really about. When Molly talks about psychology with her mother, she has no idea what psychology is or why it's something a person would want to study. So Molly and her mother have a friendly understanding: "When I left for college this fall my mother said to me 'Whatever you decide, dear, will be OK with me.' I'm pretty much on my own."

Chang's parents were very supportive of him going to college because getting a university education is a big deal in Chinese culture. I suggest to Chang that Chinese universities are very different from universities in the United States and ask him whether his parents understand what the liberal arts are. "My parents don't understand the liberal arts. Neither does my uncle. And quite frankly, I'm not sure I do either." He tells me that in China you declare what profession you plan to enter and then take the appropriate courses at university. At Queens College, in contrast, he must take lots of general education requirements. "Sometimes I think I'm wasting my time," Chang says. "On the other hand, I've been forced to take some classes I really enjoy. Well maybe not philosophy. But I love the anthropology class I'm taking."

I wonder whether first-generation students have helicopter parents like their more affluent classmates, so I ask my new friends how involved their parents are in their lives. Imran says that he hardly ever see his father, who leaves for work at 5 A.M. before Imran is up and sometimes comes back at night after he is asleep. Imran sees his mom all the time, but she's a control freak and very critical, always on him for not getting his housework done or not working. "When I'm at home all I hear about is how badly I compare to my cousins," Imran says with a note of bitterness.

Chang says that because of his current situation he will see his parents again only after he graduates. He admits that his uncle in the Bronx is really his family. "He doesn't know much about college, but he is very supportive of what I'm doing."

And what has been the biggest challenge for each of these first gens in going to college? For Molly it has been meeting the expectations of her teachers. She finds Queens College to be very difficult compared to her high school, where there was incredibly little homework. In high school everything was scheduled, whereas at Queens College she has an enormous amount of free time. Molly admits, therefore, that time management has been a big challenge for her. "Money has also been a challenge," Molly says after a pause. "My family is very poor. I wanted to live in the new residence hall but didn't have enough money so I live off campus in cheap housing."

Imran says that until he went to grade school, he mostly spoke Punjabi at home. So he struggled with English all through school and even today sometimes finds English a challenge. Fortunately his professors have been very supportive, especially his English professor. "When I got an F on my first English paper, she called me into her office and now she works with me on my essays." Imran confesses that he probably made a mistake by taking fifteen credits when most of his classmates were taking only twelve. He admits that he really wasn't prepared for this kind of heavy course load, in large part because he found high school easy. He had no AP or honors courses, no pre-calculus, and his high school teachers weren't very challenging. But at Queens College, he is struggling. "The amount of work I have to do in some of my classes is incredible," Imran says, shaking his head. "But Ms. Silverman got me back to twelve credits and she has been very supportive. She's great." Silverman smiles.

Citizenship is Chang's biggest challenge. Because he is an immigrant on a student's visa, it's hard for him to get financial aid. Chang had the grades in China to go to college anywhere in the United States—indeed, he was hoping to go to Cornell—but he didn't qualify for state and federal financial aid and couldn't afford their high tuition. The main reason Chang came to Queens College was because he was accepted into the Macaulay Honors College with a full scholarship. He tells me that he plans to join the Marine Corps immediately after he graduates so that he can become a U.S. citizen. He repeats his hope to then attend Cal Tech to do a master's in engineering.

What kind of tensions might lie in this very diverse community? Do these first gens feel comfortable at Queens College? Molly says that for the first few weeks she was terribly lonely and thought she might drop out. But then someone suggested she get involved with the Newman Center, the Roman Catholic student group at Queens. So she did, and Father Wood, the Catholic chaplain, has been a great support to her. Because the Newman Center is located on the second floor of the Student Union with all the other chaplaincies, Protestant, Muslim, and Jewish, Molly says that she's met lots of first-year students from different religious and cultural backgrounds. She admits that she never knew a Muslim before. "The second floor is a great place to hang out and make friends," Molly says. "You should meet Father Wood!"

Chang admits that he isn't the most outgoing guy and therefore initially found it difficult to make friends. But since living in the new residence hall, this has all changed for him. He tells me that his roommate comes from upstate and that he's become part of his family. "They came to visit him last week and took me out to dinner," Chang beams.

Queens College has a relatively large Asian American population—about 27 percent—so I ask Chang whether he has any Chinese friends. "Not really," Chang answers. "I want to be an American, so I'm making a special effort to meet different people."

Molly seems almost offended by my question. "You really don't see ethnic clusters like you might see on other campuses—you know, Chinese hanging out with Chinese, Koreans with Koreans," she says. "Students really connect with each other here based on their interests, *not* their ethnic or religious background." Imran agrees with Molly. He says that the campus is a very friendly environment, one in which he can make lots of friends. He feels *very* comfortable at Queens College.

What advice do Molly, Imran, and Chang have for first gens like themselves contemplating college? "I have three suggestions for first-generation freshmen," Molly says without hesitation. "First, try to get as much money as possible *before* you come to college. Look at Work Study and ask the Financial Aid Office about scholarships beyond the obvious ones. Second, take advantage of *everything* the college has to offer. And finally, realize you can't slack off. It might have been easy in high school. But college is a different matter!"

Imran: "My parents want me to become the head of our house when I graduate and support it by working. But I don't want to do this. I want to be on my own. So my advice is to make sure your family understands that this is a time when we are struggling to figure out our future. *Our* future, not theirs."

And Chang: "I made the mistake of taking all my general education courses at the same time. Because my English isn't very good and because these courses required an enormous amount of reading, I was overwhelmed. It would have been much better had I taken some of my freshman courses in physics and computer science because I already took many of these same courses back in China and they don't require as much English. So, while you learn English, balance general education courses that maybe are more difficult for a foreign speaker with ones that are familiar to you."

I jokingly ask Chang why he then didn't take Chinese. Before Chang can answer, Laura Silverman, who has been silent up to this point, jumps in: "Because Queens encourages international students to move outside their comfort zone, we discourage them from taking a class that is too easy."

What Do You Need to Know If Your Child Is the First in Your Family to Go to College?

As Molly, Imran and Chang leave, I hang back. Because of Laura Silverman's own background as a first-generation college student and her vast experience advising them, I am eager to hear her views on the special challenges they face the first year. How do first gens and their parents adapt to this new and unfamiliar environment? What are the tensions that arise in the process?

When they first arrive at orientation, can she differentiate between first gens and students whose parents attended college? Sometimes, she says. New students with college-educated parents are more or less familiar with the rationale behind a liberal arts education, namely, that it provides them with exposure to a wide variety of courses that may or may not bear a direct relationship to what they will eventually major in or to what they will become in life. For many first-generation students, conversely, this concept is foreign and odd. For them, education is meant to be utilitarian, a process whereby they absorb a quantifiable amount of useful information from their professors and then eventually do something tangible with this information. She says that this is why many first-year first gens and their parents see business, accounting, and computer science as the only options for serious study. They think these disciplines offer usable information with a reward at the end—specifically, employment. It doesn't especially matter that maybe they aren't actually interested in becoming accountants or computer programmers. "Since the liberal arts do not fit hand in hand with their idea of what college should be," she says, "we often have to start from scratch with these first gens and indoctrinate them into this brave new world of a modern American university. This means encouraging them to seek new interests where the monetary rewards are not always so obvious."

Silverman gives an example of a first gen who has been able to make this transition. Jacek, better known as Jack to his friends, is a first-year Polish American student she currently advises who was brought up in a working-class neighborhood on Long Island. Jack is much like Imran in that he spoke very little English before he entered grade school. And like Imran, Jack attended a high school with a low graduation rate and where few kids went on to college. The cards were stacked against him. Silverman says that just to get to Queens College, Jack must commute well over one hour each way. Any kid who does this *must* be dedicated.

When Silverman first met Jack at orientation, he was disoriented and confused. But unlike many of his quiet and withdrawn first-gen classmates, Jack was bold and curious. If he didn't understand something, he just kept asking questions, even if they weren't sophisticated questions. For instance, in the beginning Jack wanted to know what disciplines like anthropology or political science were, something many kids already understood. "My point," Silverman says, "is that unlike some of his first-gen classmates, Jack is inquisitive and open-minded. He really *wants* to take all those 'impractical' liberal arts courses. I really think that inquisitiveness and open-mindedness are important ingredients to college success for first-generation freshmen. And I have no doubt that Jack will do well."

In their book *Higher Education? How Colleges Are Wasting Our Money and Failing Our Kids—and What We Can Do about It*, Claudia Dreifus and Andrew Hacker (himself a Queens College professor) state that students with college-educated parents stand a five times better chance of getting a college degree.[2] Clearly, kids whose parents went to college have an enormous advantage over kids whose parents didn't. I ask Silverman to tell me more about the parents of first gens she works with.

She sees two extremes. On the one hand, some parents of first-generation students are very aggressive about their children's education and are overly involved. But more often she sees the opposite— that is, parents who are completely uninvolved.[3] She gives me examples of both.

At orientation, Silverman was giving a presentation to incoming first-year students and their parents in the Student Union. Sitting almost directly in front of her was a big burly man, presumably someone's father—the silent type with a gruff exterior, a person who reminded her of her own father. At the end, she asked if there were any questions, knowing you can tell the parents who went to college by the questions they ask. "What is the student-faculty ratio at Queens?" "How many faculty are involved in research?" "What percentage of the faculty have PhDs?" But this guy was just sitting there, arms crossed. No emotion. Stoically passive. Frowning. And, so far, no questions for Silverman.

At the end of the Q-and-A period, Silverman excused the students so that they could meet with their advisers in Kiely Hall across the main quad. She then told the parents that their portion of the program with college administrators would begin in a few minutes. During the intermission, this guy walked up to where Silverman was standing behind the podium. "Ms. Silverman," he said, "I couldn't understand a thing you said—but I liked it!" "Here is a nice dad," she says. "But unlike the more sophisticated college-educated parents present, he *really* didn't have a clue what was going on."

Silverman's second example is of the opposite extreme, what she calls the aggressive first-generation parent. At the same meeting, as the students were filing out of the Student Union to meet with their advisers and register, she found out that a Korean American mom had followed her daughter to Kiely Hall. After lurking in the hallway for an hour, she pulled her embarrassed daughter out of the classroom so that she could review the courses being planned. She then told her daughter which courses were appropriate—only science and math—and which were not—all the rest. "This mother didn't have a clue either about college or a liberal arts education," Silverman says. "But unlike the burly dad who did not understand and was quiet and nonparticipatory but appreciative, she was aggressive and intrusive. While both approaches are problematic for different reasons, at least the dad was willing to let the professionals do their job."

For many families who are not college educated there is tension between having their children go to college and just getting a job after high school. And so I ask Silverman whether this is an issue with the first gens she advises here at Queens College. Her response surprises me. She tells me that at least here in New York City the issue generally isn't work versus college. Many parents who did not go to college themselves see a college education as a ticket to the American dream, a notion in part supported by data showing that in 2005 47 percent of new first gens nationally reported that an important reason why they decided to go to college was because their parents supported them in this decision, up from 20.9 percent in 1971.[4] The problem, Silverman says, is what these first-gen parents believe the *purpose* of a college education should be. For many this purpose is very circumscribed. "In the minds of these parents," she says "the primary reason you go to college is to eventually get a job that hopefully pays better than washing dishes in a Korean restaurant or selling newspapers on Wall Street. Consequently many first-generation students are encouraged by their parents to take very narrow, vocationally oriented courses."

But children don't always follow their parent's advice. Silverman tells me about Salima, a student she advises whose story is similar to her own. Like many Pakistani and Indian students, Salima comes from a particularly traditional family that has long planned *exactly* what their son or daughter will become in life. For Salima this means becoming an accountant. And Salima has been compliant. She is dutifully taking courses that will lead to an accounting degree. But over the semester, Silverman has noticed a quiet rage building up in Salima. She has taken some political science and history. And last week, at one of their counseling sessions, Salima told Silverman that she is bored to tears in accounting and instead wants to major in international relations with the hope of eventually working for the United Nations. "Here is a young woman," Silverman says "who is brave enough to go against her parent's wishes, at least as far as her college education is concerned, and reject that narrow, utilitarian concept of education that her parents, like so many parents of first-generation students, hold." But Silverman is concerned. She isn't sure where it will end. She worries the tensions with Salima's parents will only grow as she moves forward in college.

What about first-gen attrition? What are the signs that might indicate that a first-gen advisee is vulnerable? Silverman lists difficulty engaging, failing to attend class, lack of curiosity, not knowing why they are in college, being on the cellphone or texting all the time, and constantly playing computer games.

She gives me an example of a new first gen she worried was a prime

candidate for attrition. This kid—Silverman calls him Harvey—came
into her office midway through fall semester wanting to know what
courses he should be taking in the spring. Harvey told her that he
had had it with the general education requirements. All he wanted
to do was take courses in—you guessed it—accounting and business.
When she pushed him about why he wanted to take courses in these
areas, he had no answer. When she asked him what he wanted to do
with accounting and business, he didn't know either. All he knew was
that accountants make a lot of money. So she showed him the requirements for these demanding majors. Now he was less interested. "Why
do I have to take calculus for accounting?" he wanted to know. "Why
business ethics?" "Why do I have to know about other cultures?"
"First-generation freshmen like Harvey who come in and say 'Just
tell me what to do,'" Silverman says "but demonstrate no curiosity,
no motivation, nothing, are prime candidates for attrition."

Inability to manage time is another factor in first-gen attrition.
This includes lack of prioritizing, not knowing when to start work on
a paper, and not knowing how to "kick start" oneself. With many of
these first gens, everything is done at the eleventh hour. Just before
finals, Silverman's office gets extraordinarily busy!

And what advice might Silverman give parents to help their new
first gens be successful in college? Her answer will resonate with all
first-year parents, not just the parents of first gens. "Support but do
not do. Help them to navigate but do not navigate for them. Encourage them to consult and ask questions. Help them to formulate the
questions, but do not make decisions for them. They must learn to
do this for themselves. Value education. Learn about what education
means and how it will benefit your child. Learn about the college or
university, its values, goals, mission, and history. Participate in activities and events when invited, like orientation. First-generation parents don't always do this."

Key to Laura Silverman's advice is the notion that first-gen parents
must encourage their children to be assertive. Often first-gen students not only fear questioning people in positions of authority but
they also don't know how to negotiate a college's chain of command.
But just like their middle- and upper-class counterparts who tend to
understand these things, first gens must speak up when things are
not right—when, for example, they are not getting proper academic

advice or when they are in a bad resident hall situation. And their parents must encourage them to do this. (See chap. 5 [p. 88] on how to help your child negotiate a college or university's chain of command when there are problems.)

What Is It Like to Come from a Proscribed Ethnic Community but Attend a Very Diverse College?

Most public universities are not noted for their religious life programs. But Queens is an exception. Before the 1970s the various chaplains—Jewish, Catholic, and Protestant—separately worked out of their churches or synagogues off campus. But when Queens College decided to build a student union in 1972, Father Brown (the Catholic chaplain at the time) had a vision. Knowing that the college needed funds to build this new facility, he convinced his diocesan bishop and then the Jewish and Protestant chaplains to offer the Student Activities Corporation, a private entity, a substantial sum of money in return for a long-term lease to occupy the entire second floor of the new building. A ninety-nine-year lease was arranged. Several years later, New York State bought the bond issue, owning the building outright; but they were stuck with the campus ministry because of the ninety-nine-year lease arrangement. Thus a public facility initially embraced three religious organizations (other groups like Muslims joined later), an anomaly in American public higher education. But the marriage between church and state has been a happy one in this instance.

Reflecting on Molly's comment about being lonely and discovering the Catholic Newman Center on the second floor of the Student Union—where first-generation students of all faiths hang out—I arrange to meet with Father Wood, the Catholic chaplain, and Rabbi Shur, Father Wood's counterpart at Hillel. I take the elevator to the second floor and am amazed again by the religious diversity of students who attend this institution. A young woman dressed in a black burka exits the elevator with me. I can only see her eyes. A Jewish student in a yarmulke and prayer shawl rocks back and forth in the corner of the foyer over a prayer book.

I pass the Catholic Newman Center and hang a right into Hillel, the Jewish student organization. Displayed near the entryway is a poster announcing that next week the Muslim Student Association and Hillel are cosponsoring a movie with the intriguing title *Arranged: Friendship Has No Religion*. The poster features two young women, one Muslim, one Jewish, both wearing head scarves, facing each other with big smiles. I walk through a large room of well-worn sofas and tables. Eight students are studying, seven are engaged in earnest conversation, and one is stretched out on an overstuffed couch, deep in sleep. I find Rabbi Shur's office, where he and Father Wood are sitting around a small conference table piled high with precarious stacks of papers and books.

Rabbi Shur looks just like Santa Claus . . . but with a yarmulke. His smile is contagious. He has spent his life working across religious divides. During the Civil Rights era, he worked with Dr. Martin Luther King and the Southern Christian Leadership Conference on voter registration projects in the South. A picture of this event joins several other knickknacks on a windowsill. Father Wood's face is equally jolly. He wears a full Roman collar and reminds me of Karl Malden, the actor who portrayed a New York City priest in *On the Waterfront*. Even before I engage them in conversation I sense that these two men have known each other forever and are good friends.

The Student Union is a striking scene of religious and cultural pluralism. What is it like for first gens who have lived their entire life in an ethnic New York City neighborhood to come to Queens College? Rabbi Shur responds with one word. "Shocking." He explains himself.

"Many of these freshmen have been nurtured by parents in family and neighborhood environments that are generally distrustful of American culture. So when they come to 'Planet Queens College' it's as though they landed on Mars." He continues: "Two groups of Jewish freshmen come to mind, Orthodox Jewish women, many of them just back from a year in Israel, and Bukharan Jews from Uzbekistan." Rabbi Shur gestures to a group of young women sitting on a sofa just outside the door of his office. They are all wearing head coverings and dressed so that they do not show any skin except for their faces and hands.

"Let me give you an example of both," he says. "One of my freshmen this year comes from Kew Garden, Queens. Her father went to a yeshiva—a Jewish religious training school—but not to an American university. This young woman's Hebrew name is Devorah, but at Queens College faculty and students have Anglicized her name to Debby. So now when she goes to class her professors address her as Debby and to her this is very alien. Now, last week she was in my office very upset. She is taking a political science class and one day the professor, a New Left socialist and a secular Jew, started ranting against Israel. Devorah doesn't know how to handle this distressing situation. Israel is her second home and she has never heard anyone say a negative word about it. Should she protest and risk getting a bad grade? Or should she just shut up? Devorah is a timid and rather introverted young woman who all of a sudden is confronted by an impious person who, in her eyes at least, is mouthing blasphemy. And she wants me to tell her what to do. So I have to explain to her what freedom of speech means in the university and that debates about Israel's place in the world, even among Jews, is common here. I suggest that she join a group at Hillel that teaches Jewish students how to deal with these controversial issues."

"The other example I have in mind," Rabbi continues "is a freshman from Uzbekistan, a Bukharan Jew by the name of Yosef who lives in Rego Park. Of course, he is called Joe here at Queens College. God blessed this kid with good looks and a great personality. Anyway, Yosef leaves his insular Bukharan neighborhood and comes here to a culture where everyone hangs out with everyone else, blacks, Latinos, Chinese American, you name it. Here there is both interfaith and intercultural socializing and dating. Now Yosef could date any Jewish girl he wanted to. But what does he do? He hooks up with a good looking Latino from Corona, Queens. This is a no-no in general. But in his Bukharan community, it's a no-no with capital punishment! So because of the prohibitions in both communities, these two freshmen try to keep their relationship secret. But of course, everyone knows. Yosef eventually comes to see me. He tells me that he has met the girl of his dreams. He says that they have seen the movie *My Big Fat Greek Wedding* thirteen times because it's all about *them*. But I can see the hard reality. Because of who they are and where they both come from, this relationship is in trouble, especially when the families eventually find out. So I try to tell Yoef the difference between 'Miss Right' and 'Miss Right Now.' These are real life issues that many first gens must deal with when they come to college."

Father Wood has been nodding in agreement. Does he see these same issues at his end of the second floor? "Oh yes," he says, giving Rabbi Shur a suggestive wink as though they often compare notes on the students they work with. I'm wondering whether Yosef's Latino girlfriend has been in Father Wood's office over at the Newman Center for the same reason. "Eastern European Catholics often come to Queens College from the same kind of insular background. Vira comes to mind. Vira is the Christian version of Yosef, I guess. She is a first-generation freshman whose parents are Albanian Catholics who immigrated to the U.S. two years ago and now live in Morris Park. Before college even started her father and mother made it known to me that they wanted their daughter to only meet Albanian Catholic men. But Vira has a mind of her own. She dates whomever she pleases, Jews, Christians, Muslims. She's fearless. But she has to hide it from her parents. And just like Yosef and his Latino girlfriend, her classmates know exactly what's going on." Father Wood continues: "These kids live in two different worlds. During the day they live in a modern, multicultural world here at Queens College. But when they go home in the evening, they live according to the ethnic and religious traditions and customs of their parents and the surrounding community." Rabbi Shur jumps in. "In fact, this is *precisely* why their parents send them here. They want their kids to get a modern American university education. But they also want to keep them under the watchful eye of the community. Because it's largely a commuter campus, Queens College fits the bill perfectly."

Father Wood continues, "I have been a chaplain here for almost twenty years and in all these years I have witnessed maybe twenty interfaith marriages, mostly between nonobservant Jews and nominal Christians. In the context of the general population, that is not many. Religion and culture are very powerful forces. The stronger the religious and ethnic ties at home, the more likely these first-generation Queens College students will eventually end up right back in the neighborhood they came from."

Maybe so, I'm thinking to myself, but what I'm seeing here at Queens College is an incredible demonstration of religious and cultural *mixing*. And so I ask Rabbi Shur and Father Wood to share with me ways these various groups cooperate with each other, considering the insulated backgrounds they come from.

Father Wood says that the various religious groups represented here on the second floor regularly come together around common programs that are mostly noncontroversial, at least from a religious or ethnic perspective. "Is the movie *Arranged* I see advertised here on the second floor one of these 'noncontroversial' programs?" I ask. "Well, yes and no," Rabbi Shur says. "The film is being cosponsored by us and the Muslim Student Association. It's about two young women who are public schools teachers in Brooklyn, one an Orthodox Jew like Devorah and the other a Muslim. They become friends and discover how similar they are to each other, especially because they are both going through arranged marriages. In one sense the movie is controversial. But because it is about Muslims and Jews relating to each other, in another sense it isn't."

"OK. So what about conflict? Surely there must be some interfaith friction up here," I wonder out loud, remembering an account I read in the *Knight News*, the Queens College student newspaper, about a recent incident involving the president of the Young Republicans calling Muslims terrorists. A well-known Imam, Siraj Wahhaj, was scheduled to speak at the Student Union, and the student's comments incited protest from the college's growing Muslim student population.

"If you are referring to the imam who spoke here a couple of weeks ago," Father Wood says, "he actually gave quite a good address, affirming positive relations between Muslims, Jews, and Christians and taking as his personal role model Martin Luther King. He was hardly the firebrand some thought he would be."

Rabbi Shur assures me that this incident was atypical. "Most of our students are too busy to get into spats around religion. If there is conflict, it probably takes place on Facebook or at social parties. I don't know. I just don't see it here."

A final question: "How do you interact with the parents of these first-generation students? Certainly they must fret about what goes on with their kids when they are on campus."

Rabbi says that parents want him to make sure their kids are not slacking in their religious obligations. "I remember a father who encouraged me to shadow his son to make sure he was being observant. He wanted me to do this without letting his son know of his concern."

Father Wood shares a similar story. "A freshman from a devout

Catholic family told his parents soon after he arrived here this fall that he was meeting with me on a regular basis just like he apparently had done with his priest back home. But this kid's shadow never darkened my doorstep. So I tracked him down and chastised him, suggesting that he at least be honest with his parents."

What Are the Challenges for First Gens Who Are African American or Latino?

Nationally, Black and Latino students, many of them first gens, make up 26.9 percent of the total student population attending *all* institutions of higher education, about the same as the 27 percent who attend Queens College.[5] And so I decide to explore the different challenges some of these students face as they go off to college. What's it like to move from a crowded urban neighborhood to an attractive and spacious campus? How easy is it to fit in with mostly majority white and Asian American students? What are the principal causes of minority attrition?

I wander across the Queens College campus looking for Delany Hall, where Frank Franklin, director of the Search for Education, Elevation, and Knowledge (SEEK) program, has his office. The SEEK program was implemented by the city of New York largely for first-generation New York City students with significant financial need, mostly but not exclusively American minorities. Franklin is a muscular but distinguished looking man in his early sixties. He has the arms of a weight lifter but the face of a scholar. Like Laura Silverman, he was the first in his family to go to college. But his story is somewhat different.

Franklin grew up in the Jim Crow South on a farm near Richlands, North Carolina. "Well, actually," he tells me, "the town is called Haw Branch. But nobody ever heard of it." His parents moved to New York City when he was a baby. Even though they returned to Haw Branch from time to time to visit, Franklin was really brought up by his grandmother and aunt. To get to high school in Jacksonville, North Carolina, he had to spend long hours on the school bus, almost twenty-three miles each way. During high school football season, he often didn't get home until 8 P.M.

Like a lot of rural blacks, Franklin was tracked into the high school commercial course, but his football coach saw college potential in him and got him switched to the academic track. By his own admission Franklin was not the greatest high school student, but he was nevertheless accepted as a probationary student on a football scholarship by Johnson C. Smith University, a historically black school in Charlotte, North Carolina. He knew he had to prove himself, not only on the football field where he played halfback, but in the classroom as well. And that's what he did, graduating in 1968. "What I learned from high school and college football," Franklin tells me, "is that when you get knocked down, you got to get right back up. You need persistence to get through life." That persistence, or "grit," took him through a series of ups and downs: a teaching-training assignment in Harlem just as the New York City school system was shut down by a teachers strike; a job with a California book company hawking textbooks to local New York City schools; a job working with abused children in Queens; then several jobs with SEEK at Queens College—as a financial aid counselor, financial and budget officer, and then as acting director. When the SEEK directorship came open in 2001, he applied, for the second time. This time he got the position that he's held ever since. "Coming up through college in the South," he tells me, "I learned how fortunate I really was to get a college education. And if I learned one thing at Johnson C. Smith it was that you've got to give back. That's what I'm doing with these SEEK students."

The SEEK program is a good example of the kinds of educational opportunity programs that many colleges have established for first-generation students. Created in 1965 as a way to help first generation blacks and Latinos in New York City attending the City College of New York, the oldest school in the City University system, SEEK initially served only these two minority groups. But in the 1970s not only were the parameters for participation widened—now all New York City first-year students below a certain financial level can benefit from SEEK—but SEEK itself was expanded to the other City University campuses, Queens College included.

Today, first-year students accepted into the SEEK program at Queens are supported at four levels. First, they receive funds from New York State for books and incidentals that supplement the financial aid they receive from federal and local government. Almost all

SEEK students receive full tuition. Second, they are assigned a counselor who stays with them through their four years of college. These counselors provide academic and personal counseling and advice. Each counselor also teaches a Student Life Workshop that all SEEK students are required to take first semester. Third, each student receives academic support in terms of tutoring and supplemental instruction. And finally, in conjunction with the academic programs, SEEK can select its own faculty who teach English, math, and world studies first semester and then courses in their own discipline during the second semester.

The classes affiliated with SEEK are purposefully small, between twenty and twenty-five students, and are made up of "learning communities," groupings of first-year students who take all their courses together. In addition to SEEK-specific courses, these first-year students take a writing-intensive English course and an elective taught by regular Queens College faculty. By sophomore year, SEEK students are fully integrated into the regular Queens College curriculum, still maintaining contact with their original SEEK counselor.

The program works! Frank Franklin tells me that the SEEK retention rate from first to sophomore year is 87 percent—higher than the retention rate for the college's regular students—although the four-year graduation rate of 42.6 percent is not quite as good.[6] Then again, the challenges faced by these first gens, financial and otherwise, are enormous. That so many survived at all is a testimony to SEEK's effectiveness.

It used to be that remediation was a dirty word in the vocabulary of American higher education, something colleges and universities didn't want to make too public lest it affect their ratings in various publications like U.S. News and World Report. But with 35 percent of all high school students attending a four-year college in the United States not prepared for college-level work, according to an editorial in the New York Times, remediation is considered the norm, not the exception.[7] In New York City the need for remediation is even more acute: 77 percent of New York City high school students (many of them first gens) are unprepared for college because of some weak city high schools.[8] So educational opportunity programs like SEEK have become an accepted part of the country's educational landscape. And why not? If our goal in America is to open the American dream to as many people as possible, especially to underserved populations, and if programs like SEEK can give these first-year students a head start toward academic success, who cares what the ratings say![9]

Franklin and I sit in his postage-stamp office on the first floor of Delaney Hall around a small conference desk piled high with folders, books, and other clutter that partially block my view of him. Building on what Laura Silverman said about the challenges of the first gens she advises, we discuss how these first-year SEEK students adapt to Queens College and eventually find their niche. Because most of the SEEK students he works with have absolutely no idea what college is about, they are required to attend a special summer orientation program. Some come to this program not quite sure what to expect. Others have totally unrealistic expectations about what going to college means or entails. Still others don't even know how to behave in the classroom.

"I think one of the biggest adjustments these first gens must make," Franklin says, "is to their physical surroundings. I mean, look out the window. This college looks pretty much like a country club. There are trees. There is grass. This is *not* Bedford Stuyvesant! This place is hardly what they expected and, frankly, many of them find the college intimidating." Eventually these first gens are reassured that this really is the place they want to be because they quickly see how welcoming the college is, he says; that it isn't just a bunch of buildings and broad lawns but people as well—people who care about them.

What kinds of unrealistic expectations do many SEEK students have? Franklin recently worked with a young man, LeBron, who said on his application that he wanted to become a medical doctor. On the very first day of the summer program LeBron came to Franklin's office with his mother in tow and wanted to know what he had to do to get a medical degree. Franklin had to tell LeBron and his mother that there are certain courses LeBron would have to take *before* going to medical school and becoming a physician; that you don't start out by taking some college courses and four years later get your MD. Franklin then had to break the news that, for starters, LeBron would have to improve his math skills substantially. "I could tell they didn't believe me," Franklin says. "So I had to patiently go over all the requirements for premed."

Franklin also works with SEEK students who come to Queens not knowing how to behave in class. "It's really not their fault," he says. "Many of them come from overcrowded and underfunded city high schools where they were pretty much left to their own devices. They must now learn that in class they should not be talking to friends while the professor is speaking. They need to learn how college students act. One first-year student from one of the worst neighborhoods in the Bronx, Rico, usually sat at the back of the room chatting with his friends and not paying attention. It wasn't only his professor who was complaining about Rico's behavior, but some of his classmates as well. Anyway, I had to call him into my office. 'You don't talk in class, Rico, until the professor calls on you. You bring pencil and paper and you take notes. You turn your cell phone off.' Kids from affluent high schools automatically know this."

What other challenges do first-year SEEK students face? Learning how to deal with the system is one of them. Soon after they arrive at Queens, these students must make contact with the business office, the health center, and the Financial Aid Office. And because everyone else is trying to get into these places at the same time there are long lines. Often, when they discover they don't have the appropriate documents and have to return, they just give up in disgust. Franklin tells me about Tina, an African American first gen and another one of his advisees. When Tina went to the Financial Aid Office at the beginning of the semester to clarify her financial aid package, she was told, after standing in line a good hour, that she needed to bring in her parent's income tax returns. She just knew that no way was her father going to give her this information. Not only would he be reluctant to share financial information with his daughter, but he generally distrusted bureaucracies. "So Tina ended up in my office upset and ready to quit," Franklin says. "I had to explain to her why this information is needed, that it would only be used to determine the amount of financial aid she will receive. I suggested that if her father didn't want her to know what his financial situation is, he could bring in the information himself."

Yet another challenge these students deal with is how much time they must spend studying. "In my opinion," Franklin says, "freshmen should be spending twenty or more hours *per week* doing reading assignments, writing papers and generally preparing for classes.[10] But some of these kids spend maybe an hour, *if that.* They just don't have a clue about how many hours they must devote to study in order to succeed in college."

Are the challenges African American and Latino SEEK students face different than the challenges faced by nonminority students? "Well, you have to remember," Franklin says, "that most African American and Latino students were the majority at their New York City high schools. At Queens College, on the other hand, the majority are white and Asian. So African American and Latino freshmen often feel self-conscious and out of place." He gives an example. "This fall I counseled a young African American who faced a perception issue. He wore baggy pants that fell well below his hips. He wore a 'do rag' on his head, one of those black skull caps that African American young men often wear. We try to encourage our African American freshmen not to look so stereotypical. But they do anyway. It's kind of a statement about who they are and where they come from. But it can cause others to make unwarranted assumptions about them. Anyway, this young man felt increasingly uncomfortable when he was in class with other non-SEEK students. He expressed this by being openly aggressive and confrontational. His attitude was 'no one can tell me what to do or what to look like' and this eventually got him into trouble both with his classmates and his professors." On Franklin's suggestion, this young man eventually ended up with Mr. Modeste, one of SEEK's senior counselors who spoke candidly, one black man to another, about how he looked and behaved and how people perceived him. He got the message and is now more aware of the choices he is making.

The principal causes of attrition for Franklin's African American and Latino advisees are financial. Because these students are a critical part of the family's income, they are pulled in other directions. "We recommend that SEEK students *not* work full time during the first year of college," he says. "We do this because they have skill deficiencies and really need to spend time working on them. They can't do this and work full time as well. It's really all about skills like reading, writing, and math, so that when they move into regular classes sophomore year they will survive."

Unfortunately, Franklin is fighting an uphill battle. According to the Higher Education Research Institute, 55 percent of all new first gens are expected by their families to get a job to pay college expenses. Moreover, a higher proportion of these first-year students than their peers worked twenty or more hours per week in their final year of high school, a gap that has been widening over the years.[11] As we saw at Washington College, working this amount of time can adversely affect academic performance.

Family problems are another cause of attrition. Franklin remembers a SEEK first-year student who told him that because her parents were constantly fighting with each other, she couldn't study at home. "If we hadn't worked out a way she could study here in the library," he says, "she probably would have dropped out of school altogether." Franklin pauses. "Oh yes, spending too much time having fun is another cause of attrition. Queens is not a party school, but some of our SEEK students spend far too much time hanging out in the Student Union and then don't come to class."

I ask Franklin whether being in an opportunity program creates a stigma for his SEEK students. Frank shakes his head. "In the past, SEEK was viewed as a 'black' program and if something bad happened on campus, the assumption was that SEEK students were involved. But this is no longer the case. Because Queens College is such a diverse community to begin with, and because SEEK has been here for so long, black and Latino SEEK students blend in with the rest of the community. For all intents and purposes they are simply seen as regular Queens College students. There is no stigma."

Finally, what advice might Frank Franklin have for the African American or Latino parents of first-generation students? His answer is clear and precise: "Don't push your student to work the first year because they need to focus *all* of their energies on being college students. Understand that your child's financial aid monies should only be used for school purposes. Provide a quiet place at home for homework. And most importantly, try to understand the new pressures your student is now under and be supportive."

A First Gen Talks about Surprises First Year and Challenges of Being a Minority Student on a Largely White Campus

Marita is a first-year SEEK student. Bilingual since childhood— Marita only speaks Spanish at home where she lives with her parents— her English is flawless, with a slight Queens' accent. Marita was born in Manhattan where her father works in a restaurant and does various jobs. Her mother stays at home taking care of her two younger sisters, though before coming to New York she was a cook in Mexico City. Marita has three siblings: an older brother who never went to college and two younger sisters, one in middle school and the other a junior in high school. She lives across the street from the Queens College campus.

Like all SEEK students, Marita is on full scholarship. She doesn't know yet what she wants to major in, but her father hopes that she and her sisters will get good jobs so that they can support their extended family.

Marita's biggest surprise coming to college was finances. At $6,000, Queens College's otherwise modest annual tuition would be a small fortune for her family. But as a SEEK student she gets full financial aid. She didn't even have to take out a loan. "When I was accepted into SEEK," Marita says, "and got my scholarship, my father said, in disbelief, 'You just don't get things like this for free!'"

Another surprise was Queens College's size. Even though she lives just across the street, Marita had never walked on the Queens College campus because she thought going to college was never in the cards for her. She imagined Queens to be like a city high school. But when she arrived at orientation this summer, she couldn't believe how many large buildings there were and how beautiful the campus was. "I mean this library is like a palace!" Marita says as she gazes up at the atrium under which we are seated. "I also thought that professors didn't really care about students, that you are just a number," she continues. "But they really *do* care. What a surprise *that* was!"

"Mom is absolutely proud of me." Marita says, "She's constantly bragging about the fact that she has a daughter in college. Dad's not really a man of many words, but I know he is proud as well. Actually, he played a very important part in my decision to come here after I was admitted to SEEK with a full tuition scholarship. Last year he told me, 'There's no excuse not to go to college now,' and he really pushed me to do it." She adds that her younger sisters thinks it's really cool that she is a college student, and Marita says that she now wants to be a role model because she hopes that they might go to college as well.

What special challenges does Marita face as a minority among a largely white and Asian American student body? While Marita sometimes feels awkward being Mexican American in a largely non-Latino population, she doesn't let it get to her. "I mean, I'm proud of my heritage," she says, "but I'm also proud to be an American. I guess I want to get beyond old stereotypes and just be who I am. So my feeling about the majority of students here is 'I'm here and you're here and we are both here to learn.'"

But Marita feels a very definite tension between her ethnic background and, as she puts it, being an American. "Here at Queens College, you are expected to behave in a certain way. At home, it's different. Here I speak English and eat pizza in the Student Union like all the students do. At home I speak Spanish and eat *pollo encacahuatado*, my mother's favorite dish. Here we are always rushing from class to class and to various activities. At home life is very casual." Marita says that another tension that exists between her Mexican heritage and being an American is where her parents expect her eventually to live. Her dad hopes that when she finishes college she will continue to live with the family like many grownup Mexican American children do. His plan, she says, is to buy a large five-family house so that her brother and sisters and their families can eventually live together. "But I want to experience something new," Marita says with passion. "I want to experience other places. And I know that this will create tension."

Marita wasn't sure at the start about SEEK. She found registration frustrating with all the different classes she had to choose from, and was initially flummoxed by all the free time she now has. Margarite Equizabal, her SEEK counselor, sat down with her and patiently went through everything step by step. She recommended courses and suggested what might be good for Marita to take. She also asked about her life in general. Marita tells me that she sees lots of SEEK students going into Equizabal's office and that she's always available. "I never had someone like that in high school," she says. Her comment reminds me of Dean Long's counseling session with Carla at Vassar. Dean Long was also concerned about the total student, not just the academic program they were taking.

And what does Marita want first gens and their parents to know? "First, I want them to know that there is help when you go to college and that you are not alone. Also, don't be afraid to ask questions even if you think they are dumb questions. Second, remember that while academics are important, going to college is also about making new friends. Don't miss out on life. Third, I thought classes would involve horsing around like in high school. But in college, the teachers are serious and you've got to be serious as well. Fourth, I thought college would be easy. But it is intense. Lots of homework. This is definitely not high school. Finally don't limit yourself just to things you are good at. Roam around campus. Go to events. Work hard because you're probably going to go to grad school and you want to do well in college. And get to know your professors because they can really help you in the future." Marita pauses and then adds: "As for parents: Give your kids more freedom. Let them grow up and become adults."

Some Straight Talk from an Old Hand in First-Gen Education

Bill Modeste, SEEK's senior counselor, is a thin man with a kindly face and a big grin. Mr. Modeste—out of respect, everyone addresses him as "mister"—has been around the block a few times. A native of Harlem, he is old enough to remember when Jackie Robinson, the first African American to play professional baseball in the major leagues, visited his grade school! Except for college at Shaw University in Raleigh, North Carolina, where he witnessed racial discrimination firsthand, and a stint in the U.S. Army as a medic, Modeste's entire life has been spent in New York City working with low-income kids. Before joining the army he was a counselor with New York City's Youth Board in the Bronx and then, after his army service, with the Urban League as a vocational counselor working with high school dropouts. In 1966, the year SEEK was founded (and two years before I was employed by the Education Incentive Program, also in New York City), Modeste joined the program, so he probably knows better than anyone the enormous challenges first gens face as they begin college.

Meeting with Bill Modeste presents me with a golden opportunity to ask a question that has been on my mind ever since I first came to Queens College. "What is it that makes Queens College such a special place for first gens? Is it the curriculum? The financial aid? What's the secret?"

Modeste expresses a sentiment I have heard from others at Queens College: "First-generation students who come here are all different," he says, "so there is no one reason why so many of them succeed. Having a diverse campus where everyone pretty much gets along obviously helps. So does the generous financial aid we are able to provide these students. No doubt, the way first-generation students are integrated into the Queens College curriculum is an important factor. But, if I were to identify one major reason why we are so successful here, it would be because all of us, teachers and counselors alike, show *genuine* interest in these students. When you really *care* about these kids. When you are *honest* with them. When you tell them what they must do to succeed. When they come to see that you *really* believe in them, they respond accordingly."

Modeste and his staff have almost become surrogate parents for their SEEK students, and like all good families they provide them with not only support and encouragement but also tough love. "What I mean by tough love," he says, "is telling these kids what they must do in order to succeed in life, even if it means telling them the hard, brutal truth. When they begin to waver, when they think about dropping out, we sometimes have to spell out the possible and very real consequences of quitting, like ending up in a dead-end job or even going to jail. We don't candy-coat the truth."

Modeste becomes pensive. "These kids will almost *always* rise to the level of our expectations for them. But to do this we have to create a culture and an environment here, what I call a 'citadel of positiveness and success,' that says to them 'You can make it. You can be successful.'"[12]

I am impressed with what Queens College has done with its first-generation students. But not all colleges have comprehensive programs like SEEK or staff like Bill Modeste, Frank Franklin, and Laura Silverman, who have dedicated their lives to working with these students. So what do first-gen parents do when the college their student is attending has limited support services?

Whether or not your child's college has an opportunity program like SEEK, good advising will be critical to their success, preferably from someone who understands the special needs of first gens and has worked with them in the past. If the adviser assigned your student has not had this experience or doesn't seem to know what they are doing, you should encourage your student to speak up and ask for an adviser who is more appropriate. Colleges and universities usually have a point-person in the dean of students office who works with first gens and especially first gens who are underserved students, and this person might be able to suggest such an adviser. Your student should also seek out whatever support services are available and not be embarrassed to use them. Colleges often have first-year programs designed to help students adjust to college-level academics or to college life in general. These programs are usually offered, sometimes for credit, during the academic year but also in the summer just before orientation, and they are often free. In addition, many colleges and universities have a learning and/or writing center that provides tutors in certain college subjects but also can help your student develop learning and writing skills. Finally, larger universities often sponsor a black or Hispanic/Latino student union. If your student is Latino or African American these unions will not only help them identify additional resources but also provide a place where they can socialize with classmates from similar backgrounds. Remember: encourage your student to be assertive. And strongly suggest that they use the resources available to them. Doing so might mean the difference between success and failure.

9

First-Year Students
with Disabilities

Like Phoebe and Nathan, I went off to college with high hopes and expectations, but unlike them I had not been a particularly strong student at Mamaroneck High School. When reading a book or taking a test, words often got scrambled in my mind, and as a result I was an extremely slow reader. Consequently my grades were below average and my SAT scores were deplorable. I now realize that I probably have a modest form of dyslexia, but fifty years ago comparatively little was known about this and other learning disabilities such as attention deficit hyperactivity disorder (ADHD) or even autism. I struggled through my first year of college and was even told by a professor that I wasn't very bright. Lacking any kind of support system, I thought about dropping out of college. Fortunately, we know a lot more today about students with disabilities than we did when I was a first-year student fifty years ago, and most colleges and universities have support systems in place that help insure that these students, too, can be successful.

This chapter is a very personal one for me because, in addition to the normal challenges first-year students face, those who come to college with a disability like I did must deal with unimaginable additional obstacles that most people take for granted. What are the special challenges learning or physically disabled students face the first year of college and what do you need to know in order to be supportive of them? How must they be accommodated according to the Americans with Disabilities Act? What kinds of support are available to them?

What First-Year Students with a Learning Disability Say about Going to College: The Importance of Accommodation

I'm back at Morningside College, on my way to meet with a group of first-year students who have come to college with a learning disability. As I walk past Lewis Hall, Morningside's main administration building, I notice a lone student with a cane, probably contemplating how he's going to make it up the granite stairs that lead to the front door. He is obviously sight-impaired, reminding me of a first-year student in a wheelchair I saw at Tufts, checking out an ancient building where one of his orientation sessions was to be held. I and a couple first-year students hoisted him up the steps and into the front door, but he was probably wondering whether, once he got inside, there would be elevators or accessible restrooms. I offer help to the Morningside student and then continue on my way.

I arrive at the Hickman Learning Center, a combined library and study center, where I meet with three first-year students who are willing to tell me about their learning disabilities on condition that I protect their identities and use different names. They are, for the purpose of this discussion, Jennifer from Des Moines, Iowa; Tim from Rockford, Illinois; and Tanya from Indianapolis, Indiana. They are among the 3.3 percent of all full time first-year students nationwide who have a documented learning disability.[1]

Jennifer's parents suspected there was something wrong with her when she was struggling to read in grade school. She was tested and diagnosed as having dyslexia. She says she has struggled with spelling, putting words together, and remembering names. She used to freak out whenever she had to take a timed test; the panic caused a mental block so that she focused mostly on how much time she had left rather than the test. This was especially the case with science, where she would study all night and then draw a complete blank the next day. "I thought I was freaking stupid!" Jennifer says. "I was ashamed about my disability."

Tanya, who is now rather forcefully rocking back and forth in her chair, almost shouts, "Well, I bet you've already guessed what my disability is!" We all laugh. Tanya was diagnosed in eighth grade with Asperger syndrome and auditory processing disorder. It was so difficult for her to hold a pen or crayon still in high school that she couldn't even do art. And since she could only process half of what her teachers were saying in class, she never quite got the full picture. As a consequence Tanya had to be in special classes since she was little.

Tim is next up. All through high school he struggled to concentrate. "When I took a test," he says, "I would hear random noises like the wind, clocks, the scratching of pencils. And all of these things made me lose concentration. My heart would start racing, causing me to rush to finish." Because of anxiety, Tim was ridiculed by his classmates and his grades suffered. It was only after he struggled through the first few days of college this fall that his psychology professor surmised that he might have attention deficit hyperactivity disorder and encouraged him to get tested. "When the test revealed that I indeed had ADHD," Tim says "my psych professor told me that she was amazed I had gotten through high school."

As Joanne Long, dean of freshman at Vassar, made very clear, it is extremely important for students with learning disabilities to identify themselves to the college soon after they are admitted but well before they arrive for orientation. Unfortunately, many new students fail to do this. The regrettable consequence is that they unnecessarily struggle through college. Did these three students reveal their disability to Morningside ahead of time?

Because she knew in grade school that she had dyslexia, Jennifer's parents filed a 504 Form, discussed further below, which helped determine the accommodation she would need in high school. She came to Morningside with similar documentation from a psychologist, which she shared with Karmen Ten Napel, the college's disabilities coordinator, who then determined what her accommodation would be. With Ten Napel's help, Jennifer talked to her professors about her dyslexia and the accommodation she would be receiving. She tells me that none of her classmates, except for Tim and Tanya, know about her disability and that she plans to keep it this way.

Tanya's story is similar. Because of the very visible nature of her disability, she learned how to advocate for herself in high school. So when she came to Morningside this fall she was prepared. She met with Ten Napel and shared with her documentation of her twin disabilities. They then figured out what accommodation was appropriate.

Jennifer and Tanya are using a technical word when they talk about "accommodation." It refers to what professors *must* do by law under Section 504 of the Rehabilitation Act and the Americans with Disabilities Act to create equity for students struggling with a learning disability. So what accommodations have Jennifer, Tanya, and Tim received from Morningside?

Because he gets easily distracted by what's on the walls of the classroom rather than listening to the professor, Tim is allowed to choose where to sit and, as a consequence, always arrives early to classes. (Indeed, he arrived ten minutes early for this conversation!). He also gets extended time on tests, which he can take in a private room on the second floor of Lewis Hall. Tanya is allowed to type her notes and can also tape lectures. She is warned in advance about assignments so that she can finish them on time, has no oral quizzes, and can take tests with no time limit. Like Tim, Jennifer gets extended time on tests. She also gets help with homework and if an assignment is due for a morning class, she is allowed to hand it in at the end of the day as long as she shows up for that class.

And how are they doing academically? "I am getting mostly Bs, which is really not that bad," Jennifer says. "But I'm a perfectionist and expect more of myself. I work my butt off to get these grades." Jennifer goes on to say that she's struggling with science and anything that requires extensive reading. General psychology is particularly difficult for her because lots of information is dumped on her over a short period of time and she can't absorb it all.

Most colleges have first-year requirements in science and a foreign language, which dyslexic students find difficult to master. Morningside does not waive these requirements, but Karmen Ten Napel has suggested science courses that will be less difficult for Jennifer. Thankfully foreign language, which she simply cannot do, is not a requirement for graduation.

"I'm busting my ass just to get Cs and Ds," Tim says as he shakes his head. "And I have to study four to five hours each night to get these grades! At least I know now what my problem is and I can live with it."

Tanya is smiling. She tells me that so far she's mostly getting As, but is upset about a B on a recent science quiz. "But to get these grades I have to spend all my time on homework, meaning that I really don't have a life socially." These kids have an impressive work ethic, but it comes at a price.

I ask a sensitive question: have their disabilities caused Tim, Tanya, or Jennifer to feel like second-class citizens at Morningside?

Jennifer tells me that in middle school, when she was taken out of class and given different books, she not only felt like a second-class citizen but stupid as well. "But here at Morningside," she says "classmates who know about my dyslexia—and most don't—either don't care or are understanding."

"As you can see, I'm very talkative," Tim says. "I'm also actively involved in *everything*. I'm involved with SERVE, a college service organization, write for the student newspaper, and sing in the college choir. Oh yes, and I hold down two jobs on campus. So I don't feel like a second-class citizen. But this is just a front. All these activities hide the fact that I have ADHD. I'm not complaining. I'm having a great time. But I'm not about to tell anyone that all these activities are the result of my being hyperactive."

Tanya, however, *does* feel like a second-class citizen here at Morningside because her classmates don't understand her disability and sometimes treat her like a Martian. She sometimes answers other students' questions about her Asperger's directly, but mostly she changes the subject. "I also feel weird in class," Tanya says. "For example when my biology professor asked the class to pick lab partners at the beginning of term, no one picked me. I ended up with an older, nontraditional student. At first she didn't want to be my partner, but after I talked to her she felt better." In another class a professor had problems with her accommodation; he thought she might cheat on an exam if she were allowed to take it alone in Lewis Hall. Karmen Ten Napel had to speak with him. "But not everything is bad," Tanya quickly adds. "As I said, my social life is very limited. But I'm a Methodist and religion is very important to me, so I go to weekly Bible study. I also went to the football game Saturday in Sioux Falls with a girl who lives across the hall. I loved it, though I almost froze to death!"

I admire these students. Their road to college has been difficult. But they have learned to cope.

I ask them what advice they have for high school students—and their parents—with a learning disability who are contemplating college. "Don't be afraid to get accommodation," Jennifer says. "You don't need to tell everyone about your disability, but let your professors know because most of them will work with you. Work hard. Strive to realize your potential. And parents: help your child find coping mechanisms. Get help *before* they go to college."

"If you are having problems with a class or a professor," Tim says, "make use of the disabilities office. They can intervene or at least advise you what to do. Don't fall behind. If you have ADHD like me, use it to do good. Get involved. Don't sulk in your room."

And Tanya: "Have an open mind. Know that at college you have a fresh start. Get involved and make friends who aren't going to ridicule you. And parents, let your child be who she is. Be there to provide support because if you're like me with a very visible disability, that support will mean everything."

What Do You Need to Know If Your Child Has a Learning Disability?

As I have learned, Karmen Ten Napel is a learning disabilities specialist at Morningside College and the point person for students like Tim, Jennifer, and Tanya. We meet in her Lewis Hall office where we explore a number of issues that might be on the minds of parents whose children have a learning disability. How does the administration work with students who reveal a learning disability? What are the challenges first-year students with a learning disability face? Are support classes offered? And what is the role of parents?

Ten Napel runs through the steps involved in identifying, registering, and then orienting first-year students who comes to Morningside College with a learning disability. She tries to make initial contact with students who might have a disability at the various admissions open houses that take place on campus throughout the year. While it is not a requirement, she encourages students with a disability to identify themselves to her either before or during the application process. She points out that by law colleges cannot discriminate in the application process against students with a disability. "Initially, prospective students and their parents are reluctant to reveal a disability, but once they realize that we can provide them with accommodation that will make their college experience more productive and enjoyable, they usually cooperate."

She points out, however, that just because students with a disability received accommodation in high school it is not guaranteed that they will receive accommodation in college. Indeed, colleges are required to make an independent assessment of every student who claims a disability. A qualified health professional (often a psychologist) does an in-depth evaluation and recommends appropriate accommodation. Ten Napel reviews this information, often in consultation with a professor at Morningside who teaches special education. She then individually interviews the new students so that she can personally understand the extent of their disability. Finally she contacts the professors who will teach the students and shares with them what the accommodations will be. The professors are required by law to provide this accommodation.

Depending on the circumstances, accommodation can take on several different forms. One is right next door: a lone student taking a test with extended time. The college might also provide textbooks on audio tape, readers or scribes for tests, handouts including the professor's notes, special software for computers, and preferential seating. "By taking all these steps, we attempt to level the playing field for these students," Ten Napel says.

We discuss some of the challenges students with a learning disability face when they first make the transition to college. Being a self-advocate, Ten Napel says, is huge. "When they were in high school," she says "parents were their chief advocates. But in college and even more so when they leave college to go out into the real world *they* must advocate for themselves." She tells me that if the new student doesn't self-advocate right off, she personally helps them make the transition. She asks first years to meet with their professors about their accommodations and, in some cases, even encourages the professor to initiate contact.

Do all of these accommodations cause those affected to feel singled out? In high school, Ten Napel says, students with a learning disability are often separated into special education classes and thus are very visible to their classmates, but this isn't an issue at most colleges, where classes are fully integrated. Moreover, unless students go public with their disability, no one will know except Ten Napel and their professors. "And in my experience," she continues, "even if the disability becomes known, most college classmates won't care. The

important point is for these kids to move beyond the negative feelings some had in high school and just get on with life in college."

Ten Napel shares an example of learning-disabled first-year students she has worked with who blossomed in college. This student
came to Morningside with documented auditory processing disorder. He could sit through a lecture, but once it was over forgot almost
everything the professor had said—until later that evening when it
all came back. The college accommodated this student by allowing
him to complete in-class writing assignments at the end of the day
or the next morning in Lewis Hall's special test room. Ten Napel tells
me that he has done very well after graduation and now works for a
graphic design company.

What about first-year students who have not done well? When students with learning disabilities are struggling to the point that they
simply can't do the work, they are asked to take a semester off or to
attend community college and then, if appropriate, to transfer back
in. Ten Napel says that sometimes the problem is not an inability but,
rather, an unwillingness to do the work. She tells me about a first-
year student who came to Morningside trying to use his learning disability to get out of having to work hard so that he could party. Had
she known his disposition, she would have recommended that he
take time off between high school and college to figure out what he
really wanted to do in life. "Like the general population," Ten Napel
says, "not every learning disabled student should go to college. Many
are more suited for a vocational or trade school. But students who are
unmotivated probably should not be in college."

Outside of special institutions like Landmark College in Vermont
and the Salt Center at the University of Arizona that deal exclusively
with learning-disabled students, most colleges and universities do
not have special remedial courses for students with a learning disability. "But I do send some of my students to faculty for special tutoring," Ten Napel says, reminding me of two professors when I was a
sophomore at Drew University who noticed my struggle with reading and retention and patiently worked with me outside of class. In
time I learned from them strategies that not only made me a much
better student but also got me through college. This kind of person-
alized attention for students with a learning disability is one of the
strengths of a small college like Morningside.

I ask Karmen Ten Napel what advice she might have for the parents of first-year students with a learning disability. There are two
kinds of parents, she says: those who drop their children off at orientation and with the college's help let them deal with their disability, and those who can't let go. Helpful parents are the ones who provide the college with useful information about how their children
have learned or not learned in high school—are they procrastina-
tors? poor organizers?—and then let the professionals do their job.
Unhelpful parents, by way of contrast, often jump the chain of command. When there is an issue—for example, their child didn't do well
on an exam—they call the president's office, not her. Or they e-mail
the professor directly, which isn't doing their child a favor either. "My
point is," she says, "I want parents to feel that we are the professionals
and that we know what we are doing."

Karmen Ten Napel and her colleagues are, in fact, professionals of
the highest standard. But not all colleges are as responsive to students with a disability as Morningside College is. Some are terribly
understaffed in this area. I know of a small university with a population of six thousand students that has only one person working with
disabled students! By law, all colleges and universities must comply
with the Americans with Disabilities Act, but some do only what is
minimally required. Consequently, it's imperative that you and your
student visit a campus and its disabilities office well before accepting admission. Orientation is too late to discover that a campus is
under resourced. At that point there is probably very little you can
do beyond complaining.

What Do You Need to Know If Your
Child Has a Physical Disability?

Alex Watters is a Morningside graduate who experienced a terrible accident during orientation several years ago—a parent's worst
nightmare. He went to a lake in Northwestern Iowa with some classmates and, from a boat dock, jumped head first into water that he
didn't realize was only a couple feet deep. He snapped his neck and
today must use a wheelchair.

I wanted to know what it's like to negotiate this campus in a manual wheelchair, so after obtaining one from Morningside College's nursing department, Alex took Terri Curry, vice president of Student Life, and me on a tour of the Morningside campus. It wasn't a pretty scene. Wheeling over a thin strip of tar in the parking lot was like fording a small river. Terri Curry and I found it almost impossible to get through residence hall doors lacking an automatic door opener. Alex, in his motorized wheelchair, almost got hit crossing a busy street by a distracted driver talking on her cell phone. At least Alex could accelerate to avoid a collision. I can only imagine what would have happened to Terry Curry or me in our manual chairs. And wheeling up a slight hill was so exhausting that I finally got out of my chair and walked the rest of the way.[2]

Mary Leida, associate dean of students, and Susan Burns, associate dean of academic affairs, both work directly with physically disabled students like Alex. Even though only a tiny percentage of first-year students come to college with a physical disability, what they tell me—and what I just experienced with Alex and Terri Curry—is important for all parents to know.[3] Students with physical disabilities want to participate in class activities just like any other student. "They have a general desire to be treated as equals and with respect," Susan Burns says. "They want to focus on academics and on their social life. They assume that accommodation will be taken care of."

Mary Leida tells me about a new student they are working with who is sight impaired—indeed, the student I met in front of Lewis Hall. She says that initially their concern was whether he could find his way around campus, especially since he does not have a Seeing Eye dog but instead uses a cane. So a specialist from the local rehabilitation center spent a good part of the summer working with him on strategies for negotiating the Morningside campus. Fortunately, when he showed up for orientation students were more than happy to help out. Leida says that this young man is very social and so was quickly adopted by his classmates. She worries, however, that he might become *too* dependent on them because when he leaves Morningside he's not always going to be surrounded by empathetic and helpful classmates.

So what should students with a physical disability do to get accommodation? Susan Burn's and Mary Leida's answer is very similar to the course for students who have a learning disability: they should provide documentation from a health care professional with recommendations for accommodation; set up, if possible, an interview with someone like Susan Burns before applying to the college to determine whether the accommodations the college can offer will be adequate; and finally, once accepted, arrange to meet with their professors.

Using Alex and some other students she has worked with as examples, Mary Leida tells me how a college can give "reasonable accommodation" to first-year students with a physical disability. For example, students who lack mobility like Alex must be accommodated by being assigned either to a residence hall that has an elevator or to a room on the first floor. Because Morningside doesn't have residence halls with elevators, Alex was assigned to the first floor of Roadman, a residence hall with large rooms and located just across the street from Olsen Student Center and its dining facility. Students with a physical disability must also be provided with classes and labs in buildings with an elevator or, if an elevator doesn't exist, again on the first floor. Sometimes a college will move an entire class that normally meets on an upper floor of a building to the first floor, even if only one physically disabled student is accommodated by making this change. Ramps and wheelchair accessible bathrooms, of course, must also be provided in buildings used by physically disabled students. And since Alex doesn't have complete use of his hands, automatic door openers had to be installed on all the buildings he used as well as a lever to replace the knob on his room door.

"Reasonable accommodation" is a technical and legal term. By providing a residence hall that is accessible and by holding classes and labs in buildings that either have an elevator or are held on the first floor, reasonable accommodation is achieved for students with a physical disability. But colleges are sometimes faced with *unreasonable* requests for accommodation. Mary Leida says that sometimes students (or their parents) request a full-time caregiver. She says that the college simply can't afford this. "The rule of thumb," Susan Burns adds "is that if a freshman with a disability needs something above and beyond what is legally determined to be 'reasonable accommodation'—like expensive computer software or braille readers or the salary for a personal assistant—they should pay for it."

While students with dyslexia or ADHD can often hide their disability, someone who has a physical disability can't. So how do Susan Burns and Mary Leida help their students with a physical disability have as normal a college experience as possible? Burns says that when she first meets first-year students with a physical disability, she assumes that their expectations will be the same as the professors, namely, that academic standards will not be lowered just because of their disability. At the same time, how the first-year student with a disability relates to the professor will often determine how the professor relates to the student. She says that if they go to the professor assuming that they will be treated like a second-class citizen, they could be treated this way.

"But we are their advocates," Mary Leida adds "and will run interference for them if we have to." She says that sometimes, but very rarely, a faculty member will refuse accommodation, arguing that students with a physical disability won't necessarily be accommodated in real life. She must then tell the professor that accommodation is not up for debate; that documented accommodation is a requirement by law. "Still, students with a physical disability have ownership on how they use their accommodation," Susan Burns says. "Sometimes they don't want accommodation. It's up to them." Alex, for example, is a very independent person who, when he was a student at Morningside, lived as normal a college life as possible.

What advice would they give to parents with children who have a physical disability? "E-mail me if you have concerns," Susan Burns says, "but trust your student to communicate their needs to me. They must now be self-advocates. Let your son or daughter take ownership of their lives from now on. Also, while we might not have all the facilities a larger university has, because we are a small, caring college, we can provide a personal connection to your student."

"That's right," Mary Leida says. "We are a college that has heart."

10

Growing Up

Any book about the first year must end with a fundamental question that is on the minds of most parents: What, after all, is the purpose of a college education? Is it just a matter of our children accumulating enough academic credits to get a degree? Is it only to prepare them for high-paying jobs?

While sending your children off to college *is* about having them earn enough credits to earn a degree and eventually a good job, it's much more than this. From the first year onward, college is—hopefully—about your children discovering their passion in life. It is about developing basic tools they will use not only in their chosen careers but throughout life as well: the ability to communicate clearly, to think critically, to develop a strong set of ethical principles, to have a robust understanding of the exceedingly complex, global, and highly technological society in which they will eventually live, and to develop a curiosity that promotes continuing education throughout life.

First year is when young people begin to figure out how to develop and manage their financial resources, how to live in a diverse community with total strangers, how to eventually manage the sometimes competing challenges of their social and work lives in a largely unstructured environment, and how to balance being independent adults with the continuing responsibilities of family.

From the first year onward, college is about students learning how to lead healthy life styles and how to be safe, about how to make mistakes and learn from them. It's about being part of a team and learning not only how to win graciously but also how to lose with honor. For many children, college is about learning how to overcome the disadvantages of poverty or personal disability.

In short, first year begins the process of growing up, of becoming independent and ethically responsible citizens and adults.

A College President Comments on the First-Year Growing-Up Process

I'm again at Queens College, sitting with President James Muyskens around a large conference table in his office on the twelfth floor of Kiely Hall. Muyskens is a tall man with a broad Great Plains accent (indeed, he is a graduate of Central College in Iowa)—the kind of person you would expect to be president of a small college like Morningside or Washington College rather than a large public urban university. Nevertheless President Muyskens has happily been at Queens College for many years and is one of the City University of New York's most successful presidents.

I ask President Muyskens to share his philosophy of the first year. He settles back in his chair and delivers an eloquent summary of what many of the faculty and staff I have met while writing this book have been saying. One of the major purposes of a college education, he says, is to give students a chance to know who they are. "I'm a philosopher by training, and I really subscribe to Socrates's dictum Know Thy Self." Right from the start, Queens College challenges first-year students to think outside the narrow confines of their racial or ethnic group. They are encouraged to study the medieval period, to read French literature, and to take a physics course. This is why most four-year universities like Queens are committed to the liberal arts and sciences during the first and second years. Of course, students want to know "Why take art history if my plan is to be an accountant?" President Muyskens tells me that when he talks to accountants long after they graduated from Queens, they will often mention the inspiring history course they took their first year before even mentioning accounting.

Even though it is a large institution, Queens College focuses on small classes first year so that students will get to know a dozen or so students and also their professors. "Of course," he says, "if you put a dozen random students in the same class at this institution, the class will automatically be extremely diverse, and this in itself will open the eyes of our first-year students." He says that the college works hard at writing because, by writing, first-year students often discover their inner selves. "So the purpose of the first year," he says in conclusion, "is to help students to discover both their external and internal worlds."

I share with President Muyskens a conversation I had with Manny Avila, Queens College's coordinator of judicial affairs, that perhaps illustrates what he is talking about. Avila told me about Christopher, a white student from an upper-middle-class neighborhood in Jamaica Estates, who got in trouble with alcohol soon after arriving at orientation. Christopher and some of his friends were caught red-handed drinking shots of beer and vodka at a party in the new residence hall. Christopher was then summoned to the Office of Judicial Affairs so that Avila could determine whether or not he would have to go before the judicial board. Part of Avila's job is to determine the severity of an infraction and then, after an initial conversation with the offender, decide what will happen next. So he had a one-on-one conversation with Christopher. Avila emphasized that first-year students like Christopher have a responsibility to obey the law, but if they fail to do this there will be serious consequences. He then asked Christopher whether he understood that by drinking underage he was putting his college and athletic careers in jeopardy. (Christopher had received an athletic scholarship to play on one of the college's Division II varsity athletic teams.) Christopher hadn't realized how much trouble he was in and became very upset. But after he calmed down, he responded as Avila hoped he would. He didn't make up excuses, like some do, but took full responsibility for his behavior. Avila told Christopher that he would give him a second chance, but that if this happened again, Christopher might be having this conversation with a judge, not with him.

There is a wonderful sequel to this story. Two weeks ago Christopher came back to Avila's office to thank him for the conversation they had during orientation. Christopher confided that he had been a heavy drinker in high school and that until their conversation, he had never realized how irresponsible he had been. His immature behavior was not worth getting kicked out of college and losing his scholarship. Christopher had learned from his mistake and he now wanted to become involved in some kind of community service program instead of partying all the time.

President Muyskens loves this story. It is a wonderful example of the impact college can have on young people's lives starting first year. He points out that many Queens College students come from circumstances that initially forced them to define themselves in very narrow prescribed ways. "They don't know who they really are," he says. "And they aren't happy with their situation." If someone like Manny Avila hadn't helped break the cycle Christopher found himself in, he probably would have remained a heavy drinker for the rest of his life. "But college is a secure place where professors and counselors can break that shell and show first-year students that, indeed, they *can* transform their lives."

"Let me tell you about a first-year student with whom I was personally involved," President Muyskens continues. "I think he also illustrates what we are talking about. His name is Albert, and like many of our first-year students he came to Queens College from a very proscribed ethnic neighborhood here in New York City." President Muyskens describes Albert as a duck out of water, somewhat of a nerd—odd and shy, but determined. He was very smart but also very frustrated by the situation in which he found himself. For this reason he was sometimes ridiculed by his classmates. "Albert was brought to my attention by one of his professors," President Muyskens says "and I helped him get involved with some of our clubs. I also insisted that he live in our new residence hall second semester because he needed to learn social skills."

One day Albert did something that was not what you would expect from a shy, withdrawn first-year student. He approached his math professor and told him that he was teaching a particular theorem incorrectly. Many professors would blow off this kind of impertinence, but Albert's professor took him seriously. Eventually he saw that maybe Albert had a point. They ended up writing a scholarly paper together. Albert graduated last year with a double major and is now doing a PhD at an Ivy League university. "I think one of the triggers that propel a first-year student on the way to adulthood is this kind of transformative experience," President Muyskens continues. "And these experiences in big and small ways are repeated over and over at American colleges and universities."

President Muyskens pauses for a moment. "You know what?" he says, as though he just had an epiphany. "You ought to meet Mike Goldstein, one of our more famous alumni, because his story fits the pattern we have been discussing." Mike Goldstein, like Albert, came to Queens College from extremely limited circumstances, not knowing who he was or what he was going to do with his life. In his case too, a professor triggered the maturing process, and this experience eventually led to him becoming CEO of a major U.S. corporation.

As I know well from personal experience, professors often play a key role in the maturing process![1]

A Personal Story of the First Year

Michael Goldstein is not a household name. But almost every parent reading this book has in some way been touched by Toys "R" Us, the company he ran several years ago. With over fifteen hundred stores worldwide and sales of over $11 billion when he was CEO, Toys "R" Us is the largest retailer of children's toys in the world.

We are sitting in Goldstein's office in midtown Manhattan where he now serves as chair of the board at IBD Bank. A Telly Savalas look-alike, Goldstein proudly tells me that he owes much of his success in business and life to the growing-up process that began during his first year at Queens College.

A Brooklynite by birth, he moved with his family at age thirteen to a largely lower-middle-class Jewish neighborhood in Queens. His father sold yarn to shops around the city; his mother was a bookkeeper. Neither finished high school. As a teenager, he watched his parents come home every night utterly exhausted. And for all their hard work, they made just enough money to put food on the table. So before he was fifteen, Goldstein decided that he would become a millionaire so that he wouldn't have to sacrifice and suffer like his parents had.

Goldstein modestly tells me that he was an A student in school not because he was amazingly brilliant, but because he had a strong work ethic. So in his senior year at Jamaica High School, he made the decision to attend Queens College, not far from where he lived. He chose Queens for two reasons, first because his family couldn't afford an expensive college like Columbia or New York University, and second because he was extremely shy. He felt he would feel more at home at Queens College than some university far away or even in another borough of New York City.

When Goldstein arrived at Queens College, he was uncertain about how he would achieve his goal of financial independence. Initially he thought that he could do this by becoming a lawyer. But soon he made an important observation. He saw that the smartest students at Queens College—those with the highest IQs—were interested in prelaw, premed, and engineering, while the more average students were interested in accounting or teaching. He figured that if he did prelaw he would be competing with classmates who were smarter than he was and consequently he would end up near the bottom of the pack. Accounting majors, conversely, seemed (at least to Goldstein) to be less than brilliant and also not as hardworking and motivated as he was. "So I saw an opportunity," he says "and decided that since I was good at math I would take an intro accounting course. I really liked it!"

That first accounting course was taught by Professor Lou Geller, then somewhat of a luminary at Queens College. Professor Geller not only was an outstanding teacher who made accounting exciting but also, having seen real potential in Goldstein, took him under his wing. "I got an A and ended up being the number one student in Professor Geller's class," he tells me with pride.

It soon became clear to Goldstein that he not only liked accounting but could be a star as well, rather than just one student among many. So he ended up majoring in accounting and taking more courses with Professor Geller. Goldstein had the best grades in the major and ended up graduating from Queens magna cum laude.

Mike Goldstein's story is one that I've heard over and over from successful people like him who, because of a charismatic professor teaching an exciting course (often in their first year), had their eyes opened for the first time to what they might become in life. More often than not, these professors continue to play a prominent role in their students' lives well after graduation. For example, just after graduation, none of the "elite eight" accounting firms Goldstein interviewed offered him a job, in part because they had a quota on Jews. He remembers one day returning to campus depressed and demoralized, searching for moral support from his old professor. "Lou gave me confidence," Goldstein tells me. "He told me that I was better than the students those accounting firms had hired and that I should not be discouraged." Professor Geller then helped open the door for him at S. D. Leidesdorf, a largely Jewish accounting firm in New York City. They were delighted to hire Goldstein, especially on Professor Geller's recommendation. But Professor Geller's words about being better than the others were prophetic. A few months after joining Leidesdorf, Goldstein received an award for getting the highest certified public accountant grade in New York State. The man who presented the award to him was the very person who had turned him down at one of the accounting firm he had interviewed. Vindication!

Goldstein continues:

One of the lessons I learned at Queens College freshman year that has carried through my life is that by identifying areas of mediocrity and weakness I could also identify great opportunity. I also learned that while it's important to be smart, you don't have to be super smart in order to succeed. Hard work and passion are far more important. I have given 100 percent to whatever I do and I do it with passion. And this combination has worked for me! But I also learned from Professor Geller that integrity and honesty are central not only to the profession of accounting but to life in general and that you should always do the right thing. There have been at least two major instances in my career where integrity issues came up and where it was tempting to take the easy way out. But I remembered my professor's admonition freshman year about integrity and I did the right thing both times.

Goldstein ends our conversation by telling me yet another way he grew up his first year at college. He came to Queens College from an extremely insular New York City neighborhood, but from the moment he stepped on campus, his eyes were opened. There he met Christians and Jews of all persuasions, straights and gays, rich and poor, you name it. This was also the era of the civil rights movement, and he became keenly aware of the plight of blacks and other American minorities. He began to see that another key to success is the ability to meet and relate to people who are different and to cultivate their friendships.

"But I also learned something else from the great diversity that surrounded me at Queens. I eventually achieved my goal of becoming a millionaire—many times over. But well before this happened I began to see human need and suffering. And remembering the modest circumstances I came from as a child, I discovered that the greatest thing about being wealthy is the joy of giving back. From freshman year I was destined to be a philanthropist."

Postscript

It's late spring and classes have ended. I have navigated five college campuses, exploring with faculty, staff, and students many aspects of the first year. The experience has been exhilarating—and exhausting. I feel like a rising sophomore myself! I have one last task, which is to once again visit Phoebe and Nathan, the Mamaroneck High School students who, ten months ago, were heading off to Tufts University for orientation. I want to find out what they learned and how much they have grown over the year.

This time we all meet at Phoebe's home. Both families are sitting around a large table in a breakfast nook just off the kitchen. Whereas last time, they didn't really know each other and sat together silently awaiting my arrival, now they are engrossed in animated conversation. They have clearly become part of the larger Tufts community. Phoebe is wearing the same Tufts sweatshirt she did for our first interview.

Did Nathan and Phoebe's first year of college measure up to their expectations? "Yes!" they both reply. Nathan says that one of the things he discovered is that independence has its responsibilities. "Sure, no one is breathing down your neck like in high school," he says. "And professors really don't care if you blow off their class. But if you're irresponsible—if you neglect your studies—you pay for it big time."

Phoebe makes the same point but in a slightly different way. She says that in college you can be absolutely selfish. Get up when you want to. Go to bed when you want to. Eat when you want to. Go to the gym when you want to. You can just focus on yourself. But then *you're* responsible. You can no longer blame your parents if you screw up.

Was college as perfect as they thought it would be? Nathan says that going in you think that college will be absolutely wonderful, but his first weeks at Tufts were hard. He missed his friends and his parents. But then he realized that the situation wasn't going to improve by itself. "I had to *make* college wonderful," Nathan says. "It took me some time to do this."

Phoebe agrees. "Everyone says that college will be the best years of your life," she says. "Well, hello. College won't necessarily be the *best* years of your life." Phoebe shares a comment by one of her professors who told her class that if they live to be eighty, four years in college will represent *a very small* percentage of their entire life! "There's going to be ups and downs," Phoebe says, "so don't stress out if things aren't perfect. You did well in high school. You made it into college. Now just enjoy college for what it is."

After they've agreed that they have finally discovered independence from mom and dad, I sheepishly ask them whether they didn't sometimes wish that they still had their parents around to tell them what to do. Weren't they a *little* homesick? Phoebe says no. She was too busy at Tufts with soccer and studies to be homesick. She pauses and then says, "Well, maybe I got a little homesick around finals week."

Nathan claims with a sense of pride that he did really well without his mom always telling him what to do. He was able to mix and match his wardrobe without her help, got the laundry done, and had no major breakdown. "I survived!" he says. But Nathan was homesick in two ways. "When I was at college I was sometimes homesick for my family. But after a couple days visiting at home, I got homesick for Tufts!"

How often did Phoebe and Nathan actually come home to visit their families? Phoebe came home a lot, but not only to see her parents, she says. She has a high school friend at Ithaca College, and so it was actually easier for her to drive from Medford to Ithaca via Mamaroneck. She also visited home several times on her way to Lehigh University where her brother Liam is a student. And, of course, she came home for major holidays.

Nathan says that he really wanted to cement his relationship to Tufts so only left Medford for Thanksgiving and winter break. "Tell the truth, Nathan," his father interrupts. "You traveled west a *whole* lot!" Nathan's face turns red. "OK, OK. I admit it. My girlfriend goes to Smith." Nathan's mother's fear about him not fitting in socially seems to have been unfounded.

What about stuff? Phoebe originally planned to take a lot of stuff with her, including her grandfather's disco lights, while Nathan planned only to bring a bed set and sheets. Had Nathan and Phoebe brought the right amount of stuff to Tufts last August?

Phoebe says with a sense of self satisfaction that she took exactly what she needed. "I actually slept with my 'bankie,' and used Liam's Tufts pillow. Even grandpa's disco lights came in handy." Did Phoebe need to use her mom's wardrobe after all? No, Phoebe responds, because she "closet shopped" in her residence hall. "What's *that*?" I enquire. "I never heard of closet shopping before." Because her residence hall floor was very close-knit group they all agreed that the clothes in each other's closets would be available to everyone else on the floor as long as they were returned the next day—thus closet shopping.

"What about you?" I ask Nathan. He admits that he forgot some basic necessities. Then his mother brought him far too many clothes, which had to be picked up during Parents and Family Weekend and brought back to Mamaroneck. "It's my fault," Nathan's mother admits. "I asked other parents what they were doing and ended up buying Nathan too many clothes."

One of Phoebe's biggest concerns about being a first-year student was getting along with her roommate. She says that things worked out just fine, though not without problems. Phoebe is a night person and her roommate went to bed just as she was starting to study, but they worked it out. "Most importantly, my roommate wears the same size shoes I do!" I ask whether they are rooming together next year. "Absolutely," Phoebe says.

Nathan says he lucked out on his roommate, also an engineering student. At first he was nervous that by rooming with another engineer he might not get exposure to other students. But they shared common experiences and interests, took many of the same classes, and were able to help each other out with homework. There were some irritants, like when Nathan's roommate continuously bounced a tennis ball off the wall in their living room. Also, he went to bed earlier than Nathan did. "But we worked it out," Nathan declares. "We got to respect each other's space."

Last June, Phoebe didn't have a clue what she might major in so I ask her whether she has made a decision. She says that she's still not sure but maybe economics. Why economics? Because she took an intro to economics course and really liked it. While the professor was just OK, Phoebe has a real interest in math and enjoys doing problem sets. She also liked the rigor of the course.

Sensing that Nathan is still glad that he went to engineering school, I ask him whether he still wants to be a mechanical engineer. "Probably," Nathan responds. "But I'm also taking courses in operations research, which is a mix of engineering and economics."

First and sophomore year are when students, even those in a professional program like engineering, have an opportunity to explore what they might major in or do later in life. Because she loves the rigor of economics Phoebe is considering this as a major, whereas last fall she thought she might major in math or Spanish. Nathan, who was *certain* last fall that he wanted to be a mechanical engineer, is now experimenting with other possibilities. Changing minds is quite natural and, as we have seen, encouraged first year!

I turn to Phoebe and Nathan's parents. I want to know how things worked out for them and whether college has met their expectations as parents. Phoebe's mother declares with great earnestness that Tufts has exceeded their expectations. She found Tufts's matriculation ceremony amazing, especially President Bacow's address, and she and her husband felt a real sense of community. Nathan's mother and father are vigorously nodding in agreement. "I *really* appreciated the part of President Bacow's address where he gave us permission to grieve," Nathan's mother adds. "That helped a lot!"

I ask Nathan and Phoebe's parents whether they were able to survive without their kids around. The emotion in the room is palpable. "To be honest," Phoebe's mother says with a sigh, "I was having a difficult time after we dropped Phoebe off at Tufts orientation last fall. I missed her so much. I thought I was going to melt. But I asked myself, What would the alternative be? Not having Phoebe at college? And then I realized that this is what I *really* wanted for her. But what gets to you is the realization that your child isn't gone just for awhile, but really for good."

"I've got to say," Nathan's mother tells us, "the three-hour ride home to Mamaroneck after we dropped Nathan off for orientation was miserable. And for the next several days I would go into Nathan's empty room and feel really sad. But once I knew Nathan was settled in at Tufts it became much easier for me." Nathan's father adds that initially he thought he was ready for this, but at work the next day it was like someone in the family had died. He says that it took him a couple days to get back into the swing of things.

I ask Phoebe and Nathan's parents what they learned first year that they might like to pass on to the parents of future first-year college students.

"That it's all going to work out," Phoebe's mother says.

"For your kids?" I ask.

"No, for us parents!"

Acknowledgments

In addition to the moms I met at Starbucks, I would like to thank the Mamaroneck High School parents who allowed me to interview them in the design phase of *Off to College*. They largely framed the questions I attempt to answer in the book. These parents included Holly Brookstein, Bill Foster, Amy and Ed Merians, Ellen McEvily, Danielle Schantz, Diane Schreiber, Susan Smith, and Michelle Stacey. I would also like to thank Bob Sweeney, former director of counseling at Mamaroneck High School who not only introduced me to these parents but also gave me access to hundreds of juniors and seniors at the school who I have assisted in the college admissions process and who gave me deep insight into the aspirations and fears of aspiring college students.

Others who were helpful with producing this book are Rob Holyer, former vice president for Academic Affairs, and Craig Anderson, director of counseling services, both at Randolph-Macon College in Virginia, and Jody Alesandro, an editor on the Education Life section of the *New York Times*, who provided invaluable initial edits, and Meg Wallace, who did a marvelous job preparing the index.

The presidents of each of the colleges and universities I write about gave me unprecedented access to their campuses. They are (along with the people they assigned to work with me) Lawrence Bacow, president emeritus, and James Glaser, dean of the School of Arts and Sciences, Tufts University; Catharine Bond Hill, president, and Chris Roellke, dean of the college, Vassar College; Baird Tipson, president emeritus, Washington College; John Reynders, president, and Bill Deeds, provost, Morningside College; and James Muyskins, president emeritus, Queens College of the City University of New York. Matthew Goldstein, former chancellor of the City University of New York, shared a speaking platform with me and opened the doors of Queens College for which I am deeply grateful.

I would like to thank Elizabeth Branch Dyson, acquisition editor for education at the University of Chicago Press, who saw promise in a book of this kind and whose patience and superb editing suggestions improved the original manuscript enormously. I would also like to thank Yvonne Zipter, manuscript editor, who cleaned up a few ponderous sentences and paragraphs making the manuscript far more readable, as well as Nora Devlin who kept the book on track and Lauren Salas whose promotional skills helped to deliver the book to a wider audience.

Finally, the support of Susan Martin, my wife, was incalculable. Without her encouragement this book would not have been possible.

Notes

Preface

1. If you want to know how difficult it is to say goodbye to your children as they leave home basically for good, read my *New York Times* article, "When a Dad Says Goodbye to His Daughter," *New York Times Education Life*, August 6, 2000.
2. "College Enrollment and Work Activity of 2013 High School Graduates," U.S. Department of Labor, Bureau of Labor Statistics, April 22, 2014, http://www .bls.gov/news.release/hsgec.nro.htm. While the title of this book suggests that most students who attend a four-year college or university leave home and will live in a residence hall, this is not the case for everyone. Still, whether living at home or on campus, the experiences of first-year students who attend four-year institutions will be similar.

Chapter 1

1. Cited by Gayle Ronan, "College Freshmen Face Major Dilemma," MSNBC News, November 29, 2005, http://www.nbcnews.com/id/10154383/ns /business-personal_finance/t/college-freshmen-face-major-dilemma/# .VIHUXyiWds8.
2. Barbara Hofer and Abigail Moore, *The iConnected Parent: Staying Close to Your Kids in College (and Beyond) While Letting Them Grow Up* (New York: Atria, 2010), 20.

Chapter 2

1. Christopher Drew, "Rethinking Advanced Placement," *New York Times*, January 7, 2011. John H. Pryor, Linda DeAngelo, Laura Palucki Blake, Sylvia Hurtado, and Serge Tran, *The American Freshman: National Norms Fall 2011* (Los Angeles: Higher Education Research Institute, UCLA, 2011), 9, http://heri.ucla .edu/PDFs/pubs/TFS/Norms/Monographs/TheAmericanFreshman2011.pdf.

2. General education requirements in the School of Engineering are more modest but the principle is the same, which is to say, to also give future engineers exposure the liberal arts as well as writing.

3. See Trip Gabriel, "To Stop Cheats, Colleges Learn Their Trickery," *New York Times*, July 5, 2010; Lauren Sieben, "Many Cheaters Are Overly Optimistic about Their Academic Ability, Study Finds," *Chronicle of Higher Education*, March 25, 2011. Other studies show higher figures. See Tim Clydesdale, *The First Year Out* (Chicago: University of Chicago Press, 2007), 165.

4. According to a recent HERI study, an incredible 41.2 percent of first-year students report having witnessed academic dishonesty or cheating (as opposed to having cheated themselves)! "2014 Your First College Year Survey: Institutional Profile Report" 2015. This information is unpublished but available if requested from the Higher Education Research Institute at UCLA. HERI data used in this book involves the same group of 9,168 students.

5. See Ipsos Public Affairs, *How America Pays for College 2011: Sallie Mae's National Study of College Students and Parents Conducted by Gallup* (Newark, DE: Sallie Mae, 2011), 17. This figure would probably be higher if Sallie Mae also looked at non–Work Study job income. See http://news.salliemae.com/sites/sallie mae.newshq.businesswire.com/files/publication/file/HowAmericaPays forCollege_2011.pdf.

Chapter 3

1. Our children feel the same way. In 2014, 53.4 percent of incoming first-year students said that getting a job is the primary reason for going to college. Kevin Eagan, Ellen Stolzenberg, Joseph Ramirez, Melissa Aragon, Maria Suchard, and Sylvia Hurtado, *The American Freshman: National Norms Fall 2014* (Los Angeles: Higher Education Research Institute, UCLA, 2014), 4, http://www.heri.ucla.edu/monographs/theamericanfreshman2014.pdf.

2. This is a very controversial number with little hard data to support it. What I do know from experience is that the college graduates I have been involved with seem to be doing dramatically different things every few years. The number might be, if anything, too low. See Carl Bialik, "Seven Careers in a Lifetime? Think Twice, Researchers Say," *Wall Street Journal*, September 4, 2010.

3. Increasingly, colleges are using advisers who are not members of the faculty. There is considerable debate in higher education circles over whether this is desirable. See Jeffery Selingo, "Here's Your Schedule, What's Your Hurry?" *New York Times*, April 13, 2014.

4. But see Steven Conn, "The Rise of the Helicopter Teacher," *Chronicle of Higher Education*, August 5, 2014.

5. But see Ariel Kaminer, "Princeton Is Proposing to End Limit on Giving A's," *New York Times*, August 7, 2014, where Princeton is reconsidering a cap on As.

6. See Doug Lederman, "When to Specialize?" *Inside Higher Education*, November 25, 2009.

7. "2014 Your First Year College Survey: Institutional Profile Report," HERI, UCLA (2015).

8. National Survey of Student Engagement, "Topical Modules: Academic Advising" (Bloomington, IN: Indiana University Center for Postsecondary Research, 2013), 2, 3, http://nsse.iub.edu/2013_institutional_report/pdf /Modules/2013%20Advising.pdf.

9. National Survey of Student Engagement, *A Fresh Look at Student Engagement—Annual Results 2013* (Bloomington, IN: Indiana University Center for Postsecondary Research, 2013), 22, http://nsse.iub.edu/NSSE_2013_Results/pdf/NSSE_2013_Annual_Results.pdf.

10. John Henry Newman, "Discourse 7: Knowledge Viewed in Relation to Professional Skill," in *The Idea of a University*, The Newman Reader, The National Institute for Newman Studies, rev. September 2001, http://www.newmanreader.org/works/idea/discourse7.html. For a more modern defense of the liberal arts, see Michel Roth, *Beyond the University: Why Liberal Education Matters* (New Haven, CT: Yale University Press, 2014).

11. "2014 Your First Year College Survey: Institutional Profile Report," HERI, UCLA (2015).

12. According to a study by the National Endowments of the Arts, 65 percent of first-year college students read for pleasure for less than an hour per week if at all. National Endowment for the Arts, "To Read of Not to Read: A Question of National Consequence," Research Report no. 47 (Washington, DC: NEA, November 2007), 8, http://arts.gov/sites/default/files/ToRead.pdf.

13. This is not to suggest that lectures are necessarily bad, just that lecturing without any active student involvement (such as debate or discussion) is not the best way to learn subject matter.

14. "Topical Modules, Development of Transferable Skills," in *National Survey of Student Engagement*, 2014, 2, http://nsse.iub.edu/2014_institutional_report/pdf/Modules/NSSE14%20Module%20Summary-Development%20of%20Transferable%20Skills.pdf.

15. Derek Bok, *Our Underachieving Colleges* (Princeton: Princeton University Press, 2006), 123.

16. See Dan Berrett, "Students Come to College Thinking They've Mastered Writing," *New York Times*, March 21, 2014.

17. See Richard Arum and Josipa Roksa, *Academically Adrift: Limited Learning on College Campuses* (Chicago: University of Chicago Press, 2011), 96

18. "2014 Your First Year College Survey: Institutional Profile Report," HERI, UCLA (2015).

Chapter 4

1. National Center for Educational Statistics, "Table 320: Average Undergraduate Tuition and Fees and Room and Board Rates Charged for Full-Time Students in Degree-Granting Institutions, by Type and Control of Institution: 1964–65 through 2006–07," Digest of Education Statistics, http://nces.ed.gov/programs/digest/d07/tables/dt07_320.asp. College Board, "Average Published Undergraduate Charges by Sector, 2014–15," Trends in Higher Education, http://trends.collegeboard.org/college-pricing/figures-tables/average-published-undergraduate-charges-sector-2013-14.

2. John Pryor, Linda DeAngelo, Laura Blake, Sylvia Hurtado, and Serge Tran, *The American Freshman: National Norms Fall 2011* (Los Angeles: Higher Education Research Institute, UCLA, 2011), 12. See http://heri.ucla.edu/PDFs/pubs/TFS/Norms/Monographs/TheAmericanFreshman2011.pdf.

3. Ron Lieber, "Placing the Blame as Students Are Buried in Debt," *New York Times*, May 28, 2010. For the impact of student debt on the general economy, see Neil Irwin, "How Student Debt May Be Stunting the Economy," *New York Times*, May 14, 2014.

4. See Natalie Kitroeff, "Loan Monitor Is Accused of Ruthless Tactics on Student Debt," *New York Times*, January 2, 2014.

5. Pryor, Eagan, Blake, Hurtado, Berdan, and Case, *The American Freshman*, 12.

6. Steve Cohen, "A Quick Way to Cut College Costs," *New York Times*, March 20, 2014.

7. Mark Keierleber, writing in the *Chronicle of Higher Education*, reports that in 2012, 45 percent of bachelor's degrees were awarded (but not without problems) to students who transferred from a community college. See Mark Keierleber, "Four-Year College's Views of Transfer Credits May Hinder Graduation," *Chronicle of Higher Education*, April 7, 2014. Conversely many elite colleges and universities with large endowments have eliminated loans altogether for middle- and lower-income students. Consequently, even though they have a higher "sticker price" than their public counterparts, the cost for attending one of these institutions can end up being less. For a list of the elite colleges and universities that seek out lower-income students and provide them with generous financial aid, Vassar College foremost among them, see David Leonhardt, "Behind Ivy Walls: Top Colleges That Enroll Rich, Middleclass and Poor," *New York Times*, September 8, 2014. See also Richard Pérez-Peña, "What You Don't Know about Financial Aid (but Should)," *New York Times*, April 9, 2014.

8. See David Leonhardt, "Is College Worth It? Clearly, New Data Say," *New York Times*, May 27, 2014.

9. Eduardo Porter, "Dropping Out of College, and Paying the Price," *New York Times*, June 25, 2013.

10. For an extreme example of this, see "Former College Financial Aid Head Hit with Federal Fraud Charges," *Boston Business Journal*, July 21, 2014.

11. See "2014 Your First Year College Survey: Institutional Profile Report," HERI, UCLA (2015)

12. Everyone in higher education knows that if your student has high board scores and an impressive high school GPA it's sometimes possible to bargain up the financial aid package if a competing college has offered more scholarship money. But this can only be done before accepting admissions and it does not work for students who are weaker academically or who have no needed skill (like throwing a football or playing an instrument needed in the college orchestra).

13. According to a recent survey, 45 percent of all first-year students were employed during the first semester. This breaks down to 27 percent working at on-campus jobs and 18.9 percent at off-campus jobs. "2014 Your First Year College Survey: Institutional Profile Report," HERI, UCLA (2015)

14. Of students who went on to college in 2013, 36.7 percent worked between six and twenty hours during their last year of high school. See "Almanac of Higher Education 2014," *Chronicle of Higher Education*, August 22, 2014, 36, http://chronicle.com/article/A-Profile-of-Freshmen-at/147335/.

15. Cited in Jennifer Epstein, "Will Work for Beer," *Inside Higher Education*, October 8, 2009.

16. Ipsos Public Affairs, *How America Pays for College 2014: Sallie Mae's National Study of College Students and Parents Conducted by Gallup* (Newark, DE: Sallie Mae, 2014), 56, http://news.salliemae.com/files/doc_library/file/HowAmericaPaysforCollege2014FNL.pdf.

17. See Richard Pérez-Peña, "Despite Rising Sticker Prices, Actual College Costs Stable over Decade, Study Says," *New York Times*, October 24, 2013.

18. See Scott Carlson, "Spending Shifts as Colleges Compete on Students' Comfort," *Chronicle of Higher Education*, July 28, 2014.

Chapter 5

1. Closely related to online education is what has come to be called competency-based education or the idea that what matters is not so much how you learned but what you learned. The suggestion is that time-to-degree (and thus the cost of education) can be greatly reduced by testing competencies that people have already mastered. Competency-based education (or "credit for experience") also threatens the traditional residential college. See Anya Kamenetz, "Are You Competent? Prove It: Degrees Based on What You Can Do, Not How Long You Went," *New York Times*, October 29, 2013.
2. Massive open online courses are high-quality courses produced by prestigious universities normally at no cost. They are popularly known as MOOCS.
3. Sometimes called "Velcro parents" because they seem stuck to their child.
4. "2014 Your First Year College Survey: Institutional Profile Report," HERI, UCLA (2015).
5. See Richard Arum and Josipa Roksa, *Academically Adrift: Limited Learning on College Campuses* (Chicago: University of Chicago Press, 2011), 69, where the authors show that the average college student only studies twelve hours per week.
6. I am told by fellow college presidents that this letter has appeared in many different forms throughout the years.
7. "2014 Your First Year College Survey: Institutional Profile Report," HERI, UCLA (2015).
8. Ibid.
9. "Does Living Environment (Co-ed vs Single Sex) Impact the Housing Experience?" EBI-MAP Works, November 14, 2011, http://www.webebi.com /community/research/41/does-living-environment-(co-ed-vs.-single-sex) -impact-the-housing-experience.
10. Colleges have different command chains with a key administrator at the top of each. For student affairs, campus safety, and disabilities issues, the top person is usually the vice president for student affairs; for academic or advising matters and often for athletics, the vice president for academic affairs or the provost; for financial matters, the vice president for finance or treasurer.
11. "2013 Your First Year College Survey: Institutional Profile," HERI, UCLA (2014).
12. "According to a number of studies, including one from 2008 at Ohio University, when students take part in extracurricular activities, they feel more connected to campus and are less likely to transfer or drop out. This same study also shows that students who get involved make better grades, have more friends, feel like they fit in, and adjust more easily to campus life" (https:// www.woofound.com/blog/posts/extracurricular-activities-might-be-the-key -to-the-college-experience). The Ohio study referred to is A. Michael Williford and Joni Y. Wadley, "How Institutional Research Can Create and Synthesize Retention and Attrition Information," Professional File, no. 108 (Fall 2008), http://airweb3.org/airpubs/108.pdf.
13. American College Health Association, National College Health Assessment, *Spring 2014 Reference Group Executive Summary* (Hanover, MD: American Col-

lege Health Association, 2014), 6, http://www.acha-ncha.org/docs/ACHA -NCHA-II_ReferenceGroup_ExecutiveSUmmary_Spring2013.pdf.

14. "Regular Marijuana Use by Teens Continues to Be a Concern," National Institutes of Health, December 19, 2012, http://www.nih.gov/news/health/dec2012 /nida-19.htm.

15. American College Health Association, National College Health Assessment, *Spring 2014 Reference Group Executive Summary* (Hanover, MD: American College Health Association, 2014), 6, http://www.acha-ncha.org/docs/acha -ncha-ii_referencegroup_executivesummary_fall2012.pdf.

16. Scott E. Carrell, Mark Hoekstra, and James E. West, "Does Drinking Impair College Performance? Evidence from a Regression Discontinuity Approach," NBER Working Paper no. 16330, *Journal of Public Economics* 95, no.1 (2011): 54–62, http://www.nber.org/papers/w16330.

Chapter 6

1. American College Health Association, National College Health Assessment, *Spring 2014 Reference Group Executive Summary* (Hanover, MD: American College Health Association, 2014), 13, http://www.acha-ncha.org/docs/ACHA -NCHA-II_ReferenceGroup_ExecutiveSUmmary_Spring2014.pdf.

2. "2014 Your First Year College Survey: Institutional Profile Report," HERI, UCLA (2015).

3. American College Health Association, National College Health Assessment, *Spring 2014 Reference Group Executive Summary*, 10. For the most recent figures on unprotected sex, see also American College Health Association, American College Health Assessment, *Spring 2010 Reference Group Executive Summary* (Hanover, MD: American College Health Association, 2010), 9, http://www .acha-ncha.org/docs/ACHA-NCHA-II_ReferenceGroup_ExecutiveSummary _Spring2010.pdf. The same survey reports that 20.4 percent of first-year students had unprotected sex in the past twelve months when drinking alcohol (9).

4. Kevin Eagan, Ellen Stolzenberg, Joseph Ramirez, Melissa Aragon, Maria Suchard, and Sylvia Hurtado, *The American Freshman: National Norms Fall 2014* (Los Angeles: Higher Education Research Institute, UCLA, 2014), 13, http:// www.heri.ucla.edu/PDFs/Monographs/TheAmericanFreshman2014.pdf, and *The American Freshman: National Norms Fall 2009*, 28, http://www.heri.ucla .edu/PDFs/pubs/TFS/Norms/Monographs/TheAmericanFreshman2009.pdf.

5. "2014 Your First Year College Survey: Institutional Profile Report," HERI, UCLA (2015).

6. American College Health Association, National College Health Assessment, *Spring 2014 Reference Group Executive Summary*, 15.

7. According to the National Survey of Counseling Center Directors, in 2011 (the most recent figures), only 10.6 percent of students enrolled at four-year colleges made use of a counseling center. Robert Gallagher, *National Survey of Counseling Center Directors 2011*, Monograph Series no. 8T (Alexandria, VA: International Association of Counseling Services, Inc. 2011), 4, http://college counseling.org/wp-content/uploads/2011-NSCCD.pdf.

8. "2014 Your First Year College Survey: Institutional Profile Report," HERI, UCLA (2015). "Drinking Levels Defined," National Institute on Alcohol Abuse and Alcoholism, National Institute of Health, http://www.niaaa.nih .gov/alcohol-your-health/overview-alcohol-consumption/moderate-binge -drinking

9. "2014 Your First Year College Survey: Institutional Profile Report," HERI, UCLA, 2015.
10. Robin Hattersley Gray, "95% of College Presidents Don't Want Guns on Campus," *Campus Safety Magazine*, June 13, 2014.

Chapter 7

1. According to a recent study, 35.9 percent of first-year small-college students report playing an intramural sport and 26.6 percent intercollegiate. "2014 Your First Year College Survey: Institutional Profile Report," HERI, UCLA (2015).
2. At the same time, the rate of Division I spending on intercollegiate athletics is beginning to outpace spending on academics—not a good sign! See Tamar Lewin, "Colleges Increasing Spending on Sports Faster Than on Academics, Report Finds," *New York Times*, April 7, 2014.
3. See, for example, "Higher GPA for Freshmen Who Frequent Campus Gym," *Inside Higher Education*, September 4, 2014.
4. For example, according to the American College Health Association, only 21.2 percent of college students nationally live up to the American Heart Association's standard for moderate aerobic exercise, which is thirty minutes, five to seven days a week, and only 32.9 percent live up to the standard for vigorous aerobic activity, which is twenty minutes, three to seven days per week American College Health Association, National College Health Assessment, *Spring 2014 Reference Group Executive Summary* (Hanover, MD: American College Health Association, 2014), 12, http://www.acha-ncha.org/docs/ACHA -NCHA-II_ReferenceGroup_ExecutiveSUmmary_Spring2013.pdf.
5. "How Do Athletic Scholarships Work?" National Collegiate Athletic Association, June 21, 2011, http://www.ncaa.org/sites/default/files/NCAA%2BAthletics %2BScholarships.pdf.

Chapter 8

1. Victor B. Saenz, Sylvia Hurtado, Doug Barrera, De'Sha Wolf, and Fanny Yeung, *First in My Family: A Profile of First-Generation College Students at Four-Year Institutions since 1971* (Los Angeles: Higher Education Research Institute, UCLA, 2007), 6–7, http://www.heri.ucla.edu/PDFs/pubs/TFS/Special /Monographs/FirstInMyFamily.pdf; "Almanac of Higher Education 2014," *Chronicle of Higher Education*, August 22, 2014, 36, http://chronicle.com /article/A-Profile-of-Freshmen-at/147335/.
2. Claudia Dreifus and Andrew Hacker, *Higher Education? How Colleges Are Wasting Our Money and Failing Our Kids—and What We Can Do about It* (New York: St. Martin's Press, 2011), 185.
3. See Jake New, "The Opposite of Helicopter Parents," *Inside Higher Education*, August 13, 2014.
4. Saenz, Hurtado, Barrera, Wolf, and Yeung, *First in My Family*, 15.
5. See "Almanac of Higher Education 2014," *Chronicle of Higher Education*, August 22, 2014, 36, http://chronicle.com/article/A-Profile-of-Freshmen-at/147335/. Data is for the fall of 2013.
6. Still, the 42.6 percent four-year graduation rate for SEEK students at Queens compares favorably to the national average for all students. Only 34 percent of all students who attend four-year colleges graduate within four years. See

Richard Arum and Josipa Roksa, *Academically Adrift: Limited Learning on College Campuses* (Chicago: University of Chicago Press, 2011), 54.

7. "Where Schools Fall Short," *New York Times*, December 4, 2011.

8. Sharon Otterman, "Most New York Students Are Not College-Ready," *New York Times*, February 7, 2011.

9. According to recent data, 53.6 percent of first-year students report having taken a course or first-year seminar to help them adjust to college-level academics. See "2014 Your First Year College Survey: Institutional Profile Report," HERI, UCLA (2015)

10. Data from the National Survey of Student Engagement show that first-year students averaged fourteen hours of study per week, far below the two hours per classroom hour suggested by most faculty. See National Survey of Student Engagement, *A Fresh Look at Student Engagement—Annual Results 2013* (Bloomington, IN: Indiana University Center for Postsecondary Research, 2013), 9, http://nsse.iub.edu/NSSE_2013_Results/pdf/NSSE_2013_Annual_Results.pdf.

11. Saenz, Hurtado, Barrera, Wolf, and Yeung, *First in My Family*, vii.

12. For data supporting the value of positive intervention with first gens as articulated by Mr. Modeste, see Paul Tough, "Who Gets to Graduate?" *New York Times Magazine*, May 15, 2014.

Chapter 9

1. The percentage of first-year students nationwide who have a documented learning disability is from 2008, the most recent figure. Joseph Madaus and Stan Shaw, "College as a Realistic Option for Students with Learning Disabilities," Council for Learning Disabilities, January 2010, http://www.council -for-learning-disabilities.org/publications/infosheets/college-as-a-realistic -option-for-students-with-learning-disabilities.

2. I wrote about this tour in the *New York Times*. See my "Campus as Obstacle Course," *New York Times Education Life*, October 30, 2012.

3. According to the U.S. Government Accountability Office, in 2008 (the most recent figures) about 11 percent of all postsecondary students had a disability. Most had a learning disability but 15.1 percent (of the 11 percent) had an orthopedic or mobility impairment, 6.1 percent had a hearing challenge, and 2.7 percent were blind or visually impaired. *Higher Education and Disability: Education Needs a Coordinated Approach to Improve Its Assistance to Schools in Supporting Students*, Report to the Chairman, Committee on Education and Labor, House of Representatives ([Washington, D.C.]: Government Accountability Office, 2009), 8, 38, http://www.gao.gov/new.items/d1033.pdf.

Chapter 10

1. This notion is supported by a Gallup survey of over twenty-nine thousand college graduates, 63 percent of whom strongly agreed with the statement "I had at least one professor who made me excited about learning." This was by far the highest percentage response to questions that included internship experiences and extracurricular involvement. Julie Ray and Stephanie Kafha, "Economy: Life in College Matters for Life after College," Gallup, May 6, 2014, http://www.gallup.com/poll/168848/life-college-matters-life-college.aspx.

Index

athletics and physical fitness (*continued*)
142; retention and graduation rates and,
135; scholarship athletes, 146; spending on
intercollegiate athletics and, 213n2 (ch. 7);
sports-related illness and injuries and, 145,
146; stress reduction and, 138; students' opinions about, 140–42; study abroad for athletes
and, 15, 142; substance use and abuse and,
144–45; teams as fraternities and, 94, 148;
time management and, 14, 52–53
Avila, Manny (Queens College coordinator of
judicial affairs), 193–94

Bacow, Larry (Tufts University president), 7–8,
88, 202
Bell, Andrew, 151
Benson, Shari (Morningside College director of
new students), 80–83, 92
Bergen, Debbie (Washington College accounts
receivable manager), 66–69, 70–71
Beverly, Sharon (Vassar College athletics director),
133–35
Bok, Derek, 55–56
Bonds, Barry, 28
Brown, Burton (Washington College public safety
officer), 124–28
Burns, Susan (Morningside College associate
dean of academic affairs), 188–90

campus shootings. *See* safety and campus
security
careers: athletes and, 129, 141; declaration of
major and, 44, 49–50; double majors and, 73;
first-generation students and, 151–52, 153,
157–58, 159–60; general education requirements and, 33; importance of writing for, 56;
internships and, 73; job market for graduates
and, 69; liberal arts and, 47–48, 73; number
of careers in a lifetime and, 33, 208n2 (ch.
3); professors' recommendations and, 197;
reasons for attending college and, 33, 208n1;
time management consulting and, 20. *See
also* employment during college
Carter, Stephen, 91
Chomsky, Noam, 151
choosing a college: student athletes and, 135, 139;
students with disabilities and, 187, 189
choosing a major. *See* declaration of major
City College of New York, 168
City University of New York, 149
class size: advantages of small classes and, 28–29;
large lecture classes and, 55–56; at Vassar, 37
Clery Act, 128
college administration, chain of command in, 88,
211n10
communications, student e-mail and, 71
community colleges. *See* two-year colleges
competency-based education, 211n1

Cooperative Institutional Research Program
(UCLA), xiv
counseling services and mental health: access
to counseling and, 115; chaplaincy and,
91–92; confidentiality and, 10, 106; declining
emotional health and, 112–13; depression
and, 37, 81, 112–13; disclosing disability and,
9–10; disclosing health issues and, 105–6;
eating disorders and, 105–7; encouragement
to use, 6; first-generation students and,
177–78; homesickness and, 113–14; illegality of
discrimination and, 106; orientation and, 9–10;
percentage of students using counseling
services and, 212n7; reasons for counseling
center visits and, 113; students' opinions
about, 111–12
course distribution requirements, 23
course load, 155
course selection, 18–19, 23–24, 34, 45–46
credit for experience, 211n1
crime and criminal prosecution. *See* safety and
campus security
Curry, Terri (Morningside College vice president of
student life), 188
Czula, Roman (Vassar College fitness center director), 136–38

Davis, Gene (Washington College campus safety
officer), 126
declaration of major: advising and, 44, 46; career
and, 49–50, 73; double majors and, 50, 73;
end-of-first-year thoughts about, 202; first-
generation students and, 157–58; students'
indecision and, 1–2, 44; timing of, 44
depression. *See* counseling services and mental
health
disabilities: academic performance and, 186;
academic standards and, 190; accessibility
of physical environment and, 180, 187–89;
accommodations and, 34, 181–85, 188–89;
ADHD and, 181–84; advice for parents and,
184, 185, 187; advising and, 34; anxiety
and, 181; Asperger syndrome and, 180–83;
auditory processing disorder and, 180–83,
186; author's personal experience with, 179;
choosing a college and, 187, 189; college
application process and, 184; colleges
specifically for students with learning
disabilities and, 186; confidentiality and,
185–86; disclosure of, 9–10, 34, 181, 183–84,
189; discrimination and, 184–85; dyslexia
and, 179, 180, 181, 183, 189–90; 504 Form and,
181–82; in high school versus college, 184–85;
orientation and, 9–10; percentage of students
with disabilities and, 180, 214n3; refusal of
accommodations, 190; self-advocacy and, 181,
185; sight impairment and, 188; stigmati-
zation and, 183, 185–86, 188–89; students